Switched and Fast Ethernet:
How It Works and How to Use It

Switched and Fast Ethernet: How It Works and How to Use It

Robert Breyer and Sean Riley

Ziff-Davis Press
Emeryville, California

Copy Editor	Kelly Green
Project Coordinator	Ami Knox
Technical Reviewer	Dave Brooks
Cover Illustration and Design	Regan Honda
Book Design	Paper Crane Graphics, Berkeley
Screen Graphics Editor	Paul R. Freedman
Word Processing	Howard Blechman
Page Layout	Alan Morgenegg
Indexer	Carol Burbo

Ziff-Davis Press books are produced on a Macintosh computer system with the following applications: FrameMaker®, Microsoft® Word, QuarkXPress®, Adobe Illustrator®, Adobe Photoshop®, Adobe Streamline™, MacLink®*Plus*, Aldus® FreeHand™, Collage Plus™.

For information about U.S. rights and permissions, contact Chantal Tucker at Ziff-Davis Publishing, fax 212-503-5420.

If you have comments or questions or would like to receive a free catalog, call or write:
Ziff-Davis Press
5903 Christie Avenue
Emeryville, CA 94608
800-688-0448

ISBN 1-56276-338-5

Manufactured in the United States of America
10 9 8 7 6 5 4 3 2

■ Contents at a Glance

■ Table of Contents

■ Acknowledgments

Co-authoring our very first book has been an exciting experience for both of us. Right now no other books cover either Fast or Switched Ethernet, so we feel like we are charting new territory here. Of course it helped to be writing about high-speed Ethernet—one of the hottest subjects in networking today. Authoring a technical book has been rewarding; we thought we knew Ethernet inside out, yet we learned that there was much we didn't know (and still don't).

Certain people provided us with invaluable information and feedback that have made this book what it is today. Many thanks go to Robert Metcalfe, Ron Crane, Bob Galin, Ron Schmidt, and Howard Charney for filling in the details regarding the history of Ethernet (the knowledge stored in these minds is enough material for ten books). Many thanks also go to our technical reviewers: Dave Brooks, the world's busiest IT manager; L.D. Weller, one of the country's specialists in desktop management (L.D. co-authored Chapter 9); Mr. IEEE, also known as Rich Bowers (Rich is a coworker and is a senior member of the 802.3 Fast Ethernet working group); Keith and Fred from Bay Networks; and Mark Fletcher from Teknon. Lastly we want to thank our editor, Kelly Green, and our project coordinator, Ami Knox, for their patience and determination.

We wish you luck with your new Switched and Fast Ethernet networks. We hope you learn as much from reading this book as we did from writing it.

—Sean Riley (Sean_Riley@ccm.jf.intel.com)
—Robert Breyer (Robert_A_Breyer@ccm.jf.intel.com)
Portland, Oregon

■ Introduction

Today Ethernet is more than just another type of LAN; it is the de facto standard for local area networking hardware. Switched and Fast Ethernet will ensure that Ethernet remains the top-selling LAN technology for another decade. That's because Switched and Fast Ethernet are evolutionary, standards-based, affordable, and supported by almost every networking vendor in the business. This is in stark contrast to many other high-speed technologies that are completely new, unproven, or proprietary.

This is not an academic book that will inundate you with theory and specifications. We have taken a hands-on approach in this publication—we focus on using Switched and Fast Ethernet products. Our objective is to teach you the practical aspects of upgrading to, building, managing, and troubleshooting a high-speed Ethernet network.

We combined the topics of Switched and Fast Ethernet in one book because the two go hand in hand. One without the other could still exist, but it's the combination of Switched *and* Fast Ethernet that will continue to make Ethernet so attractive as a high-speed networking choice for years to come.

■ Is This Book for You?

This book is designed for Ethernet users. We have made various assumptions about you: We assume that you already have some experience with LANs in general and Ethernet in particular; that you believe network infrastructure is a fundamental, necessary long-term investment to ensure your company's competitiveness; and that you are or will be experiencing performance bottlenecks in your existing LAN.

If you can identify with one of the following descriptions, then this book is for you!

- You are the chief information officer (CIO) of a large company putting together a strategic plan for your high-speed LAN that will be rolled out over the next five years.

- You are a LAN administrator that has to upgrade a severely overloaded network segment next weekend. You have two days to decide what equipment to purchase.

- You are a network manager that needs to devise an upgrade plan for your company's shared 10BASE-T LAN to a high-speed LAN.

- You are a management information systems (MIS) director that is evaluating different consultant and vendor proposals for upgrading your existing network, which has become overloaded. You need to decide which consultants' recommendations to follow.

- You are merely interested in high-speed networking technology, but know a fair amount about networking.

■ Overview

The first five chapters serve primarily as educational background. Chapter 1 discusses how Ethernet has evolved from a wireless 4,800-bps radio transmission network 25 years ago into today's 100-Mbps LAN. Chapter 2 contrasts Switched and Fast Ethernet with some of today's other high-speed technologies. Chapter 3 delves into the topic of Fast and Switched Ethernet standards and how these two high-speed variants differ from the proven 10-Mbps shared media version. Cabling is a subject that is often overlooked by LAN managers, and Chapter 4 is dedicated to the subject of UTP (unshielded twisted pair) and fiber cabling requirements, test equipment, and certification. Chapter 5 discusses bandwidth. Bandwidth is what this book is really all about, and this chapter will describe how to measure it and how much traffic your network is actually capable of handling. We will also talk about some of the applications that are using up more and more precious bandwidth.

Chapters 6 through 10 are the hands-on part of this book, focusing on the installation, usage, management, and troubleshooting of Fast and Switched Ethernet networks. Chapter 6 introduces the various network building blocks, and the features to look for when buying network adapters, repeaters, switches, chassis hubs, and routers. Chapter 7 describes a step-by-step approach to upgrading an existing 10-Mbps shared media Ethernet network to a new high-speed Ethernet network. Chapter 8 discusses four real-world case studies to illustrate the step-by-step upgrade method discussed in Chapter 7. Network management in a switched environment works differently than in today's shared network, and Chapter 9 contrasts some of the differences. In addition, we have included a section on desktop management. Chapter 10 provides some tips and insights into troubleshooting a high-speed Ethernet LAN.

Two appendixes follow. Most LAN hardware vendors today sell Ethernet Switching gear. 100BASE-T, being relatively new, is not yet as widely supported as Switched Ethernet, and so Appendix A is a list of companies selling 100BASE-T equipment today. Appendix B contains additional references that we found to be useful during the course of writing this book.

Please note that you do not need to read this book cover to cover. Each chapter has been written to stand alone, so you can easily use this book as a reference guide. If you are using Ethernet today and want to learn about next-generation high-speed Ethernet options, then this book belongs on your bookshelf.

1

The History of Ethernet

OVER THE COURSE OF 25 YEARS, ETHERNET HAS EVOLVED FROM A 4800 bps contention-based radio channel transmission system to the most popular local area networking standard, capable of transmitting 100 million bits per second over unshielded twisted-pair telephone cable.

The development history of Ethernet is fascinating from a personal as well as a technical perspective—companies were started, fortunes were made, and in fact, entire industries were created based on the concept of connecting different computing devices.

We would like to share some of the history of the last 25 years with you. We also believe that Fast Ethernet, today's state-of-the-art Ethernet version, isn't going to be the last chapter.

■ The Origins of Ethernet: The ALOHA Radio System (1968–1972)

The key concept of Ethernet is the use of a common shared transmission channel. The idea of a shared data transmission channel had its beginnings at the University of Hawaii in the late 1960s, when Norman Abramson and his colleagues from the University of Hawaii developed a radio network called the ALOHA system. This ground-based radio broadcasting system was developed to connect the university's IBM 360 mainframe, located on the main campus on the island of Oahu, with card readers and terminals dispersed among different islands and ships at sea.

The original speed of this system was 4800 bps, and was later upgraded to 9600 bps. The system was unique in that it used an inbound as well as an outbound radio channel for two-way data transmission. The outbound (that is, a mainframe to remote island) channel was fairly straightforward in that the destination address was put in the header of the transmission and decoded by the appropriate receiving station. The inbound channel (that is, remote island or ship to mainframe) was more interesting because it used a method of randomized retransmission. An island station would send its message or packets off after the operator had hit the Return key. This station would then wait for the base station to send back an acknowledgment. If this acknowledgment was not returned on the outbound channel within a certain period of time (200–1,500 nanoseconds), the remote stations would assume that two stations had attempted to transmit simultaneously and that a collision had occurred, corrupting the transmitted data. At that point, both stations would choose a random backoff time, after which both stations would attempt to retransmit their packet again, with a very high probability of success. This kind of network is called a *contention-based network,* because the different stations are competing or contending for the same channel.

Two of the implications of this contention-based network were

- This scheme allowed multiple nodes to communicate over the exact same frequency channel in a simple and elegant manner.

- The more stations that utilized the channel, the more collisions were likely to occur, resulting in transmission delays and reduced throughput.

Norman Abramson published a series of papers on the theory and applications of the ALOHA system, including one in 1970 detailing a mathematical model for calculating the theoretical capacity of the ALOHA system. This model is now known as the classical ALOHA model, and it estimated the theoretical capacity of the ALOHA system to be 17 percent of the theoretical efficiency. In 1972, ALOHA was improved through synchronized access to become slotted ALOHA, more than doubling the efficiency.

The work done by Abramson and his colleagues has become the foundation for most packet broadcast systems in use today, including Ethernet and various satellite transmission systems. In March 1995, Abramson received the IEEE's Kobayashi award for his pioneering work in contention-based systems.

■ Building the First Ethernet at Xerox PARC (1972–1977)

Ethernet as we know it today started in July 1972, when Bob Metcalfe, a recent graduate from the Massachusetts Institute of Technology, went to work at the Computer Science Laboratory of the Xerox Palo Alto Research Center (PARC). PARC is the world-famous Xerox research facility located south of San Francisco, close to Stanford University. In 1972, PARC researchers had already invented the world's first laser printer, called EARS, and the first PC with a graphical user interface called ALTO (as in Palo Alto). Metcalfe was hired by Xerox as PARC's networking specialist, and Metcalfe's first job was to connect the Xerox ALTO computer to the Arpanet. (The Arpanet was the predecessor of the Internet.) In the fall of 1972, Metcalfe was visiting the Arpanet program manager in Washington, D.C., and stumbled across Abramson's earlier work on the ALOHA system. While reading Abramson's famous 1970 paper on the ALOHA model, Metcalfe realized that Abramson had made some questionable assumptions and that through optimization, the efficiency of the ALOHA system could be increased to almost 100 percent. Metcalfe later received his Ph.D from Harvard for his work on packet-based transmission theory.

In late 1972, Metcalfe and David Boggs designed a network to connect the various ALTO and later NOVA computers to the EARS laser printer. During the development cycle Metcalfe referred to his work as the ALTO ALOHA network, because it was based on the ALOHA system and connected numerous ALTO computers. The ALTO ALOHA Network, the world's first local area network for personal computers, first ran on May 22, 1973. That day Metcalfe wrote a memo announcing that he was changing the name to Ethernet, after the "luminiferous ether through which electromagnetic radiation was once thought to propagate." The original experimental PARC Ethernet ran at 2.94 Mbps (megabits per second), a rather odd number. This speed was chosen because the first Ethernet interfaces were clocked using the ALTO system clock, which meant sending a pulse every 340 nanoseconds, translating to 2.94 Mbps. Ethernet was a big improvement over the original ALOHA network—it featured *carrier-sense*, meaning that a station would listen first before transmitting its own data stream; and an improved retransmission scheme, allowing a network utilization of almost 100 percent.

By 1976, the experimental Ethernet had grown to connect 100 nodes at PARC, running over a 1,000–meter-long thick coaxial cable. Xerox, which was busy trying to turn Ethernet into a product, called it the Xerox wire; but in 1979, when DEC, Intel, and Xerox got together to standardize it, the name reverted back to Ethernet. In July of that year, Metcalfe and Boggs published the now-famous paper called "Ethernet: Distributed Packet Switching for Local Area Networks" in the Communications of the American Computing Machinery (ACM). On December 13, 1977, Metcalfe, Boggs, C.P.Thacker, and B.W.Lampson received U.S. Patent No. 4,063,220 for their "Multipoint Data Communication System with Collision Detection." Ethernet was born.

■ DEC, Intel, and Xerox Standardize Ethernet (1979–1983)

By the late 1970s, dozens of different local area network technologies had emerged, and Ethernet was only one of them. Besides Ethernet, the most prominent were Data General's MCA, Network Systems Corporation's Hyperchannel, Datapoint's ARCnet, and Corvus's Omninet. What made Ethernet the ultimate victor was not technical superiority or speed, but Metcalfe's vision to turn Ethernet into an industry standard.

In early 1979, Metcalfe, having recently rejoined Xerox PARC again after a two-year absence, received a phone call from Gordon Bell at Digital Equipment Corporation. Bell wanted to talk about how Digital and Xerox could work together on building Ethernet LANs. At this point, working together with different vendors to promote Ethernet seemed like a good idea, but Metcalfe's hands were tied since Xerox, being notoriously protective of its patents, restricted him from working with DEC. Metcalfe suggested that DEC directly approach Xerox management about turning Ethernet into an industry standard. Xerox went for it.

One of the obstacles to getting DEC and Xerox working together on an industry standard was antitrust legislation. Howard Charney, an attorney and a friend of Metcalfe's from the MIT days, recommended that Metcalfe turn over the actual Ethernet technology to a standards organization. (Later that year Charney would become co-founder of 3Com, and today he is CEO of Grand Junction Networks.)

On a trip to the National Bureau of Standards (NBS) in Washington, D.C., Metcalfe met up with engineers from Intel Corporation, who were visiting the NBS to find new applications for its state-of-the-art 25-MHz VLSI NMOS integrated circuit process technology. The fit was obvious—Xerox would provide the technology, DEC would add systems engineering capability and become a supplier of Ethernet hardware, and Intel would provide Ethernet silicon building blocks. Soon afterwards, Metcalfe left Xerox to become a full-time corporate marriage broker and entrepreneur. By June 1979, DEC, Intel, and Xerox were contemplating trilateral meetings; in the fall of 1979, the first meetings actually took place. On September 30, 1980, Digital Equipment Corporation, Intel, and Xerox published the third draft of "The Ethernet, A Local Area Network: Data Link Layer and Physical Layer Specifications, Version 1.0." This became the now-famous Ethernet Blue Book, also known as the DIX (for *DEC*, *Intel*, *Xerox*) Ethernet V1.0 specification. The experimental Ethernet originally ran at 2.94 Mbps, then DIX specified 20 Mbps, and then the speed was reduced to 10 Mbps again. Over the next two years DIX refined the standard, culminating with the Ethernet Version 2.0 specification, which was published in 1982.

During the same time that DIX started work on Ethernet, the Institute of Electrical and Electronic Engineers (IEEE), a worldwide professional organization, formed a committee to define and promote industry LAN standards, with a focus on office environments. This committee was called Project 802. The DIX consortium had produced the Ethernet specifications, but not an internationally accepted standard. In June 1981, the IEEE Project 802 decided to form the 802.3 subcommittee to produce an internationally accepted standard based on the DIX work. One-and-a-half years later, on December 19, 1982, 19 companies announced the new IEEE 802.3 draft standard. In 1983, this draft was finalized as the IEEE 10BASE5 standard. 802.3 is technically different from DIX Ethernet 2.0, but the differences are minor. Today Ethernet and 802.3 are considered synonymous. In the process Xerox turned over its four Ethernet patents to the IEEE, and today anyone can license Ethernet for a fixed fee of $1,000 from the IEEE. In 1984 the U.S. Federal Government adopted 802.3 as FIPS PUB 107. International recognition for the IEEE standard 802.3 came in 1989 when the International Organization for Standards (ISO) adopted Ethernet as standard number IS88023, assuring world-wide presence.

■ 3Com Productizes Ethernet (1980–1982)

While DEC, Intel, and Xerox engineers were still finalizing the Ethernet specifications, Metcalfe was already pursuing other entrepeneurial interests. Metcalfe even turned down Steve Jobs's offer to join Apple Computer to develop networks. In June 1979, Metcalfe, Charney, Ron Crane, Greg Shaw, and Bill Kraus founded the Computer, Communication and Compatibility Corporation, better known today as 3Com Corporation.

In August 1980, 3Com announced its first product, a commercial version of TCP/IP for UNIX. The product shipped in December 1980. A business plan was written, and in February 1981, 3Com received venture capital funding. By March 1981, 18 months before the official standard was published, 3Com was already shipping its first 802-compliant hardware product, the 3C100 transceiver. Later on in 1981, the company started selling transceivers and cards for DEC PDP/11s and VAXes, as well as Intel Multibus and Sun Microsystems machines.

The original business plan that Metcalfe had presented to his venture capitalists in 1980 was based on the concept of developing Ethernet adapters for the new personal computers that were sprouting up all over the world. By 1981, Metcalfe was talking to all of the major PC companies about building Ethernet adapters, including IBM and Apple. Steve Jobs at Apple was quick to say yes, and 3Com's first Ethernet product for Apple shipped a year later. The Apple Ethernet devices, called Apple Boxes, were unwieldy boxes connected to the Apple II's parallel port; they were a market failure. IBM, which had made history that year by announcing the original IBM PC, said no to 3Com because the company was busy inventing its own Token Ring network. However, 3Com decided to proceed without IBM's cooperation, and started developing the EtherLink ISA adapter. Eighteen months later, on September 29, 1982, the first EtherLink shipped, along with the appropriate DOS driver software.

The first EtherLink was a technical breakthrough for many reasons:

- The EtherLink network interface card was made possible through advances in silicon technology. In 1981, 3Com had entered into a silicon partnership with a start-up called Seeq Technologies. Seeq had promised its VLSI technology could deliver a chip that would contain most of the discrete controller functions on one single chip, reducing the number and cost of the components on the board, and freeing up sufficient space so that the transceiver could be integrated on board. In mid-1982, the EtherLink became the first network interface card (NIC) to incorporate an Ethernet VLSI controller chip—the Seeq 8001.

- The Seeq chip meant lower cost, so 3Com was able to price the EtherLink at $950, which was far less than other card and transceiver combination had previously sold for.

- More importantly, the EtherLink became the first Ethernet adapter for the IBM PC; this represents a milestone in the history of Ethernet, because the Ethernet transceiver is included on the adapter card itself. This radical concept, called Thin Ethernet, was invented by the EtherLink design engineer Ron Crane and became a de facto standard soon afterwards. It had numerous benefits: It eliminated the need for an external transceiver and transceiver cable, was cheaper, and made networking much more user friendly, since thin coaxial cable was easier to install and use.

Metcalfe's decision to focus on the IBM PC paid off handsomely for 3Com. IBM had designed the IBM PC to be primarily a home computer. Instead, companies started buying the PC, not home users. Demand for the PC exceeded expectations—by 1982, the IBM PC was shipping 200,000 units a month, three times the company's original forecasts, and it took IBM's factories over 2½ years to catch up with demand. By early 1983, the IBM XT shipped, and IBM captured 75 percent of the business market for PCs. What IBM failed to realize early on was that companies would want to network their personal computers. By 1983, EtherLink sales were booming; and in 1984, 3Com was able to file for its first public offering of stock.

3Com, ICL (International Computers Limited), and Hewlett-Packard later submitted the concept of Thin Ethernet to the IEEE, which adopted it as an official standard in 1984, calling it 10BASE2.

■ StarLAN: A Great Idea, Except for Its Speed (1984–1987)

Thin Ethernet was superior in most ways to regular Ethernet—thin Ethernet replaced the expensive thick yellow coaxial cable with a cheaper, thinner, and more manageable coaxial cable. In addition, most thin Ethernet NICs had the transceiver built in, translating into easier installation and lower costs.

But thin Ethernet still had some major drawbacks. For example, if the coaxial cable was accidentally severed or otherwise disconnected by a user (something that occurred pretty regularly), the entire network would come to a halt. In addition, proper termination at both ends of the network was required. Network reconfiguration in particular was a problem—if a user physically moved, the network cable had to be rerouted to follow the user. This was often inconvenient and disruptive to other users.

In late 1983, Bob Galin from Intel started working with AT&T and NCR to cooperate on running Ethernet over unshielded twisted-pair (UTP) telephone cable. NCR proposed a bus topology similar to that of thin Ethernet, but AT&T, being a telephone company, favored a star configuration, similar to the existing telephone wiring infrastructure. In early 1984, 14 other companies started participating in the UTP Ethernet initiative. Lots of discussions followed, mainly centered around how fast Ethernet would be able to run over UTP wire. Bob Conte from AT&T's Bell Labs in New Jersey was able to prove that a slower version of Ethernet, around 1–2 Mbps, could be run over Category 3 wiring and still meet EMI regulations and crosstalk limitations.

Some vendors were strongly opposed to this reduction in speed to 10 percent of regular Ethernet and quickly lost interest. 3Com and DEC, two leaders in Ethernet, were among them. Other participants argued that 1 Mbps was fast enough for PC networks featuring IBM PC and XT machines. After many heated technical discussions the group voted to scale Ethernet back to 1 Mbps.

Ten companies decided to proceed with 1 Mbps Ethernet and approached the IEEE. The IEEE 802 group chartered the StarLAN task force, chaired by Galin. By the middle of 1986, 1BASE5 was approved as a new IEEE 802.3 standard (StarLAN could support distances of up to 250 meters from hub to node, and the *5* in *1BASE5* stands for 500 meters node to node).

The Demise of StarLAN

By 1986, numerous vendors, lead by Hewlett-Packard and AT&T, were shipping StarLAN hubs and NICs. StarLAN actually shipped several million connections in the 1980s, but many vendors, including 3Com and DEC, had decided early on that 1 Mbps was too slow—in an industry that was getting used to doubling performance every two years, some customers and vendors perceived 1 Mbps Ethernet as a step backwards. (In 1984, IBM had announced the PC AT, based on Intel's 80286 microprocessor. Two years later in 1986, the year that the StarLAN/1BASE5 standard was approved, Intel had already introduced the 80386 microprocessor, a 32-bit CPU that was many times more powerful than the previous-generation 80286.) As a result, StarLAN was never able to gain significant enough industry or market momentum to get off the ground properly. The final demise of StarLAN came in 1987, when SynOptics introduced LATTISNET and delivered full-speed 10 Mbps Ethernet performance over regular telephone wire. Soon afterwards, LATTISNET was standardized by the IEEE as Twisted Pair Ethernet, also known as 10BASE-T; StarLAN's days were numbered.

Credit needs to be given to StarLAN and Galin for pioneering the concept of Ethernet over unshielded twisted pair and star-shaped wiring.

■ The History of 10BASE-T and Structured Wiring (1986–1990)

By the mid-1980s, the PC revolution really had picked up steam. By 1986, personal computer sales were booming as applications began to drive demand. Lotus 1-2-3 had become the "killer application" for the IBM PC AT—every business had to have it. Apple's Macintosh, launched in 1986, was starting to sell briskly because it offered an unparalleled graphical user interface. People wanted to print their spreadsheets and desktop publishing creations on the expensive shared laser printers, so networking sales were booming as well.

Two events occurred that gave Ethernet another boost. In 1985, Novell started shipping NetWare, a high-performance operating system designed exclusively for networking IBM-compatible personal computers. The other event was, of course, 10BASE-T, full-speed 10-Mbps Ethernet running over unshielded twisted-pair telephone wire.

Fiber Ethernet and UTP Ethernet

The first Ethernet network, invented by Metcalfe and Boggs at the Xerox PARC in 1973, utilized a thick coaxial cable. A few years later, Metcalfe and Eric Rawson proved that a CSMA-type signal could be run over fiber-optic cable.

In the early 1980s, fiber optic cabling experienced a surge in popularity; Xerox decided to investigate running Ethernet over fiber optic cable after Ethernet was standardized in 1983. Eric Rawson was appointed as the project leader for Fiber Ethernet, joined by Ron Schmidt soon afterwards. Rawson and Schmidt discovered that Ethernet could indeed be run over fiber, but only in a star configuration, not the typical Ethernet-bus topology. The star configuration was a breakthrough in its own right, because it allowed for structured wiring, where a single wire connects every node to the central hub (Figure 1.1). This has obvious advantages in terms of installation, troubleshooting, and reconfiguration, reducing cost of installation and ownership for the entire network.

Figure 1.1

A structured cabling system with nodes arranged in a star configuration around a central hub.

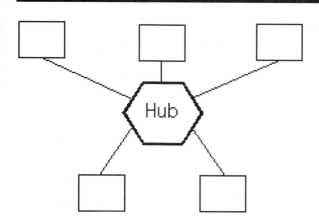

Structured Wiring: StarLAN and Token Ring

In 1985, IBM started shipping its 4-Mbps Token Ring LAN—six years after Metcalfe had originally approached IBM about building Ethernet network adapters for the IBM PC, and almost three years after the first ISA Ether-Link shipped. Although Token Ring was less than half the speed of 10-Mbps Ethernet, it had one major advantage over Ethernet—it was based on a structured cabling system, which incorporates a central concentrator or hub and shielded twisted-pair (STP) wire to connect to the nodes.

By 1986, StarLAN, which also utilized a structured cabling system, was shipped. Unfortunately StarLAN ran at only 1 Mbps, 10% of Ethernet speed, and was not a viable replacement for regular 10-Mbps Ethernet or 4-Mbps Token Ring. However, the appearance of Token Ring and StarLAN made it clear that the future was in twisted-pair wiring and centralized wiring hubs. In 1985 Schmidt at PARC modified the Fiber Ethernet hardware to run over STP as well. The disadvantages of IBM's STP cable were its cost and bulkiness when compared with regular UTP wiring. Later that year Schmidt did some experiments showing that Ethernet could also be made to run over regular UTP cable.

SynOptics Communications Is Founded

Back in 1983, Schmidt had started searching for a business unit within Xerox to make a product of Fiber Ethernet, but his search was unsuccessful. However, Schmidt's search for a product group was successful in another respect—he found a business planner at Xerox by the name of Andy Ludwig. By the summer of 1985, Schmidt and Ludwig had come to an agreement with Xerox whereby the two of them could start their own company, with Xerox being a minority shareholder. Venture capital was secured, and in November 1985 eight Xerox employees, led by Schmidt and Ludwig, left the company to start ASTRA communications in order to sell structured wiring Fiber and STP Ethernet hubs. (The name ASTRA didn't last very long, as NEC had already trademarked the name and was threatening to sue the new company for trademark violations. The name *SynOptics Communications* was proposed by one of the board's directors after browsing through a dictionary and coming across the word *synopsis*.)

10BASE-T Is Approved as an IEEE Standard

In 1986, SynOptics started working on 10-Mbps Ethernet over UTP telephone cable. The first SynOptics products, called LATTISNET, shipped on August 17, 1987, the same day that the IEEE 802.3 working group got together to discuss the best way to implement 10-Mbps Ethernet over UTP, later to be called 10BASE-T.

In addition to the SynOptics LATTISNET scheme, many competing proposals were submitted, the most notable being from 3Com/DEC and Hewlett-Packard. For over three years, engineers from around the world met regularly under the IEEE 802.3 umbrella to find the best implementation of 10-Mbps Ethernet running over UTP. In the end, the IEEE agreed to a standard that was based on Hewlett-Packard's multiport repeater proposal and an improved version of the SynOptics LATTISNET technology. On September 28, 1990, the new 802.3i/10BASE-T standard was officially adopted. The next year, Ethernet sales nearly doubled, fueled largely by new 10BASE-T repeaters, twisted-pair medium attachment units (MAUs), and NICs.

The advent of the star wiring configuration was a significant milestone for Ethernet. First of all, Ethernet started looking more and more like a telephone system, with a central switch located in the wiring closet and dedicated wires running to each node. Secondly, IBM's Token Ring had lost two of its advantages—the structured cabling approach and use of twisted-pair wiring. Until as late as 1992, many industry and market research analysts erroneously predicted that Token Ring would one day outship Ethernet. The truth is that Token Ring's future was dealt a fatal blow when in December 1987, an eight-person start-up called SynOptics shipped its first Ethernet hubs to Texas Instruments and the Boeing aircraft company.

Novell NetWare: The Networked "Killer Application"

In the early 1980s, a small software company in Provo, Utah called Novell developed a network operating system called NetWare. Almost overnight NetWare became the "killer app" for offices, allowing PCs to access shared printers, send e-mail, exchange files, and access central databases.

In 1989, Novell sold its NIC business; but at the same time, it started licensing its Novell Engineering (NE) Ethernet adapter card designs to anybody that wanted them, thereby enabling a huge NE2000 clone business to emerge similar to the IBM PC clone industry. All of a sudden, companies operating out of their garage could get into the NIC business by buying the chips from National Semiconductor and licensing the name, the design, and the appropriate software from Novell. Some companies didn't even bother licensing the design, and just bought the 8390 chips from National Semiconductor and shipped the cards without software, labeling them "NE2000-compatible." Fierce competition among the NE2000 clones on the one hand and 3Com on the other drove prices down radically. By 1988, there were literally dozens of NE2000 card manufacturers in business, and Ethernet NICs could be purchased for as little $200, whereas IBM's Token Ring cards cost over $1,000. By 1990, some NE2000 vendors such as Western Digital (later SMC) and a consortium of Taiwanese companies even started cloning the National 8390 Ethernet chip itself. The result was that Ethernet sales just kept on growing, fueled by lower prices, broader vendor availability, and innovation resulting from the pressure of competition.

The Demise of Token Ring

By the late 1980s, not even IBM could ignore Ethernet any more; the company started selling Microchannel Ethernet adapters for its personal computers and AS/400 minicomputers, providing customers with connectivity options they had been asking for for almost ten years. Another example of how IBM had to adapt to the changing world was the RS/6000 engineering workstation line. Sun Microsystems, the workstation leader, had long ago adopted Ethernet as the standard, building it into every machine. In 1991, IBM's Austin, Texas workstation division did the unthinkable and adopted Ethernet as its standard—the RS/6000 machine came equipped with an Intel 32-bit Ethernet coprocessor built in.

Only in the 1990s did IBM's networking division come to the realization that Token Ring would not replace Ethernet and that its strategy had failed. At this point, Ethernet was outshipping Token Ring by a ratio of 3:1, and the trend was accelerating. In a last-minute attempt, IBM tried to stop the market share erosion by copying the Novell NE2000/National 8390 clone strategy. In 1992, the company licensed its Token Ring chipset to National Semiconductor to generate a broad-based, cheap clone industry. But by 1992 it was all over for Token Ring—Ethernet had become the de facto standard for local area networks in small and large companies around the world. In four years, Ethernet sales had grown tenfold, from 1 million units in 1988 to 10 million units in 1992—a phenomenal growth rate.

Some view IBM's Token Ring strategy as one of the company's biggest strategic mistakes, comparable to the company's disastrous attempts to distance itself from the clones with the PS/2 and the Microchannel architecture.

■ Ethernet Switching and Full-Duplex Emerge (1990–1994)

Three market factors were driving the network infrastructure in the late 1980s:

1. More PCs were added to networks, resulting in higher traffic levels.

2. More PCs and faster PCs were sold, also resulting in more traffic.

3. Multiple Ethernet LANs were being connected. Due to the shared media technology of Ethernet, joining up these different LANs increased traffic significantly.

Two-port bridges (connecting only two LANs), which are almost as old as Ethernet itself, became popular during this time to connect LANs while keeping traffic levels manageable. By the late 1980s, a new type of bridge was emerging—the intelligent multiport bridge. Alantec, Synernetics, Racal-Milgo, Clearpoint, and others were selling intelligent multiport bridges, but in 1990, a radically different bridge appeared—the Kalpana EtherSwitch EPS-700.

The EtherSwitch was very different from most other bridges at the time for a number of reasons.

- The EtherSwitch used a new bridging technology called *cut-through* (versus the store-and-forward technology conventional bridges used). This improved delay times through the switch by an order of magnitude.

- The switch consisted of an architecture that allowed for multiple simultaneous data transmission paths, just like a telephone switch, improving overall throughput significantly.

- What ultimately made Kalpana famous is the fact that the company founders Vinod Bhardwaj and Larry Blair took a very different approach to marketing their product. The EtherSwitch was sold as a networking switch to boost LAN performance, rather than as a bridge to interconnect different LANs. The differences were subtle, but almost overnight the EtherSwitch created a new market category—the network switch.

Full-Duplex Ethernet

In 1993 Kalpana fostered another breakthrough—full-duplex Ethernet. Regular shared-media Ethernet works only in half-duplex mode. A station is either transmitting or receiving, but not doing both at once. Shared Ethernet depends on a single shared media connection for all users, and simultaneous transmitting and receiving is technically not possible. A switched or point-point 10BASE-T connection, on the other hand, can be operated in such a way as to make simultaneous transmitting and receiving possible. The benefits of full-duplex were obvious—transmitting and receiving simultaneously can theoretically double the data transmission rate. Kalpana added this feature to its hubs, and full-duplex is likely to become a standard for switching hubs and server NICs in the future. The IEEE 802.3 working group is currently investigating full-duplex as an official standard, and this work should be complete by the end of 1995.

■ Fast Ethernet Emerges (1992–1995)

Network switches were excellent devices for reducing network congestion, but each Ethernet switch could only deliver a maximum of 10-Mbps throughput per port. The only serious contender for applications requiring more than 10-Mbps throughput was Fiber Distributed Data Interface (FDDI), an expensive

100-Mbps-fiber-based LAN. Administrators of larger networks were starting to implement FDDI network backbones and FDDI server connections; and, in some instances, they were even connecting clients or workstations to an FDDI ring. In the 1980s, companies like Digital Equipment Corporation, Advanced Micro Devices (AMD), National Semiconductor, and IBM poured millions of dollars into FDDI semiconductor and product development. In 1991 Sun Microsystems even considered adding an FDDI connection to every SPARCstation machine (All Sun SPARCstations already have a 10-Mbps Ethernet connection built in). Unfortunately, FDDI never achieved the volumes necessary to drive prices down enough. At the same time Ethernet prices continued to plummet, driven by phenomenal growth. Some networking companies started building switching hubs that contained both high-speed FDDI and Ethernet ports. Crescendo Communications was one of these—it built a workgroup switch that featured both FDDI and switched 10BASE-T ports.

In August 1991, Howard Charney, now retired from 3Com Corporation; David Boggs, co-inventor of Ethernet; Ron Crane, inventor of Thin Ethernet and lead engineer of the first EtherLink network adapter at 3Com; and Larry Birenbaum, also an ex-3Com engineering vice president, were brainstorming the idea of founding a new company. The idea was to start selling networking test equipment, but during the conversation Birenbaum asked if Ehternet could be run at ten times its original speed. Crane, having researched this concept before, answered "Yes, it can!" Boggs agreed. The rest is history—on February 28, 1992, Charney, Birenbaum, and others founded Grand Junction Networks to design, build, and market high-speed Ethernet equipment. On the board of directors were Metcalfe, Charney, and three venture capitalists. The company was located in Fremont, California, about 20 minutes from the Silicon Valley. Grand Junction immediately began work on 100-Mbps Ethernet.

By late 1992, word was starting to spread that a startup company in California was working on 100-Mbps Fast Ethernet technology. Grand Junction hence decided to make public its work on 100-Mbps Ethernet in September 1992.

The IEEE 802.3 100-Mbps Standards Wars

On November 9, 1982, the IEEE project 802 convened in San Diego for its plenary meeting. One of the agenda items was the topic of higher-speed networks. Two technical proposals were presented: one was from Grand Junction Networks, which proposed retaining the existing Ethernet protocol. This approach was endorsed by 3Com Corporation, Sun Microsystems, and SynOptics. The second proposal came from Hewlett-Packard and detailed a completely new MAC (medium access) protocol for 100-Mbps transmission. This marked the start of the "Fast Ethernet wars."

During 1993, the IEEE's high-speed study group continued its work on 100 Mbps. Various proposals were made, but the main issue was still to be re-solved—would the 802.3 group adopt a new MAC as proposed by Hewlett-Packard, or would the Ethernet CSMA/CD MAC be retained? Most mem-bers of the group were in favor of retaining Ethernet, but the required major-ity of 75 percent could not be garnered, so the debate continued. Grand Junction, Intel, LAN Media, SynOptics, Cabletron, National Semiconductor, Standard Micro Systems (SMC), Sun Microsystems, and 3Com soon grew tired of the endless debates and political gridlock in the IEEE standards and got together to pick up the pace. As a result, the Fast Ethernet Alliance was founded "to advance 100-Mbps Ethernet solutions based on the original Ethernet standard." This pitted the entire industry against Hewlett-Packard and AT&T.

Unfortunately, Hewlett-Packard and AT&T refused to retain the CSMA/ CD Ethernet protocol for 100-Mbps transmission, insisting that its demand-priority protocol was the better way to go. To clear the impasse the IEEE al-located a new group called 802.12 for the Demand Priority Access Method. The events below followed:

- In October the FEA published its 100BASE-X interoperability specifica-tion, today known as 100BASE-TX. That same month Grand Junction became the first company to ship the first world's Fast Ethernet hubs and NICs—the FastSwitch 10/100 and FastNIC100.

- In May 1994, Intel and SynOptics announced and demonstrated Fast Ethernet equipment.

- For most of 1994, the IEEE 802.3 group was busy working on other parts of the 100-Mbps Ethernet standard, such as 100BASE-T4, MII, re-peater, and full-duplex.

- During the same year, the fast Ethernet Alliance, an industry group chartered with advancing Ethernet as a technology, grew to over 60 members. Numerous initial supporters of the new 802.12 technology also abandoned Demand Priority altogether or publicly endorsed both technologies.

- By late 1994, Intel, Sun Microsystems, and Networth started shipping 100BASE-TX-compliant products.

- In the first quarter of 1995, Cogent, 3Com, Digital Equipment Corpora-tion, SMC, Accton, SynOptics/Bay Networks, and others followed.

- In March 1995, the IEEE 802.3u specification was approved by its mem-bers and the Executive committee. Fast Ethernet had arrived.

Table 1.1 illustrates the evolution of the Ethernet standard over the last 13 years.

Table 1.1

The Evolution of the
Ethernet Standard

ETHERNET STANDARD	IEEE SPEC	YEAR APPROVED	SPEED
10BASE5	802.3	1983	10 Mbps
10BASE2	802.3a	1988	10 Mbps
1BASE5	802.3c	1988	1 Mbps
10BASE-T	802.3i	1990	10 Mbps
10BROAD36	802.3b	1988	10 Mbps
10BASEF/FOIRL	802.3i	1992	10 Mbps
100BASE-T	802.3u	1995	100 Mbps

Table 1.1

The Evolution of the
Ethernet Standard
(continued)

STATIONS/ SEGMENT	TOPOLOGY	SEGMENT LENGTH (M)	MEDIUM SUPPORT
100	Bus	500	50 ohm coaxial (thick)
30	Bus	> 185	50 ohm coaxial (thin)
12/hub	Star	250	100 ohm 2-pair Cat3
12/hub	Star	100	100 ohm 2-pair Cat3
100	Bus	1,800	75 ohm coaxial
	Star	2,000	2 strands multimode or mono-mode fiber
1024	Star	100	2-pair 100 ohm Cat5 or 150 ohm Cat1
		100+	4-pair 100 ohm Cat3/4/5
		2,000	2 strands multimode fiber

- *The Contenders*
- *Migration Issues*
- *Comparing the Technologies*
- *Conclusion*
- *What If I Am a Token Ring User?*

2

The Future of
High-Speed Communications

T ODAY YOU AS A LAN MANAGER ARE FACED WITH AN ABUNDANCE of technologies and standards, some proven and some still very immature. FDDI, TCNS, Switched Ethernet, Fast Ethernet/100BASE-T, isoEthernet, ATM, 100VG-AnyLAN, Switched Token Ring—which one is really for you? Different vendors are all advocating different solutions, claiming that theirs is the logical choice. The reality is that these different technologies have created a tremendous amount of confusion in most people's minds, and it has become quite a challenge to distinguish vendor hype from reality.

This chapter will start off with a brief overview of the different high-speed technology choices available today. Choosing the right high-speed technology to migrate to is a strategic decision that requires careful consideration. The second part of this chapter will discuss the different selection criteria that you as an Ethernet LAN manager need to think about when selecting your next-generation high-speed LAN standard. The last section of the book will discuss in more detail each of the different high-speed options and how we rate each of them in terms of being a viable upgrade options for an overloaded Ethernet network.

This book has been written from the perspective of an Ethernet user. We have included a short section for Token Ring LAN managers at the end of this chapter.

■ The Contenders

This section will briefly introduce the high-speed technologies available today. A more in-depth discussion follows later on in the chapter.

In today's shared Ethernet networks, multiple users or devices have to share the same bandwidth. Reducing the number of stations by subdividing or bridging the network increases the bandwidth available to each station. Taken to the extreme, the entire network bandwidth becomes dedicated to one particular client or server. This is known as *Switched, point-point, private,* or *personal Ethernet.* A Switched Ethernet hub uses the existing NICs and a new switching hub to provide each client or server with dedicated 10-Mbps bandwidth.

Moving from a shared Ethernet network to Switched Ethernet is easy as it involves only replacing the hub—the existing NIC and cabling can be used. As a result of this easy migration, Switched Ethernet has become the most popular high-speed technology for servers and power users. Switched Ethernet hubs have been shipping since 1990.

100BASE-T is 10-Mbps Ethernet that has been modified to run at 100 Mbps. 100BASE-T uses the same framing format as 10-Mbps Ethernet, supports shared media as well as switching, and has a star configuration similar to that of 10BASE-T. 100BASE-T utilizes STP or UTP cabling of up to 100 meters, and fiber with lengths of up to 2 kilometers. 100BASE-T was standardized by the same IEEE group that developed Ethernet. Shared and switched 100BASE-T products have been shipping since late 1993.

Fiber Distributed Data Interface (FDDI) is a stable and proven 100-Mbps LAN technology that was developed in the late 1980s and is now an official American National Standards Institute (ANSI) standard. FDDI was developed as a high-speed network with a focus on reliability and fiber cabling. FDDI is very similar to Token Ring in that it uses a token-passing protocol.

For added reliability, a second redundant counterrotating ring is part of the standard. FDDI was developed at a time when people thought that fiber would replace copper wiring, but twisted pair wiring became so popular that FDDI now supports STP and UTP also. FDDI has become the de facto standard for new high-speed backbone installations. FDDI, just like Ethernet and Token Ring, can be switched, but the only FDDI switching hub we know of is made by Digital.

TCNS, which stands for *Thomas-Conrad Networking System*, is a proprietary 100-Mbps solution from Thomas-Conrad Corporation in Austin, Texas. TCNS is based on the ANSI 2.5Mbps ArcNET 878.1 specification. TCNS supports fiber, coaxial cable, STP and, since late 1994, UTP as well. TCNS products have been shipping since 1990.

100VG-AnyLAN is a new 100-Mbps shared-media technology that was developed by HP and AT&T Microelectronics from 1991-1994. 100VG supports Category 3 UTP, but requires four pairs of wire. 100VG uses a new protocol that incorporates a priority access method allowing time-critical applications to transmit ahead of others. 100VG is an official IEEE 802.12 standard. 100VG products first started shipping in 1994.

ATM, or *Asynchronous Transfer Mode*, is a technology whose origins can be traced to work done in the late 1970s and early 1980s by the research arms of AT&T and the Baby Bells. ATM is an attempt to combine the best features of telephone switching networks with the best features of packet-based data networks. The standardization of ATM is being undertaken by the Consultative Committee for International Telephone and Telegraph (CCITT, the group that standardized ISDN) and the ATM Forum. Numerous vendors have announced and are shipping ATM products, but the ATM standards are too loosely defined at this point and still prevent widespread interoperability among different vendors' products. ATM can run at speeds from 25 Mbps to 622 Mbps and more.

■ Migration Issues

You are the network manager for a LAN that is running out of bandwidth and want to migrate or move your users, servers, and peripherals to a higher-speed network. Unfortunately the number of competing high-speed technologies has created a lot of confusion in the marketplace. Some of these technologies are complementary, while others clearly compete with each other. The following section will outline all the most important issues that you as a network manager ought to consider before deciding on a high-speed technology.

Consider the following issues when considering your options.

Connection Cost

The cost of a new LAN technology should be measured in terms of connection cost, which includes the cost of the NIC and the hub port. Factor into this calculation the cost of network management software and any other new equipment that needs to be purchased.

Performance

Since you purchased a book about high-speed Ethernet options, performance is probably your number one concern. Different vendors measure performance in various ways; here are a few thoughts on how to measure performance.

Wire Speed and Average Throughput Rate

There are different ways to measure performance in shared media networks such as Ethernet. The *wire speed* is the maximum data transmission rate for the network. For Ethernet, it is 10 Mbps, and equals the speed of the data transmission once the node gets onto the network. But since most networks have more than one user, the *average* throughput is significantly less for each user. One way to calculate average throughput is to take the wire speed number and dividing it by the number of stations that share the network. For example, a fully-loaded Ethernet segment that has 200 users contending for the same 10-Mbps channel delivers only 10 Mbps/200 = 0.05 Mbps of average throughput per station. This of course assumes that all stations generate the same traffic all the time, which in reality is never the case. In addition, this assumes a 100 percent efficiency and a 100 percent loading capability, neither of which applies to Ethernet. Due to the chaotic nature of shared Ethernet networks, the average utilization is limited to less than 40 percent, which means that the average throughput rate is limited to about 4 Mbps for a large Ethernet network. For switched networks, the average throughput can approach wire speed, since a switched network does not share the random nature of a shared network.

Full-Duplex (FDX) Throughput

Full-duplex means that data can be simultaneously transmitted and received, effectively doubling the nominal throughput. Full-duplex is a relatively new phenomenon for data networks, having been made possible by twisted-pair and fiber cabling where one pair sends and the second pair receives data. Co-axial cable, on the other hand, uses one wire for either transmitting or receiving, and hence cannot accommodate full-duplex traffic. Many Ethernet vendors now advertise FDX as a feature and claim 20 Mbps throughput. While this is true in theory, the reality is that today's network operating systems, protocol stacks, and device drivers all still work in the half-duplex mode, an inheritance from the coaxial cabling days. The other point to note is that full-duplex works only in a switched environment where both stations can support this capability. Switch-switch connections operating in full-duplex mode can yield close to a 100 percent improvement, but shared media or server connections will show hardly any improvement at all. This will change over time as networking software is upgraded.

Quality of Service

Quality of Service, or *QOS*, is a relatively new buzzword in the LAN industry, but has been in existence in the communications industry for quite some time. QOS means that the recipient of the data gets the data *when* and *where* they need it. Telephone companies measure QOS in terms of delay time, signal-to-noise ratio, echo, wrong numbers dialed, and so on. QOS never used to be important for data networks and with today's networked applications it is mostly not an issue. Take a very busy Ethernet network as an example, where a user is trying to send an e-mail over the network. The sender wants to transmit their data stream right away, but cannot because the LAN is busy. At some point a time slot becomes available on the wire and the transmission occurs. This process is transparent to the receiver, who doesn't care or know that the e-mail message has arrived a fraction of a second later.

QOS is becoming more important because today's data networks are increasingly utilized for time-critical applications like real-time voice and video transmissions. Latencies are acceptable for time-critical applications as long as they are relatively small and *constant*—for example, a voice transmission with a constant delay of 0.1 second from sender to receiver will not be noticed. *Variable* delays are difficult for multimedia transmissions. A changing *latency* is not acceptable because it will make the audio transmission sound like a tape recorder whose speed is varying permanently, a sign of bad quality. Video picture quality in particular is susceptible to variable latencies.

In general, dedicated connections provide the best quality of service, allowing for guaranteed bandwidth and constant delay times. All shared media technologies inherently exhibit variable latencies, because the transmission channel is shared with other users.

Ease of Migration

To assure an easy migration, ask yourself these five questions:

- Can my cabling plant support the higher-speed networking technology?

- How do I upgrade my existing users to give them a performance boost with minimum cost and disruption?

- How do I connect new users or servers to the new network infrastructure?

- How do I join up the new section of my network with the older part?

- What happens to the replaced equipment? Can I use it somewhere else in my LAN?

Let's talk about these one at a time.

Before you decide to purchase high-speed networking hardware, make sure you understand the capabilities of your cabling plant. Your investment in cable, conduits, wiring closets, patch panels, and so on can exceed the cost of the networking hardware itself! You need to make sure that your new high-speed networking gear can run on your existing wiring wherever possible. If that's not the case, factor in potentially huge additional costs for upgrading your cabling plant to accommodate the new LAN standard.

Most LAN managers will want to keep as much of their existing equipment as possible since it's working, proven, and already paid for. Replacing equipment is always disruptive and time-consuming and should be avoided wherever possible. For example, replacing network adapters should be avoided at all cost—while the cost of a new NIC alone may not seem that high, the cost of installation, configuration, and associated user disruption often exceeds the cost of the NIC itself. If the performance of the network can be increased by replacing a single hub instead, choose that way.

Replacing equipment prematurely should also be avoided. Networking gear is part of a company's capital budget, meaning that the equipment needs to last for a period of five years before it is in effect paid for. Your accountants will tell you that replacing equipment before the five-year depreciation period is over can be prohibitively expensive because the equipment needs to be depreciated in one go for those purposes, a costly undertaking.

When you add new users to your network, you will want to choose the best available equipment at the time. These new users will likely have faster machines, requiring a higher-speed network connection.

New users and servers will need to be integrated seamlessly into the existing network. Will you need to bridge or route? Will this task cause user disruption or server downtime? Don't forget network management—make sure your new networking gear can blend seamlessly into your existing network management map.

Another point to consider when upgrading to a new high-speed LAN is what to do with the old equipment. Often new high-speed equipment is added one step at a time, replacing at least some existing equipment. Your cost analysis needs to comprehend if the replaced equipment can be used somewhere else or if it becomes obsolete.

Familiarity and Maturity of the New Technology

Sometimes it pays to buy something completely new, but remember that there's a steep learning curve associated with every new technology. LAN management is a time-consuming job—stick with what you know as much as possible.

All these new high-speed networking products are great stuff. Unfortunately, history has proven that when new technology debuts, vendors worry first about getting it to market. Maturity, true compatibility, interoperability, and performance optimization only come later, sometimes years later. Only buy state-of-the art equipment if you absolutely have to—if it's a choice of buying proven, five-year old technology for a few bucks more, then absolutely buy the old stuff. Let someone else discover the vendors' bugs.

If you absolutely have to buy state-of-the art equipment, product or technical support from your vendors' engineering department becomes mandatory. Any time you buy new technology you need to factor in additional in-house support costs, as more of your time will be spent with this new equipment.

Multivendor Support

Make sure that whatever you buy is supported by as many vendors as possible. Below are some reasons why you should buy products that are manufactured by multiple vendors.

Lower Prices

Multivendor support means you have choices, and the more choices you have, the better. Vendors are likely to compete more aggressively, ensuring lower prices for you. There's another reason popular technologies will be cheaper—economies of scale. The cost of manufacturing hubs, switches, routers, and NICs decreases radically as the volume of product manufactured increases. That's why good products and standards often become so entrenched in the market—they develop an early lead, prices decline, and the lead widens. Sometimes nothing else short of a technological breakthrough can ever compete again.

Innovation

Choices means that your supplier needs to work harder to earn your dollars. Innovation is just as important as lower prices, because it ensures that future products will provide more features, higher performance, and other improvements that will benefit you in the long run.

Availability of the Necessary Building Blocks

A network consists of many building blocks—hubs, bridges, routers, NICs, clients, servers, MAUs, management software, and so on. No single vendor can supply you with all the building blocks, no matter what they tell you. Choosing technologies with broad vendor support means that you will be able to buy all the building blocks you need for your network, not just some of them.

Single vendor products should be avoided at all cost. Consider for example, what would happen if your single-source vendor decided to stop shipping their product. You would be in trouble because next time you wanted to add or replace a piece of networking hardware you could no longer buy it!

■ Comparing the Technologies

The next section will compare the high-speed technologies available today, and discuss their strengths and weaknesses.

Fiber Distributed Data Interface (FDDI)

FDDI was first developed over ten years ago by mainframe companies such as Sperry, Burroughs, and Control Data Corporation. FDDI was standardized by the ANSI X3T9.5 committee in 1990. FDDI incorporates many features of IBM's Token Ring technology, such as the Token Ring frame format and a shared media ring architecture. FDDI also has sophisticated management, control, and reliability features that are not found in Ethernet or Token Ring. An optional second counterrotating network ring improves overall reliability. This ring is called DAS (dual attached station, as opposed to SAS or single attached station). FDDI supports cable lengths of up to 2km for multimode fiber.

FDDI products first appeared in 1988, and sales have grown steadily ever since. Until recently, FDDI was the only viable high-speed backbone technology available, and some LAN managers have already started connecting servers or even power users to FDDI LANs.

FDDI was created at a time when scientists and engineers were still predicting that fiber cabling would reach every office and home by the year 2000. One of the inventors of FDDI claims that he chose the data rate of 100 Mbps to make FDDI so fast that no copper-based LAN technology would ever be able to match its speed. This is ironic, considering the fact that most FDDI equipment sold today uses UTP wire as a medium. That's because twisted-pair wiring and structured cabling systems replaced coaxial cable as the most popular LAN media almost overnight, preventing fiber cabling from becoming widely accepted. In addition, engineers figured out a way to run FDDI over twisted-pair wiring. This technology is called *TP-PMD*, short for *twisted-pair physical media dependent*. The ANSI TP-PMD standard uses a transmission scheme called *MLT-3*, short for *Multi-Level Transmission 3*. The standard requires two pairs of Category 5 data grade wire and supports a maximum distance of 100 meters. Crescendo Communications named this technology CDDI, short for Copper Distributed Data Interface. IBM and other vendors are also selling FDDI products capable of running on STP cabling, which is predominately used in Token Ring installations. This technology is called SDDI (Shielded Distributed Data Interface).

Strengths of FDDI/CDDI are

- FDDI delivers 100-Mbps throughput capability with little overhead. FDDI is a shared media technology, but unlike Ethernet FDDI does not use a collision-based access method, so there is no performance degradation at high usage rates.

- The FDDI standard was in the making for almost 10 years. Products have been shipping for over five years. So the technology is proven, mature, and well understood.

- FDDI has broad multivendor support. Hundreds of companies from all over the world manufacture FDDI equipment. All the major networking suppliers such as Bay Networks, Cabletron, 3Com, and Cisco offer FDDI products. FDDI chipsets from Motorola, AMD, and National Semiconductor provide a source of semiconductor building blocks to the industry.

Until recently, FDDI has been the only high-speed LAN standard to deliver true 100-Mbps performance. As a result, users, resellers, and manufacturers have all accepted FDDI as the de facto standard for high-speed networking needs.

The weaknesses of FDDI/CDDI are

- FDDI is still very expensive. In 1995, NIC prices range from $500–$1,000 for a SAS CDDI card, and up to $2,000 for a DAS card. An FDDI hub can cost anywhere from $450 to $1,900 per port. The price of FDDI products has remained stubbornly high over the last seven years, and only with the introduction of CDDI have prices started declining. However, compared to newer 100-Mbps technologies, FDDI equipment is still considerably more expensive.

- Customers wanting to upgrade from Ethernet to FDDI face numerous migration issues—in all cases expensive routers are required.

- People view FDDI as a super-high-performance technology that is expensive, and only usable for backbones. While prices have come down, the perception of the technology hasn't. This perception has made customers leery of buying it as a desktop technology.

- FDDI only supports Fiber and Category 5 cable. A large portion of the installed base is still Category 3, which has limited sales, especially within the workgroup.

FDDI II

FDDI II is a standard in the making that is a superset of FDDI. FDDI II offers improved support for multimedia data transmissions. (FDDI II features isochronous data transmission, which means predictable and guaranteed access time. In addition, FDDI II includes a prioritization scheme to ensure low latency, which is nice to have for video transmission in particular). No FDDI II-compatible products are shipping at this point.

We doubt whether any FDDI II products will ever appear on the market as the networking industry focuses on Fast Ethernet and ATM instead.

If you have started installing FDDI/CDDI backbones you should continue to buy CDDI/FDDI equipment. We expect FDDI/CDDI sales to peak in 1995 and decline thereafter as customer chooses 100BASE-T or ATM for installations.

TCNS

TCNS is a proprietary 100-Mbps solution from Thomas-Conrad in Austin, Texas. TCNS is based on the ANSI ArcNET 878.1 specification and uses a token-passing bus access method and operates in a shared media mode. TCNS supports fiber cable of 900 meters, coaxial cable of 150 meters, and STP or UTP of 100 meters. Thomas-Conrad started shipping TCNS NICs and hubs in 1990, and in 1993 over 20,000 TCNS NICs were sold, representing a significant share of the high-speed NIC market. No other vendor builds TCNS-compatible equipment.

Strengths of TCNS are

- It is a proven, mature technology. TCNS has been in production for five years, with an installed base of over 100,000 nodes. Thomas-Conrad is a reputable vendor and delivers products that work.

- It's affordable. Traditionally, TCNS equipment has sold for half the price of FDDI equipment.

Weaknesses of TCNS are

- It has no Category 3 wiring support. Almost 50 percent of the installed base of wiring is Category 3. Until recently TCNS supported fiber and coaxial cable; only last year was UTP Category 5 added. Lack of Category 3 support severely limits widespread desktop deployment.

- Thomas-Conrad is the only vendor selling TCNS equipment today. This makes TCNS a proprietary technology, which has numerous drawbacks. Customers buying single-vendor products put themselves at significant risk, since there is always the possibility that Thomas-Conrad could stop supporting the technology altogether.

- Thomas-Conrad only sells ISA, EISA, and MCA NICs as well as small repeaters. Thomas-Conrad does not offer many critical network building blocks such as PCI, PCMCIA, SBus, and NuBus NICs, routers, chassis hubs, switches, and management software. (The reality is that no single vendor today can offer all the building blocks of a reasonably sized network.) Since customers cannot buy all the elements of a network that are typically needed in order to deploy the technology widely, TCNS will remain a niche product.

- There is no upgrade path from Ethernet. TCNS deployment requires that both NICs and hubs be replaced altogether. This is expensive and time-consuming.

To date, TCNS has been purchased by customers wanting 100-Mbps performance at an affordable price. With the arrival of more affordable, industry-standard, standards-based high-speed solutions, TCNS customers will likely migrate to 100BASE-T over the next few years.

ATM

ATM is a new type of cell-switching technology that is currently under development. ATM is clearly the buzzword of the 1990s, much like ISDN was ten years ago. In fact, ATM is based on Broadband ISDN (B-ISDN) work done at Bellcore and Alcatel Bell in the late 1970s and early 1980s.

ATM, which stands for *Asynchronous Transfer Mode*, is very different from all other common LAN technologies on the market today. Ethernet, Token Ring, TCNS, and FDDI use variable-length packets to transmit data from source to destination. ATM uses fixed-length 53-byte cell-switching to transmit data, voice, and video over both LANs and WANs.

The Consultative Committee for International Telephone and Telegraph (CCITT, the same group that standardized ISDN) and the ATM Forum are in the process of standardizing ATM. Numerous vendors are shipping ATM products, but for the time being the standards allow for too much interpretation by individual vendors, making interoperability a major issue.

ATM is emerging as a strategic and state-of-the art technology for the following reasons:

- ATM is a switching technology; thus it does not suffer from the latency problems of shared media and packet-based transmissions. ATM switching provides dedicated bandwidth to the connection, making ATM ideally suited for emerging time-critical applications such as voice and video.

- ATM will enable virtual LANs, guaranteeing flexible bandwidth when and where it is needed. Easy management, reconfiguration, and trouble-shooting are also going to be part of ATM.

- ATM scales easily. ATM will be available in many different speeds for different applications. The ATM Forum is discussing various proposals that would run at 25, 51, 155, and 622 Mbps. These different options will allow ATM to connect desktops, servers, backbones, and WANs.

- ATM will allow for a seamless integration of LANs and WANs, since the same data types can be used everywhere. This will make networks seamless, rendering obsolete many of today's routers.

ATM does have several weaknesses:

- Most industry analysts see ATM as a long-term, strategic technology, and that ultimately all LAN roads will lead to ATM. However, ATM is such a radical departure from today's LANs that many concepts will take years to be standardized. By contrast, FDDI, which borrowed heavily from Token Ring, took almost ten years to become a standard. Many vendors and most customers are taking a "wait-and-see" attitude until the final standard is at least within sight. We recommend that you do the same.

- Some people will pay a lot for leading technology, but for the time being, current high-speed technologies like FDDI and Fast and Switched Ethernet are delivering proven performance at prices that ATM products will not be able to match for quite some time. Only once ATM shipments reach significant volumes will vendors costs come down to match today's technologies.

- Not all the building blocks for ATM networks are available yet. ATM works very differently from today's shared or even switched packet-based LANs. For example, today's network operating systems and protocol stacks in particular will require significant modifications in order to support ATM.

- ATM does not provide for easy upgrades from today's legacy LANs. As with any completely new technology, ATM networks will require replacement of almost everything on the network. This is going to be very expensive, disruptive, and time consuming.

ATM has been hyped to the point that everyone expects it to be the holy grail of LANs, effective tomorrow. ATM will be broadly deployed, but not tomorrow, and maybe not even five years from now. ATM reminds us of ISDN back in the early 1980s—at the time, everyone thought that ISDN was going to take over the world in a year! Ten years later we are finally seeing ISDN becoming popular. ISDN, being a wide-area technology, was dependent on telephone switches supporting it. This proved to be a major barrier, as it took the large telephone companies ten years to implement ISDN. ATM faces similar challenges, although of a lesser magnitude.

We think that ATM will become a viable WAN and high-speed backbone technology over the next two years. However, widespread deployment within the workgroup or to the desktop will not be viable until standards have been properly set, leaving little room for vendor interpretation. At that point, interoperability will no longer be an issue, and prices will decline to Ethernet levels. That process will take a few years, meaning that ATM to the desktop will become a reality only by the turn of the century.

IsoENET

Busy shared 10-Mbps Ethernet LANs are unsuitable for multimedia applications. National Semiconductor has proposed a new standard to the IEEE for isochronous Ethernet called IsoENET. This technology would combine the best of both worlds—an Ethernet channel for noncritical data transmission, and additional support for up to 96 ISDN B channels (64 Kbps each, or 6.16 Mbps total) to carry time-critical (isochronous) data. IsoENET is being investigated by the IEEE 802.9 committee.

No major networking or telecommunications vendor seems to be backing IsoENET—only a division of IBM and National Semiconductor have announced plans to bring IsoENET products to market. IsoENET is supposed to provide quality of service in a shared Ethernet environment. Unfortunately, IsoENET requires both new NICs and new hubs as well. If you are upgrading both NIC and hub, you may opt for ATM, since IsoENET delivers only slightly more raw throughput than regular Ethernet. (By the time IsoENET becomes a reality, 25-Mbps ATM will likely be available also). Another option would be to buy a Switched Ethernet hub today, which delivers far superior voice and data throughput with existing NICs. If you want the ISDN capability, we recommend that you install separate ISDN adapters and cables and retain your Ethernet infrastructure. IsoENET is a technology that was dead before it even got off the ground.

Switched Ethernet

Switched Ethernet is based on regular Ethernet and provides each node with a private Ethernet connection, ensuring dedicated 10-Mbps performance on that segment. Switched Ethernet consists of two elements—a standard 10-Mbps NIC on one end and a switching hub on the other end. Over 500,000 Switched

Ethernet ports were shipped in 1994, compared with 100,000 FDDI ports, making Switched Ethernet the undisputed market leader.

There are several advantages to Ethernet Switching. First of all, the existing infrastructure is preserved. Nobody likes throwing away equipment that still works. Switched Ethernet utilizes most or all of the existing infrastructure and allows you to add more performance when and where it is needed. For example, the existing NICs can be used, saving both money and time. The cost of installing a new NIC in particular is often underestimated by LAN managers, since the cost of a new NIC also involves the installation cost and the associated cost of user disruption during installation. The cost of user downtime can often outweigh the price of the NIC itself!

Also, Ethernet switches have a wide variety of applications—in conjunction with existing repeaters, switches can be used to segment an existing overloaded network; or a switch can be added to create server farms or to create a new backbone. All of these applications retain the existing equipment.

In addition, the technology has been proven and is well understood. Ethernet Switching is based on Ethernet. Since Ethernet is a household technology and well-understood by everyone in the industry, switching requires little training. That means customers and vendors understand the technology, how it works, and how to apply it.

Ethernet switching hubs are being offered by all major networking vendors. Switching hub sales are currently booming, attracting many new entrants and startups, which will mean more choices, innovation, and lower prices.

High-performance Switched Ethernet networks can be built using standard 10-Mbps ISA NICs that cost less than $100 and hubs that start at $250 per port, a connection cost of $350. (For existing installations, the price of Ethernet switching is unbeatable, since the NIC is already present). More hub vendors and increasing sales volumes are going to lead to substantial price declines over the next year, and hub prices will probably drop by 30 percent per year in the short term.

Shared Ethernet LANs experience performance degradation due to collisions when the traffic and number of users increase beyond a certain point. Switched Ethernet, on the other hand, does not exhibit these symptoms, as there are no other users to collide with, guaranteeing true 10-Mbps performance—100 percent efficiency. Switched Ethernet can also be operated in full-duplex mode, boosting performance even beyond the traditional 10-Mbps limit.

Ethernet switching can offer dedicated service to every node. This is ideal for applications that require dedicated, guaranteed bandwidth with low latencies, such as videoconferencing and other natural data type applications.

Switched Ethernet provides the broadest media support. Because Switched Ethernet is Ethernet, it runs on the same cabling that today's repeated Ethernet runs on—Category 3 UTP, fiber as well as coaxial cable. Fiber Ethernet in particular makes Switched Ethernet very useful for backbones.

Switched Ethernet is a jack of all trades. It can be used for improving client performance by providing each node with a dedicated 10-Mbps private Ethernet. It can be used to segment a large shared LAN into smaller groups. It can be used to improve server throughput. Switched Ethernet, running on UTP or fiber, can even be used as a backbone LAN. In short, Switched Ethernet can be used to boost performance when and where you need it, to improve the performance of existing overloaded networks, or to build new high-performance networks.

The disadvantage of Switched Ethernet is that sometimes 10 Mbps is not enough. Switched Ethernet can still only deliver 10-Mbps wire throughput, which may not be sufficient for certain applications. Since backbones aggregate traffic from an entire LAN, they often require significantly more than 10-Mbps throughput. Today's servers are also capable of delivering much more than 10-Mbps sustained output, and certain desktops already demand more than 10-Mbps wire throughput.

100BASE-T/Fast Ethernet

100BASE-T was officially adopted by the IEEE as the 802.3u standard in early 1995. 100BASE-T is Ethernet operating at ten times the speed. Just like regular Ethernet, 100BASE-T can be used in a shared or switched environment. 100BASE-T is easy to understand, can be switched to deliver superior quality of service (QOS), and can operate in full-duplex mode without collisions.

The advantages of Fast Ethernet are as follows:

- The Fast Ethernet standard is being supported by all major networking vendors, including Bay Networks (SynOptics/Wellfleet), Cabletron, Intel, Cisco/Kalpana, 3Com, Sun Microsystems, SMC, National Semiconductor, LANNET, Grand Junction Networks, Chipcom, Networth, and hundreds of other vendors.

- 100BASE-T hubs and NICs deliver ten times the performance of regular Ethernet at only a small price premium. For example:

  - 10/100 NICs today sell for about twice the price of 10-only NICs. That's ten times the performance for twice the price! By 1996, 10/100 NICs will sell for little more than 10-only NICs, effectively rendering obsolete 10-Mbps-only NICs. FDDI NICs by comparison still cost ten times as much as 10BASE-T NICs, which explains the slow adoption rate of FDDI in general.

- 100BASE-T repeaters are already available for $200 per port, or about four times the price of 10-Mbps repeaters. Fast Ethernet hub prices are expected to drop significantly, and LAN managers will see the delta between 100-Mbps and 10-Mbps hub ports narrow substantially over the next year.

- Because 100BASE-T is 10BASE-T at ten times the speed, upgrading to 100BASE-T is relatively easy. 10/100 NICs are expected to become the de facto standard in two or three years, much like 16/4 NICs made 4 Mbps-only NICs obsolete in the Token Ring market a few years ago. This means that upgrading the client becomes a no-brainer. On the hub side, migrating from 10BASE-T to 100BASE-T requires only bridging. On the other hand, migrating from 10BASE-T to a new technology such as 100VG-AnyLAN requires routing, a much more complex and expensive technology. 10/100BASE-T hubs are already available, allowing existing 10-Mbps LANs to be seamlessly connected to new 100Mbps LANs. Alternatively, specific clients or servers can be upgraded when and where it is needed.

- Ethernet is well understood, and running shared or switched Ethernet at ten times the speed requires no change in thinking at all. In addition, network management and analysis tools work seamlessly with 100BASE-T, an important factor to consider.

- 100BASE-T supports Category 1, 3, 4, and 5 twisted-pair wiring, as well as fiber cabling for extended distances. In most cases your existing wiring infrastructure can be used without modifications.

Disadvantages of Fast Ethernet are

- While network adapter cards, low-end switches, and repeaters have been shipping since 1993, backbone switches and routers are still in short supply two years later. If 100BASE-T were a brand-new technology this would be cause for concern, but since 100BASE-T is an evolutionary technology where very little has changed, it is safe to buy and deploy 100BASE-T now.

- Even 100-Mbps throughput may not be enough for some applications. Full-duplex will help, but some backbones will require even more throughput. These kinds of applications are likely to move to 622-Mbps ATM soon.

- Very large 10BASE-T networks can be built by cascading numerous repeaters together (most vendors specify a limit of five). Shared 100BASE-T allows for only two repeaters to be connected together. Stackable repeaters connected by a fast bus will alleviate this issue somewhat, but ultimately switches will be required to extend the network diameter.

- The IEEE did not include any coaxial wiring support in its 100BASE-T 802.3u standard. That means customers wishing to upgrade from thin Ethernet to Fast Ethernet will need to rewire. However, most installations are moving to UTP wiring anyway, so this issue will diminish over time.

For the next few years Ethernet customers are going to be best served by a combination of 10BASE-T switching and 100BASE-T. These two mature and well-understood technologies offer high throughput capability; the broadest vendor support; easy, cost-effective and seamless upgrades, excellent price performance, and support for emerging multimedia applications.

100VG-AnyLAN

100VG-AnyLAN is a brand-new 100-Mbps shared-media technology jointly developed by Hewlett-Packard and AT&T's Microelectronics Division from 1991 to 1994. 100VG incorporates a new protocol that incorporates a priority access method, allowing time-critical applications to transmit ahead of other noncritical packets. 100VG-AnyLAN was standardized by IEEE within the new 802.12 committee. 100VG products first appeared in 1994.

Advantages of 100VG are

- Like TCNS, 100VG uses a shared-media token-passing bus architecture. Because 100VG does not use the CSMA/CD protocol, collisions do not occur, allowing 100VG to achieve very high throughput rates in heavily loaded shared media networks.

- 100VG can utilize either Ethernet or Token Ring frame formats. That means manufacturers can offer either 10BASE-T/100VG or Token Ring/ 100VG combo products, providing both Ethernet and Token Ring users with an easy migration path to 100VG. (High-speed options for Token Ring users are discussed at the end of this chapter.)

- 100VG features a protocol called *demand priority*, allowing time-critical multimedia transmissions to be prioritized over regular traffic. Unfortunately, the scheme is not effective, since only two demand priorities are available, too few to properly prioritize data in a busy heterogeneous network. More importantly, demand priority requires software applications to be rewritten in order to take advantage of this feature. Given 100VG's limited overall appeal and small market share, software developers are unlikely to modify their products to take advantage of 100VG's capability.

- 100VG can run on Category 3 wiring. Most of today's installed wiring is still Category 3, and many other products like 100BASE-TX, CDDI require Category 5 wiring.

The disadvantages of 100VG-AnyLAN (100VG) are

- Theoretically, 100VG networks can be built the same way that 10BASE-T networks are built today—by cascading multiple repeaters together in a random, large tree. 10BASE-T allows for five repeater hops, adequate for most installations. 100BASE-T, the main competitor of 100VG-AnyLAN, specifies a maximum of only one or two repeater hops, depending on the type of hub. In theory, 100VG can do five repeater hops like 10BASE-T, but in reality 100VG hub manufacturers like Hewlett-Packard recommend a limit of three repeater hops. This makes 100VG only marginally better than 100BASE-T in this respect, and definitely inferior to 10BASE-T.

- 100VG supporters, Hewlett-Packard in particular, have tried to promote it as the evolutionary next step after 10BASE-T. However, technically speaking, 100VG is not Ethernet. The IEEE 802.3 committee, in charge of Ethernet technology, chose Fast Ethernet as the successor to Ethernet. 100VG supporters were asked by the IEEE to form a separate committee to work on 100VG (802.12), making it clear that 100VG is not Ethernet.

- 100VG can run on Category 1, 3, 4, and 5 wire, but requires four pairs of wire. While most installations contain four pairs, sometimes only two pairs are terminated. Most new wiring is Category 5 anyway, and 100BASE-T can run on only two pairs of Category 5 or 4 pairs of Category 3/4/5. In addition, 10BASE-T, 100BASE-T, and FDDI can be run over fiber at lengths of up to 2km. 100VG only runs over UTP, making it unsuitable for extended distances, noisy environments or backbones. (Hewlett-Packard has, however, announced intentions to support both two-pair Category 5 and Fiber cabling in the near future.)

- Hewlett-Packard is the only significant vendor that is fully committed to 100VG. Some second-tier companies such as Thomas-Conrad are hedging their bets and building both 100BASE-T and 100VG products. However, all the major hub and NIC manufacturers (Bay Networks, Cabletron, 3Com, SMC, and Intel) are only supporting 100BASE-T. This makes 100VG-AnyLAN a de facto H-P-proprietary technology, similar to Thomas-Conrad TCNS.

- No 100VG switching products are available. This means that it can only operate in a shared media mode, and hence provide limited QOS (quality of service). This makes 100VG unsuitable for a high-speed backbone.

- Unlike 10BASE-T and 100BASE-T, 100VG does not support full-duplex, limiting its speed to 100 Mbps.

Hewlett-Packard has attempted to position 100VG as a mainstream 100-Mbps LAN technology, pitting it squarely against 100BASE-T and causing tremendous confusion in the market. The truth is that 100BASE-T offers similar throughput for less money, with easier upgrade capabilities. In most cases, technologies survive because they offer something unique in terms of performance or features. Some customers will of course buy 100VG purely because it is sold by Hewlett-Packard, a very reputable company with a long tradition of technical excellence. History has proven time and again that it takes standards, good technology, and multivendor support to win in a competitive marketplace. 100VG may be an IEEE standard, but we think that 100VG will not exist beyond a market niche because it offers neither improved throughput nor specialized functions to warrant its existence.

■ Conclusion

Now that we have discussed all the different high-speed options, we would like to summarize this discussion. Table 2.1 below compares the products discussed in this chapter based on several criteria.

Table 2.1

Making Sense of High-Speed Communication Technologies

Technology/ Feature	FDDI/ CDDI	Switched 10BASE-T	100BASE-T	ATM	TCNS	100VG-AnyLAN
Standard	ANSI X3T9.5	Uses IEEE 802.3	IEEE 802.3u	Evolving - CCITT, ATM Forum	Proprietary	IEEE 802.12
Major vendors promoting	All	All	Bay, Cabletron, Intel, SMC, 3Com	All	Thomas-Conrad	H-P
Ease of migration from 10BASE-T	New NICs, new hubs	Very easy	Easy	New NICs, new hubs	New NICs, new hubs	New NICs, new hubs
Quality of service	No	Yes	Yes (switched)	Yes	No	OK
100-Mbps performance	Yes	No	Yes	Yes	Yes	Yes
Price/ Performance	Expensive	Excellent	Excellent	Very expensive	Good	Good
Type of technology	New	Ethernet	Ethernet	Completely new	New	Completely new

Table 2.1

Making Sense of High-Speed Communication Technologies (Continued)

Technology/ Feature	FDDI/ CDDI	Switched 10BASE-T	100BASE-T	ATM	TCNS	100VG-AnyLAN
Support for existing cabling infrastructure	No	Yes	Yes	No	No	Mostly
Shipping since	1988	1990	1993	1993	1990	New
Maturity of technology	Proven	Proven	Partially proven	Completely new	Proven	Completely new

Many vendors are offering products with both 10- and 100-Mbps modes. For example, we know of only one vendor building a 100-Mbps-only Fast Ethernet NIC; we expect this company to add a 10-Mbps mode soon. The main selling point of Fast Ethernet is its easy upgrade path from Ethernet. Our conclusion is that 10-Mbps Ethernet Switching will accommodate most requirements. For applications such as servers, backbones, or users requiring more than 10 Mbps of wire throughput, repeated or Switched Fast Ethernet will be the right choice.

Most industry analysts will agree with our conclusion that for the next five years, Switched and Fast Ethernet are the logical choices for upgrading an Ethernet network. Figure 2.1 shows a forecast from International Data Corporation in Framingham, Massachusetts. IDC predicts that Switched and Fast Ethernet combined will account for most of the sales of high-speed networking equipment.

■ What If I Am a Token Ring User?

If this is a book for Ethernet and about Ethernet, why are we talking about Token Ring? Token Ring makes up about 15 percent of all network installations, a significant share. Many enterprise networks contain a Token Ring domain here or there, so we thought you may have a need for information about the Token Ring upgrade options available.

Many Token Ring users are rightly concerned about the future of Token Ring as a technology. While many new options are available to Ethernet users, today's Token Ring customers have far fewer choices. IBM in particular seems to have abandoned Token Ring altogether as a technology, focusing its research and development on ATM instead. Should you start replacing your

Figure 2.1

International Data
Corporation, a well-
respected market
research and forecasting
firm, predicts that high-
speed networking
connections will grow
from fewer than 2,000
connections in 1995 to
over 20,000 in 1999, a
tenfold increase.
According to IDC, the
combination of Switched
and Fast Ethernet will
comprise over 80 percent
of new high-speed
shipments.

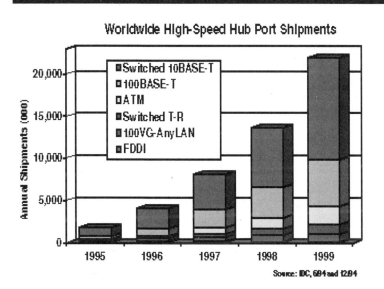

Token Ring network, then? Not yet. You do have some options for improving the speed of your Token Ring network.

Your first option is to upgrade existing users with Token Ring switches. Token Ring is a shared-media technology, just like Ethernet. Switched Token Ring uses the existing NICs and requires a new switching hub that provides a dedicated connection, allowing for dedicated 16 Mbps of bandwidth for each node. Token Ring switches are relatively new. In 1994, SMC was the only vendor to ship a Token Ring switch, but by mid-1995 dozens of vendors realized the huge potential of this market and are now shipping Token-Ring Switches.

Hewlett-Packard is trying to capitalize on the lack of a Fast Token Ring technology and is positioning 100VG as a viable option. Hewlett-Packard has announced plans to ship 16/100VG NICs, supposedly making migration from Token Ring to VG easy. This, of course, applies to new installations only, unless you want to replace your existing NICs also. You would still have to route from your existing Token-Ring segment to the new 100VG segment. From a market perspective, 100VG looks like it will become the next-generation Token Ring, with a relatively small market share and only one strong proponent, so we recommend against this option.

A third option is to keep existing users on a Token Ring LAN but start connecting new users with Ethernet. Routing from Token Ring to Ethernet has become very easy and cost effective, especially through larger chassis hubs. This way you can slowly migrate to Ethernet or Fast Ethernet.

- *Ethernet and the OSI Model*
- *10-Mbps Ethernet MAC and PHY Standards*
- *100BASE-T/Fast Ethernet*
- *Ethernet and Fast Ethernet Repeaters*
- *Ethernet Switching Standards*
- *Future Ethernet Enhancements*

3

Switched Ethernet and Fast Ethernet Standards

THIS CHAPTER WILL DISCUSS THE THEORY AND STANDARDS OF Ethernet, Switched Ethernet, and Fast Ethernet. The goal of this chapter is to educate you as a LAN manager or IT professional about key differences between shared 10-Mbps Ethernet and these new technologies. We have tried to focus on aspects of Switched and Fast Ethernet that are relevant to you, and not get into too much detail. This chapter serves as a precursor to the hands-on implementation section of this book, Chapters 6 through 10. Once you have understood the key differences between today's shared Ethernet and Switched and Fast Ethernet, evaluating products and building a network with these products should be relatively easy.

The chapter is split into six sections:

- The first section, "Ethernet and the OSI Model," discusses the OSI reference model and how Ethernet relates to the PHY and MAC layers of the OSI model.

- The second section, "10-Mbps Ethernet MAC and PHY Standards," delves into the 10-Mbps Ethernet MAC in more detail, and also discusses the various Ethernet physical layer implementations available today—thick, thin, twisted pair, and fiber Ethernet. You may elect to skip this section if you are very familiar with Ethernet—we have included it as a "refresher" in order to set the stage for our discussion of the new Fast Ethernet standard and switching technology.

- The third section of this chapter, "100Base-T/Fast Ethernet," introduces the new IEEE 802.3u Fast Ethernet standard, and how it differs from today's 10BASE-T standard. This section will discuss the Fast Ethernet MAC and PHY standards in more detail.

- "Ethernet and Fast Ethernet Repeaters" talks about Ethernet and Fast Ethernet repeater standards and contrasts network design rules.

- "Ethernet Switching Standards" discusses bridging and introduces different Ethernet Switching methods. A switched connection is really just segmentation down to a 2-station network, such as a hub to a single PC or hub-hub connection. Ethernet Switching in itself is not a standard, but is merely bridging technology applied to hubs.

- The last section of this chapter, "Future Ethernet Enhancements," discusses full-duplex, which is a de facto industry standard for 10-Mbps Ethernet hubs and network interface cards (NICs). The IEEE is working on a Switched Fast Ethernet standard.

We have tried to keep this chapter as short as possible because we didn't want to inundate you with too much networking theory. Numerous excellent books on the theory of networks and Ethernet are available, and we have listed some of our favorites in Appendix B.

■ Ethernet and the OSI Model

Most data communications protocols in use today are defined in terms of a layered model called the Open Systems Interconnection (OSI) Reference Model. This model is shown in Table 3.1, along with a commonly used example of that layer.

Table 3.1

The ISO/OSI Reference Model has become widely accepted in the data communications world

LAYER NAME	NUMBER	EXAMPLES	COMMENT
Application	Layer 7	Lotus cc:Mail	Layers 5–7 are often not clearly defined and vary by operating system.
Presentation	Layer 6	Microsoft Windows 95	
Session	Layer 5		
Transport	Layer 4	Novell IPX, TCP/IP	A protocol stack transports the actual data.
Network	Layer 3	Ethernet to FDDI Routing	Dissimilar LANs communicate through Layer 3 routing
Data link	Layer 2	Ethernet—CSMA/CD	Bridges are Layer 2 devices. AUI interfaces between Layers 1 and 2.
Physical	Layer 1	10BASE-T: Manchester encoding, RJ-45, and so on	Specifies the electrical and coding characteristics on the cable. Repeaters operate at this level.

Both ANSI and the IEEE have used this seven-layer model in the past for good reason. Breaking down a technology into different layers allows a given layer to be changed without impacting the remainder of the model. For example, the IEEE was able to add unshielded twisted-pair support to Ethernet while still keeping Ethernet's core intact, just as different software protocols such as IPX, TCP/IP, or NetBeui can be used with the same hardware because each component forms an independent layer. In this way interoperability between network applications is greatly improved.

Layer 1—The Physical Layer (PHY)

The physical layer protocol or PHY layer defines the electrical signaling, symbols, line states, clocking requirements, encoding of data, and connectors for data transmission. An example of a PHY layer is 10BASE-T. Ethernet uses Manchester encoding to transmit data. Repeaters are layer 1 devices in that they only retransmit signals without decoding them. All higher layers talk to the physical layer through a predefined interface. For 10-Mbps Ethernet, this is the Attachment Unit Interface (AUI), and a DB-15 connector can be used to connect Layer 1 to Layer 2. 100-Mbps Ethernet calls this interface the Medium Independent Interface (MII). Layer 1 interfaces to the actual cable by means of the Medium Dependent Interface (MDI). For example, the MDI for 10BASE-T is the RJ-45 connector.

Layer 2—The Data Link Layer

The data link layer actually consists of two separate pieces, the Medium Access Control (MAC) and the Logical Link Control layer (LLC). Only the MAC layer is of interest to us in this book, since the LLC function happens at a higher level—it is encoded by software into the actual data. The MAC describes how a station schedules, transmits, and receives data in a shared-media environment. The MAC ensures reliable transfer of information across the link, synchronizes data transmission, recognizes errors, and controls the flow of data. Example MACs are Ethernet/802.3 or Token Ring/802.5. In general, MACs are only important in shared-media environments where multiple nodes can connect to the same transmission medium.

Bridges are used to link different LANs of the same MAC type. For example, a Thinnet segment (10BASE2) can be connected to a TPE segment (10BASE-T) by means of a bridge. These types of data transfers occur at the MAC level and are therefore often called layer 2 functions.

Layer 3—The Network Layer

The network layer is responsible for setting up the connection between source and destination. Larger networks often consist of different types of MAC standards; for example, a company may have an Ethernet network in the engineering department and a Token Ring network in the finance department. The network layer software would know how to set up the best connection between the different Ethernet and Token Ring networks. In general, data transmission among dissimilar MAC standards involves the network layer. This function is known as routing, or a layer 3 function.

■ 10-Mbps Ethernet MAC and PHY Standards

Ethernet is based on a layered OSI model. As a result the Ethernet MAC can be easily combined with different PHYs. This section discusses the 10-Mbps Ethernet MAC standards, and the four major baseband PHY specifications.

The Ethernet CSMA/CD MAC

First let's discuss the Ethernet MAC technology called *carrier-sense multiple access with collision detection*, or *CSMA/CD*. CSMA/CD works very much like human conversation and is described in the following seven steps.

1. Carrier-sense—A station wanting to transmit a packet of information has to ensure that no other nodes or stations are currently using the shared media, so the station listens to the channel first (*listen before talking*).

2. If the channel is quiet for a certain period of time called the interframe gap (IFG), the station may initiate a transmission (*talk if quiet*).

3. If the channel is busy, the channel is monitored continuously until it becomes free for the minimum IFG time period. At this point transmission begins (wait for quiet before talking).

4. Collision detection—A collision may occur if two or more stations listen while waiting to transmit, then simultaneously determine that the channel is free and begin transmitting at almost the same time. This event would lead to a collision, and destroy both data packets. Ethernet continuously monitors the channel during transmission to detect collisions (*listen while talking*).

5. If a station detects a collision during transmission, that transmission is immediately stopped. A jam signal is sent to the channel to guarantee that all other stations detect the collision also and reject any corrupted data packet they may have been receiving (*one talker at a time*).

6. Multiple access—After a waiting period (called *backoff*) a new transmission attempt is made by the stations that wish to transmit. A special random backoff algorithm determines a delay time that the different stations will have to wait before attempting to send their data again.

7. The sequence returns to step 1.

Figure 3.1 illustrates the CSMA/CD flow.

Ethernet uses *frames* or *packets* of data to transmit the actual information, also known as payload, from source to destination. Ethernet and most other LANs in existence today transmit a frame of variable length. The length of the frame changes because the payload or data field can vary. The Ethernet frame is generated by the transmitting MAC controller. Figure 3.2 shows an Ethernet 802.3 frame (the DIX Ethernet frame, also known as Ethernet Type II frame, looks slightly different).

The different fields of an 802.3 Ethernet packet are described in more detail below.

- The preamble is sent to allow the receiver to synchronize to the incoming transmission and locate the start of the frame. The preamble includes a byte called the Start Of Frame Delimiter (SFD) to indicate that the MAC frame is about to commence. The SFD octet is specified to be 10101011.

Figure 3.1

Flow diagram illustrating
the CSMA/CD medium
access method

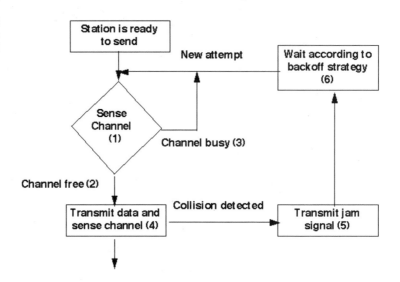

Figure 3.2

The Ethernet 802.3
frame structure

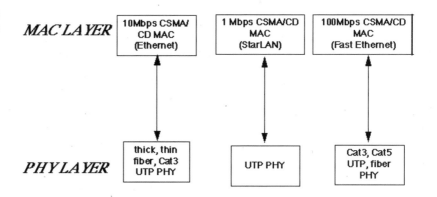

- The source address denotes the sender. Each node has a unique address. The first three Bytes of the address are called the Block ID and identify the manufacturer of the equipment, and are assigned by the IEEE. For example, Intel is identified by the 00AA00 (hex) address. The other three Bytes are called the Device ID and are assigned by each manufacturer. These are always unique.

- The destination address specifies where the frame is to be sent to.

- The largest field specifies the total length of the data that will be transmitted.

- The protocol header is actually part of the data field and contains information that a higher level, layer 4, embeds in the data field itself. For example, the protocol headers for IPX and TCP/IP are about 30 bytes long.

- The data itself can vary from 0 to about 1,200 bytes in length. If the actual data is less than a minimum length required, the MAC will add a variable pad in order to maintain a minimum total frame size of 64 bytes. If the data is longer than 1,200 bytes, Ethernet, then a higher layer, typically the protocol stack, /Layer 4, will split up the payload into different frames.

- Lastly, a frame check sequence is done to ensure accurate transmission. The cyclical redundancy check method (CRC) is used to check for invalid frames.

Ethernet and all other popular LAN standards in existence today use a variable-length frame or packet method to communicate. Newer voice/data transmission technologies such as ATM or ISDN use a fixed-length frame size, or *cell*, to transmit voice and/or data.

Table 3.2 lists all the relevant Ethernet MAC frame parameters in terms of bit times, or microseconds (μs).

Table 3.2

Most 10-Mbps Ethernet/ 802.3 MAC Parameters are listed in bit times.

PARAMETER	VALUE (BIT-TIMES)
slotTime	512 bit times
InterFrameGap	9.6 μs (minimum)
attemptLimit	16 (tries)
backoffLimit	10 (exponent)
jamSize	32 bits
maxFrameSize	1518 octets (bytes)
minFrameSize	512 bits
addressSize	48 bits

The Ethernet MAC is inherently scalable. With the exception of the interframe gap, all the parameters can be measured in terms of the time taken to transmit one bit of data, or bit-times. Note that the actual speed of

Ethernet (10 Mbps) is not mentioned in the specification at all. This makes it very easy to run Ethernet at different speeds. Calculating the time to transmit one bit for 10-Mbps Ethernet transmission becomes very easy.

$$1 \text{ bit-time} = \frac{1 \text{ bit}}{10 \text{ MHz}} = 0.1 \text{ μs or } 100\text{ns}$$

For 1-Mbps Ethernet/StarLAN, the frame looks exactly the same; the only thing that changes is the interframe gap, which becomes ten times as large—that is, a minimum of 96 μs. The bit time for StarLAN is 1/1MHz = 1 μs or 1,000 ns. Fast Ethernet works exactly the same way: The frame is identical again, but the interframe gap has been reduced to 1/10—a minimum of 0.96 μs. The bit time for Fast Ethernet is also reduced to 1/10th, or 10ns.

Ethernet PHYs

The next section will look at the different PHY implementations for 10-Mbps Ethernet (Figure 3.3). There are officially five different ways of transmitting 10-Mbps Ethernet. 10BASE5 is the original thick Ethernet coaxial cable standard, dating back to the early 1970s. 10BASE2, also known as thin Ethernet, was added in the early 1980s and uses a thinner coaxial cable. In 1990, Ethernet over unshielded twisted pair, known as 10BASE-T, was standardized. 10BASE-F, although less well known, is very important because it utilizes fiber cabling to carry Ethernet over extended distances. The physical layers mentioned so far all use baseband transmission methods, meaning that the entire frequency spectrum is used to transmit the data. 10BROAD36 is different from all the other Ethernet PHY standards in that it uses broadband transmission technology to transmit. This allows different channels to communicate simultaneously on the same cable. 10BROAD36 is far less popular and no similar 100-Mbps PHY exists yet, so we will not discuss 10BROAD36 in this book.

10BASE5: Thicknet

10BASE5 is the original Ethernet 802.3 standard. 10BASE5 utilizes a thick coaxial cable with a diameter of 10mm. The cable has to be terminated with a 50 Ohm/1W resistor. Up to 100 stations per segment are allowed.

10BASE5 utilizes a bus topology, as all stations are connected via one single continuous coax cable. The maximum length of one coax segment is 500m, a function of the quality of coaxial cable.

Stations using a network interface card are attached with a DB-15 connector to the short attachment unit interface (AUI) cable. The AUI cable in turn connects to a medium attachment unit (MAU) that is bolted to the coax

Figure 3.3

The different 10-Mbps
Ethernet/802.3 PHYs

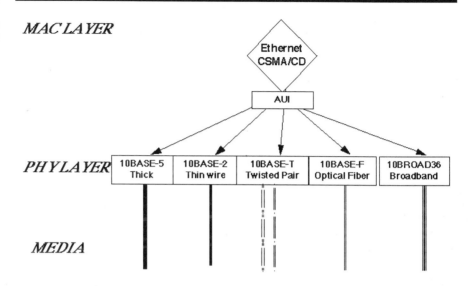

cable by means of a device commonly called the vampire connector. The MAU contains the actual transceiver that connects to the coaxial cable.

For proper CSMA/CD operation, one end node needs to be able to sense that a collision has occurred at the other end of the wire. The maximum network diameter of an Ethernet network is limited by the time it takes for a signal to travel from one end to the other, called the *propagation delay*. The network diameter for 10BASE5 is limited to 2500m, consisting of five 500m segments with four repeaters.

10BASE5 derives its name from the MAC 10-Mbps signaling rate (*10*) and baseband transmission (10*BASE*), and the maximum 500m distance between stations on one segment (10BASE*5*).

10BASE5 uses Manchester encoding to transmit data This encoding scheme translates a logical '1' to a '10' bit pattern, while a logical zero is sent as a '01' bit pattern.

10BASE2: Thin Ethernet (Also Known as Cheapernet)

10BASE2 is similar to 10BASE5, and was invented primarily to reduce the cost and complexity of installation of 10BASE5. The differences between 10BASE5 and 10BASE2 are as follows.

- Only 30 nodes per segment are allowed for 10BASE2, versus 100 nodes for 10BASE5.

- The maximum length of a 10BASE2 segment has been reduced to 185m, as opposed to 500m for 10BASE5.

- 10BASE2 retains the 4 repeater/5 segment rule from 10BASE5, allowing a maximum network diameter of 5*185m = 925m. If no repeaters are used, the maximum length of the single segment can be extended to 300m.

- This standard uses a cheaper, thinner RG-58 50 Ohm coaxial cable than 10BASE5, hence the name Cheapernet or *Thinnet, short for Thin Ethernet.*

- 10BASE2 integrates the functions of the MAU and the transceiver/AUI cable onto the NIC itself.

- The AUI or DB-15 connector on the NIC is replaced by a BNC barrel connector.

When compared with Thick Ethernet, Thin Ethernet was much easier to install, stations were easier to add, and reduced the cost significantly. As a result, Thinnet became very popular, effectively replacing thick Ethernet as a workgroup cabling solution.

10BASE-T: Twisted-Pair Ethernet

In 1990, the IEEE adopted 10BASE-T, a completely new physical layer standard for Ethernet (see Figure 3.4). 10BASE-T is very different from coaxial thick and thin Ethernet in a number of respects:

- 10BASE-T utilizes two pairs of unshielded twisted-pair telephone type cable, one pair of wiring to transmit data and a second pair to receive data. Eight-pin modular plugs, type RJ-45, are used as connectors.

- Just like the other Ethernet PHY standards, 10BASE-T uses Manchester encoding, but with predistortion of the electrical signal to allow transmission over UTP. The signaling frequency is 20MHz, and UTP cable (Type 3 or better) must be used.

- 10BASE-T incorporates a feature called Link Integrity that makes installation and troubleshooting cabling problems a lot easier. Both hub and NIC send out a heartbeat pulse every 16 ms, and both hub and NIC look for this signal. Receiving the heartbeat signal means that a physical connection has been established. Most 10BASE-T equipment features an LED indicating that the link is good. LAN managers typically start troubleshooting wiring problems by looking at the state of the Link LED on both ends of the wire.

- The maximum segment length is 100m, which is in accordance with the EIA 568 wiring standard. Repeater-repeater links are also limited to a maximum of 100m. (10BASE-T wiring is discussed in greater detail in the next chapter.)

Figure 3.4

The three most popular Ethernet standards are 10BASE5, 10BASE2 and 10BASE-T.

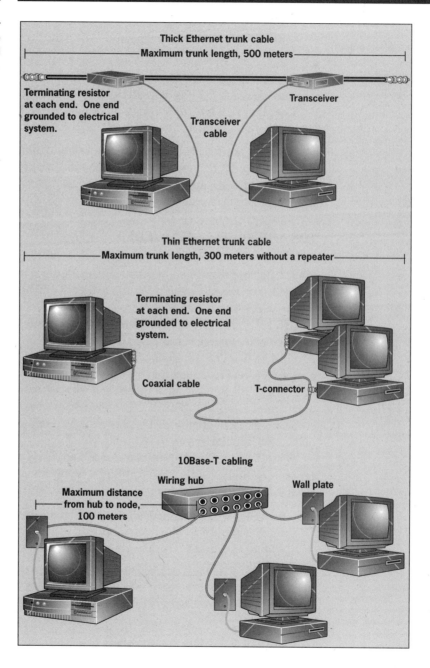

- The topology is changed to a star, and only two nodes per segment are allowed (the station and the repeater, or repeater-repeater).

- 10BASE-T retains the 4 repeater/5 segment rule from 10BASE5.

- External MAUs are allowed, but most 10BASE-T equipment integrates the functions of the MAU in the data terminal equipment (DTE) or the hub itself. (A *DTE* is defined as an Ethernet node that has a layer 2 function; that is, a NIC or a bridge or switch. A repeater is a layer 1 device and is not a DTE.)

Twisted-pair Ethernet represented another major advance in Ethernet technology, and today represents over 90 percent of Ethernet sales. 10BASE-T became popular because of its low cost and increased flexibility that only a structured wiring star topology allows.

10BASE-F: Fiber Ethernet

Only recently did 10BASE-F become an official IEEE standard, although Fiber Ethernet equipment has been available for a number of years. 10BASE-F is based on the Fiber Optic Inter-Repeater Link (FOIRL) specification, which was created to interconnect repeaters using an extended distance fiber optic cable link. 10BASE-F is essentially an extension of FOIRL allowing stations to be connected over fiber as well.

10BASE-F utilizes duplex fiber (2 strands of multimode or singlemode glass fiber), one to transmit and one to receive. Multimode fiber media of 62.5/125µm diameter is most often used with 10BASE-F to carry infrared light from LEDs. The IEC BFOC/2.5 miniature bayonet connectors have become the de facto standard. This device is also known as the ST connector, which was popularized by AT&T.

The IEEE 10BASE-F standard (see Table 3.3) actually defines four different sets of fiber optic specifications, and modifies the original FOIRL one as well. These four different specifications are described below.

1. 10BASE-FP specifies a passive star configuration—that is, no separate power is required. The overall network diameter is 1,000m, or up to 500m per segment. The MAUs are integrated into the repeater or DTE.

2. 10BASE-FB specifies a backbone or repeater fiber system, where the MAU is again integrated into the repeater. No DTE connections are allowed. The link length is 1,000m, and multiple repeaters can be cascaded in series.

3. The new FOIRL standard differs from the original one in that it now allows for DTEs to be connected as well, that is, it allows for one-to-one repeater-repeater links or one repeater connecting to a number of

DTEs. Link segment length is unchanged from the original FOIRL standard and is 1,000m.

4. 10BASE-FL is based on FOIRL and is backwards-compatible with FOIRL. It can only be used to link repeaters and requires external MAU transceivers. 1,000m or 2,000m link segments are allowed.

Table 3.3

Summary of IEEE 802.3
10BASE-F Standard

	10BASE-FP	10BASE-FB	10BASE-FL	OLD FOIRL	NEW FOIRL
DTE Connection?	Yes	No	No	No	Yes
Segment Length	500m	2,000m	1,000 or 2,000m	1,000m	1,000m
Cascaded Repeaters	N/A	Yes	No	No	Yes
Network Diameter	2,500m	2,500m	2,500m	2,500m	2,500m
MAU	Embedded	Embedded	External	External	Embedded or External

Table 3.4 provides a summary of the 10-Mbps Ethernet/802.3 PHY standards.

Now that you have become familiar with 10-Mbps Ethernet, we can move on to discuss the new 100-Mbps Ethernet MAC and PHY standards.

■ 100BASE-T/Fast Ethernet

100BASE-T is a 100-Mbps version of today's proven Ethernet standard. The IEEE officially adopted Fast Ethernet/100BASE-T as a new specification in May 1995. It is officially called the IEEE 802.3u standard and is a supplement to the existing IEEE 802.3 standard.

• The new 100BASE-T MAC uses the original Ethernet MAC operating at ten times the speed.

Table 3.4

Summary of the different 10-Mbps Ethernet/802.3 PHY Standards

	10BASE5	10BASE2	10BASE-F	10BASE-T
Maximum segment length	500m	185m	500, 1,000 or 2,000m	100m
Topology	Bus	Bus	Star	Star
Medium	50 Ohm thick coax	50 Ohm thin coax	Multimode fiber	100 Ohm UTP
Connector	NIC—DB-15	RG-58	ST	RJ-45
Medium attachment	MAU bolted to coax	External or on NIC	External or on NIC	External or on NIC
Stations/segment	100	30	33 for 10BASE-FP, 2 repeaters for FB. FL or FOIRL	2 (NIC and repeater)
Maximum Segments	5	5	5	5

- The new 100BASE-T standard is designed to include multiple physical layers. Today there are three different 100BASE-T physical layer specifications. Two of these physical layer specifications support unshielded twisted pair of up to 100m in length; a third one supports multimode or singlemode fiber. A fourth UTP specification is under consideration.

- Like 10BASE-T and 10BASE-F, 100BASE-T requires a star-wired configuration with a central hub.

- 100BASE-T also includes a specification for a Media-Independent Interface (MII), a 100-Mbps version of today's AUI. The MII layer interfaces between MAC and PHY and allows for external transceivers.

The differences between 10BASE-T and 100BASE-T are in the PHY standards and network design areas. That's because the new IEEE 802.3u 100BASE-T specification contains many new rules for repeaters and network topology. Figure 3.5 provides an overview of the new IEEE 802.3n standard.

Figure 3.5

Overview of the 100BASE-T 802.3u standard showing MAC, MII, and the three official PHY standards

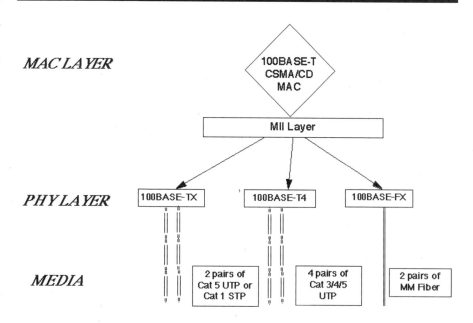

The Fast Ethernet CSMA/CD MAC

The 100BASE-T MAC is almost identical to the 10-Mbps "classic" Ethernet MAC. As mentioned earlier, the 802.3 CSMA/CD MAC is inherently scaleable, which means that it can be run at different speeds and be interfaced to different physical layers. StarLAN/1BASE5 took advantage of this scalability to run Ethernet at 1 Mbps. Table 3.5 compares 10-Mbps and the new 100-Mbps Ethernet MAC standards.Note that the 100-Mbps Ethernet MAC retains all of the 10-Mbps Ethernet MAC parameters except for InterFrameGap, which has been decreased to one-tenth its original value, from 9.6 µs to 0.96 µs. A Fast Ethernet packet has the same framing format as a 10-Mbps Ethernet frame, except that it gets transmitted across the wire at ten times the speed.

The time taken to transmit 1 bit of data, also known as the bit time, for 100-Mbps Ethernet transmission can be calculated as follows:

$$1 \text{ bit-time} = \frac{1 \text{ bit}}{100 \text{ MHz}} = 10\text{ns}$$

Some network adapters and hubs include an MII connector, but MII will not become as popular as AUI. AUI became popular because Thick Ethernet

Table 3.5

10-Mbps and 100-Mbps
Ethernet MAC Parameters
are identical except for
the IFG

PARAMETER	ETHERNET/802.3	FAST ETHERNET/802.3U
slotTime	512 bit times	same
InterFrameGap	9.6 µs (minimum)	0.96 µs (minimum)
attemptLimit	16 (tries)	same
backoffLimit	10 (exponential number)	same
jamSize	32 bits	same
maxFrameSize	1518 octets	same
minFrameSize	512 bits (64 octets)	same
addressSize	48 bits	same

was the first-generation Ethernet and AUI was the only connector for it. With 100BASE-T, most hardware manufacturers have decided to skip MII and offer different products that integrate the physical layer transceiver already. For example, NIC manufacturers often sell the same basic design in a 100BASE-TX and in a 100BASE-T4 version. You have to choose up front which media type you need. Think of it as Thinnet-only or 10BASE-T only products, as opposed to combo or AUI-only cards using external transceivers.

Fast Ethernet PHYs

As with 10BASE-T, 100BASE-T combines the CSMA/CD MAC with different physical layer specifications. There are currently three different physical layer specifications that are approved by the IEEE. A fourth one is under discussion, which is covered at the end of this section.

- Most of today's installed wiring and almost 100 percent of new wiring is unshielded twisted pair, with coaxial cable becoming less and less important. As a result the IEEE chose to focus its efforts on unshielded twisted pair and not coaxial cable. The 100BASE-TX physical layer supports Fast Ethernet transmission over two pairs of Category 5 unshielded twisted pair or Category 1 shielded twisted-pair wiring. The 100BASE-T4 physical layer supports Fast Ethernet transmission over four pairs of Category 3, 4, or 5 unshielded twisted-pair cabling.

- Fiber cabling has numerous advantages that make it useful for carrying data over long distances and noisy environments. In order to make 100BASE-T useful as a backbone technology, a fiber wiring standard has also been adopted, allowing Fast Ethernet transmissions of up to 2km in length.

- Like 10BASE-T and 10BASE-F, all 100BASE-T PHY specifications require a star-wired configuration with a central hub.

100BASE-TX: Fast Ethernet for Category 5 UTP

100BASE-TX is based almost entirely on the ANSI-developed copper FDDI Physical Layer Dependent sublayer technology (TP-PMD), also known as CDDI.

- 100BASE-TX has numerous similarities to 10BASE-T. It utilizes two pairs of data grade Category 5 unshielded twisted-pair cable with a maximum segment length of 100m. This complies with the EIA 568 wiring standard that has become commonly accepted for office LANs. As in 10BASE-T, one pair of wiring is used to transmit data; the second pair is used to receive data.

- 10BASE-T uses Manchester encoding, whereas 100BASE-TX uses a more elaborate encoding method called 4B/5B. This results in a serial bitstream of 125MHz, which is used to transmit the data.

- The signaling frequency for 10BASE-T is 20MHz. 100BASE-TX uses Multi-Level Transmission-3 (MLT-3) waveshaping to reduce the signaling frequency. MLT-3 waveshaping in effect divides the 125MHz signal by a factor of 3, creating instead a 41.6 MHz data transmission. Due to this high frequency 100BASE-TX requires EIA 568 Category 5 data grade or IBM Type 1 STP wiring, popular with Token Ring installations.

- The same eight-pin RJ-45 connector used for 10BASE-T is also used for 100BASE-TX. The very same conductors are also used, making it possible to use the same cable and connectors for 10BASE-T and 100BASE-TX.

100BASE-TX products have been shipping since early 1994, a year before other PHY products were available. As a result, 100BASE-TX is the most widely used physical layer specification for 100BASE-T today. A very broad range of 100BASE-TX products are being sold today, including NICs, repeaters, switches, and routers.

100BASE-FX: Fast Ethernet for Fiber Optic Cabling

- 100BASE-FX is targeted at applications that are considering use of fiber cabling and/or FDDI technology today—high-speed backbones, extended distance connections, or environments subject to electrical interference, or networks requiring higher security links. 100BASE-FX (like 100BASE-TX) borrows its physical layer from the ANSI X3T9.5 FDDI Physical Layer Dependent (fiber PMD) standard.

- Just like FDDI, 100BASE-FX can utilize two strands of multimode (62.5 or 125 μm) or singlemode fiber cabling.

- 100BASE-FX permits the use of the MIC/FDDI as well as the ST connectors that have become popular with 10BASE-F and FDDI, but recommends the lower-cost SC connector.

- The maximum segment length for fiber connections varies. For a multimode switch-switch or a switch-adapter connection, 412m is allowed. This number can be increased to 2,000m if the link is full-duplex. 100BASE-FX repeater segment lengths can typically be 150m, but actually vary depending on the type and number of repeaters used. (Single mode fiber, which is higher quality than multimode fiber, allows for connections of 10 km and beyond. This requires a full-duplex link. Check with the vendor for details.)

- 100BASE-FX uses the same encoding method as 100BASE-TX—4B/5B.

100BASE-T4: Fast Ethernet for CAT3 UTP

100BASE-T4 is the only completely new PHY standard, as both 100BASE-TX and 100BASE-FX are based on ANSI FDDI technology. 100BASE-T4 essentially caters to the huge installed base of Category 3 voice grade wiring.

- 100BASE-T4 utilizes four pairs of voice or data grade unshielded twisted-pair Category 3, 4, or 5 cable. Since the signal frequency is only 25MHz, voice grade Category 3 wiring can be used as well.

- 100BASE-T4 uses all four pairs of unshielded twisted-pair wire. Three pairs are used to transmit data at one time, while the fourth pair is used as a receive channel for collision detection.

- Unlike 10BASE-T and 100BASE-TX, no separate dedicated transmit and receive pairs are present, so full-duplex operation is not possible.

- The same eight-pin RJ-45 connector used for 10BASE-T is also used for 100BASE-T4.

- The maximum segment length for 100BASE-T4 is 100m. This again complies with the EIA 568 wiring standard that has become commonly accepted for office LANs.

- 100BASE-T4 uses 8B/6T encoding, which is more elaborate than the 10BASE-T Manchester encoding.

Table 3.6 illustrates how 100BASE-T4 is able to transmit 100 Mbps over Catagory 3 cabling.

Table 3.6

10BASE-T and 100BASE-T4 Throughput Comparison

IMPROVEMENT OVER 10BASE-T	IMPROVEMENT FACTOR
More pairs of wires (3 versus 1)	3.0X
Improved coding efficiency (8B6T versus Manchester)	1.33X
Increased baud rate (25Mbaud versus 10Mbaud)	2.5X
Total throughput increase (3.0 × 1.33 × 2.5)	**10X**

Table 3.7 compares 10BASE-T with the three new 100BASE-T Physical Layer specifications.

Table 3.7

Comparison of the 100BASE-T Physical Layers

	10BASE-T	100BASE-TX	100BASE-FX	100BASE-T4
Encoding	Manchester	4B/5B	4B/5B	8B/6T
Cabling required	UTP Cat.3/4/5	UTP Cat.5 or STP Type	Multimode or Single mode Fiber	UTP Cat.3/4/5
Signal Frequency	20MHz	125MHz	125MHz	25MHz
Number of pairs required	2	2	2	4
Number of transmit pairs	1	1	1	3
Distance	100m	100m	150/412/2000m*	100m
Full-duplex capable?	Yes	Yes	Yes	No**

*   150m for repeater-DTE, 412m for DTE-DTE, 2,000m for full-duplex DTE-DTE, 10,000 for single mode full-duplex DTE-DTE.

**We have heard about some companies attempting to build full-duplex-capable T4 product, but these products would be proprietary as there are currently no IEEE standards activities underway in this area.

Fast Ethernet MII

The 100BASE-T standard calls out a media-independent interface, similar to the attachment unit interface (AUI) for 10-Mbps Ethernet. The MII layer defines a standard electrical and mechanical interface between the 100BASE-T MAC and the various PHY layers. This standard interface works like AUI in the classic Ethernet world in that it allows manufacturers to build media or wiring-independent products, with external MAUs being used to connect to the actual physical cabling. The electrical signals differ between MII and AUI, the AUI being a stronger signal capable of driving 50m cable lengths, while the MII signals are digital logic type signals able to drive 0.5m of cable. MII uses a 40-pin connector, similar to the SCSI connector, although it is smaller (Figure 3.6).

Figure 3.6

The LANCAST MII 100BASE-FX Fiber Transceiver; note the 40-pin MII connector. which is similar to the SCSI-2 connector.

The Auto-Negotiation Scheme

With the advent of 100BASE-T, it is no longer safe to assume that a typical Ethernet RJ-45 connector is carrying 10BASE-T. Instead, any one of five different Ethernet signals could be present: 10BASE-T, 10BASE-T full-duplex, 100BASE-TX, 100BASE-TX full-duplex, or 100BASE-T4 all use the same RJ-45 connector.

The IEEE came up with a scheme that will simplify your life as a LAN manager tremendously. The IEEE's auto-negotiation scheme, commonly known as nWAY, can tell what speed the other end of the wire is capable of. The hub or NIC will then automatically adjust its speed to the highest common denominator, that is, the fastest speed that both are capable of.

- Both hub and NIC need to contain the auto-negotiation logic (we expect that by 1996 all Fast Ethernet equipment will contain the logic).

- Auto-negotiation is an enhancement of the 10BASE-T Link Integrity signaling method and is backwards-compatible with Link Integrity.

- Connecting 10BASE-T and 100BASE-TX may actually cause network disruption, as the electrical signal levels are incompatible. Auto-negotiation will eliminate this possibility as it will not allow dissimilar technologies to connect or interfere with each other.

- New equipment incorporating the auto-negotiation feature will still allow you to manually select one of the possible modes.

Before auto-negotiation was officially adopted by the IEEE as a 100BASE-T feature, some vendors started shipping proprietary auto-sensing network adapters. Table 3.8 illustrates how different hubs and NICs will interoperate with and without the auto-negotiation scheme.

This technology has several benefits. Assume a cable is connected into a 100BASE-TX hub port, and you are at the other end of the wire trying to connect the RJ-45 to a network adapter, but you have no idea what the hub speed is. You might assume that it's still connected to a 10BASE-T hub port, or it could be a 100BASE-TX hub. If your hub and the 10/100 network adapters support the auto-negotiation scheme, hub and card will automatically adjust their speeds to run at 100 Mbps.

Another scenario would be where you would want to upgrade a user from a 10-Mbps connection to a 100BASE-T4 hub. You had the foresight of installing 10/100T4 NICs a few years ago, but only now are you installing a new 100BASE-T4 repeater. All you need to do is exchange the hub, and away you go.

Auto-negotiation uses a series of Fast Link Pulses (FLP), similar to the 10BASE-T Link Integrity (LI) pulses. Both hub and NIC send out this sequence of pulses, which allow the other end of the wire to identify the type of Ethernet connection the host is capable of (Figure 3.7).

■ Ethernet and Fast Ethernet Repeaters

Repeaters are used to extend the length and topology of a network by joining multiple segments into a larger segment. A repeater works at the physical layer (Layer 1) of the OSI model, it does not look at the data itself, but

Table 3.8

Interoperability of Pre-Standard Auto-Speed and Auto-Negotiation Hubs and NICs Is Not Assured.

NIC\Hub	10BASE-T only hub	100BASE-TX-only hub	1st -generation 10/100TX hub (no auto-sensing)	Auto-negotiation 10/100 hub
10BASE-T only NIC	No choices can be made.	Better buy a new NIC!	Hub manually set to 10 mode (with management software).	Hub auto-negotiates to 10 mode.
Pre-standard auto-sensing 10/100TX NIC ·	NIC automatically selects 10 mode.	NIC automatically selects 100 mode.	Manually set hub to 100 mode, NIC will automatically adjust to 100 mode also.	Manually set hub and NIC to 100 mode.
New auto-negotiation 10/100TX NIC	NIC auto-negotiates to 10 mode.	NIC auto-negotiates to 100 mode.	Manually set hub and NIC to 100 mode.	Both hub and NIC auto-negotiate to 100 mode.

*   Many of today's 10/100 adapters feature a proprietary auto-sensing mode. For example, Intel's first-generation Ether-Express PRO/100 adapter operates at 10 or 100 Mbps and auto-senses the hub speed automatically. First the NIC looks for a 100 Mbps Link Integrity pulse. If it doesn't find it, it selects 10-Mbps operation. You can override the auto-speed feature with device-driver command-line options. Other NICs work differently, some requiring you to run the setup software or changing connectors. A pre-standard auto-speed sensing hub or NIC should be manually set to the correct speed when connected to an auto-negotiation hub or NIC.

**   For example, the SynOptics 28115 hub will operate at either 10 or 100 Mbps, but does not automatically adjust its speed. The speed adjustment has to be done via the hub's management software..

Figure 3.7

The Auto-Negotiation Fast Link Pulse (FLP) is similar to the 10BASE-T Link Integrity pulse.

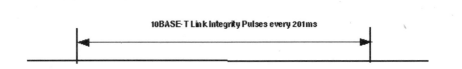

10BASE-T Link Integrity Pulses every 201ms

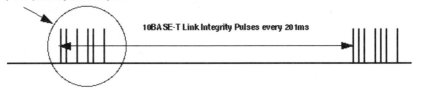

Fast Link Pulse Burst containing Information on 10/100, TX/T4, Half-duplex/Full/duplex

10BASE-T Link Integrity Pulses every 201ms

merely cleans up signals for retransmission. The new IEEE 802.3u Fast Ethernet standard contains a new specification on Fast Ethernet repeaters. One big difference between Ethernet and Fast Ethernet repeaters is the maximum network diameter, which has been reduced from 2500m to 205m. Don't be too alarmed by what appears to be a rather restrictive specification. Stackable repeaters and switching hubs will provide you with the building blocks necessary to maintain your current network topology. The other difference is that 100BASE-T allows for two different *classes* of repeaters, Class I and Class II. This section will explain the basic concept of a repeater, and then contrast 10BASE-T and 100BASE-T repeaters.

How Repeaters Work

All Ethernet repeaters work as follows.

1. An encoded signal is sent from a node (DTE) to the wire.

2. The repeater then receives the data on one port. This signal has been electrically "degraded" because it has to travel some distance from source to the repeater over less-than-perfect cable.

3. The repeater then cleans up the incoming signal; that is, it recreates a perfect signal from the degraded one.

4. Lastly, the cleaned-up signal is retransmitted to all ports.

The Repeater Collision Domain

Repeaters propagate all network traffic (and collisions) occurring on one segment to all other segments interconnected by means of other repeaters. All segments interconnected by means of repeaters are in one *electrical collision domain*.

Electrical signals take a certain time to travel across a cable. In addition, all repeater hops introduce a small delay or latency. This is the time delay between which an incoming signal is received and a retimed signal is transmitted again to all ports. This forwarding delay and its impact on Ethernet collision detection is the key factor for determining Ethernet and Fast Ethernet network design and diameter rules.

All collisions occurring in a single collision domain must be detected by the nodes causing the collision before they stop transmitting; otherwise the nodes would never know that their transmission had been corrupted. This means a transmitted data packet must be long enough so that the transmission is still in progress even though the collision has already occurred, allowing the collision signal to propagate back to all senders. This has to be true for all nodes on the network, including the ones at the farthest end of the network.

As a result, the Ethernet network diameter is directly related to the minimum packet size, which is 512 bits. The network diameter is decreased by latencies introduced by end-stations, repeaters and cable segment delays.

Take for example two stations connected to an Ethernet LAN, stations A and B. Station A starts transmitting a packet after sensing that the network is empty. The signal starts traveling down the wire, when station B senses the wire, and determines that it is empty because the signal from A is still en route. B starts transmitting also. At this time the transmission from A is still in progress. In the worst case, B starts transmitting at the point where the signal from A reaches it. A collision occurs, and B has to send a collision signal back to A before A stops transmitting. Since the minimum packet size for A is 512 bits, B needs to send a collision signal before A has transmitted more than 256 bits, or 256 bit-times after the start. That way the collision from B can be returned to A in another 256 bit-times, which equals a round-trip delay of 512 bit-times.

10-Mbps Ethernet Repeater Rules

The 10BASE-T golden rule can be easily memorized as the *5-4-3-2-1* rule:

- *Five* segments are allowed (of 500m diameter each).

- This implies *four* repeater hops in the data path.

- *Three* of these segments may be populated with nodes.

- *Two* segments cannot be populated but are only interrepeater links.

- All of this makes *one* large collision domain with a maximum of 1,024 stations, total network diameter can be up to 2,500m.

Figure 3.8 illustrates this 5-4-3-2-1 design rule, which applies to 10-Mbps Ethernet only.

This 5-4-3-2-1 rule is only a rough guideline, but for most cases this rule works very well. Actual numbers vary by manufacturer—we have seen from 4 to 7 repeater hops being specified. The Ethernet standard always needs to be taken into consideration—the round-trip collision delay cannot exceed 512 bits! 1 bit time for 10-Mbps Ethernet corresponds to 0.1µs, so 512 bit times equals 51.2µs. One can always calculate the timing delay for a network by summing up the delay times of the different components of the network. These are the cable, repeater units, MAUs, and DTEs. Adding up the total delay, multiplying it by two to obtain a round-trip number yields the round-trip collision diameter, which should not exceed 512 bit times (Figure 3.9).

For example, many manufacturers specify the latency of their repeaters. A typical 10BASE-T repeater has a port-port latency of 2µs or 20 bit times (which equals 4µs or 40 bit-times round-trip). A typical NIC has a similar

Figure 3.8

The Ethernet 5-4-3-2-1 repeater rule stipulates a maximum of five repeaters and four segments.

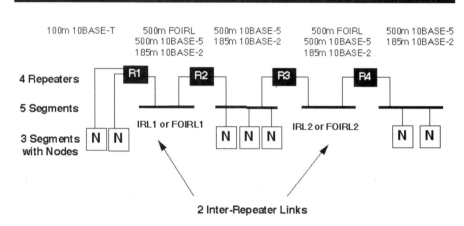

1 Single Collision domain of max. 1024 nodes

delay time. A 100m cable segment introduces a delay of 0.55 µs or 1.1µs round-trip. If the following calculation holds true then your network will work fine.

```
(Total repeater delays) * 2 + (Total cable delays) * 2 +
(total DTE delays) * 2 + (total MAU delays) * 2 < 51.2 µs
```

The factor 2 accounts for round-trip delays. As you can tell 51.2µs allows for quite a few repeaters, cable segments, and MAUs to exist without exceeding the collision domain restrictions. In most real-world networks you will find it very difficult to exceed this number.

Figure 3.9

Timing delays in an Ethernet network are generated primarily by cables, NICs, and hubs.

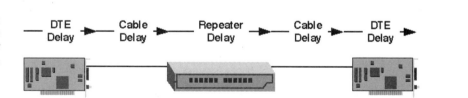

100BASE-T Repeater Rules

Regular Ethernet and Fast Ethernet repeaters work exactly the same way; the only difference between regular Ethernet and Fast Ethernet is the speed of the data transmission. In a 100BASE-T network, the 512 bit-time limitation still applies. However, 512-bit times equals only 5.12 μs, as speed of the 100-Mbps signal has been increased a factor of 10.

This decreases the overall network diameter by a factor of about 10 as well, illustrated in Table 3.9. The equation that was mentioned previously to calculate the 10-Mbps network diameter applies to 100BASE-T also—all you need to do is change the round-trip number to 5.12 μs:

```
(Total repeater delays) * 2 + (Total cable delays) * 2 +
(total DTE delays) * 2 + (total MAU delays) * 2 < 5.12 μs
```

Cabling delays for 100 Mbps are exactly the same as for 10 Mbps—a 100m section still takes about 0.55μs one-way (or 1.1 μs round-trip). 100-Mbps repeaters forward at a slightly faster rate than 10-Mbps equivalents, between 0.35 and 0.7 μs. This provides some added flexibility. DTE delays are also improved—a NIC delay is about 0.25 μs. By adding those numbers and multiplying the result by two to calculate the round-trip delay, you may realize that 100BASE-T only provides a bit budget sufficient for two 100m cable segments and room for about one or maybe two repeater hops.

Table 3.9

The Collision Diameter for 100 Base-T Has Been Reduced to about One Tenth, or 705m.

	10-MBPS	100-MBPS
Collision diameter (bit-times)	512 bit-times	512 bit-times
Bit-time (μs)	0.1 μs	0.01 μs
Maximum round-trip delay (μs)	51.2 μs	5.12 μs
Network diameter (m)	2500m	205m

The IEEE repeater rules have hence been significantly changed for 100BASE-T. The IEEE now defines different kinds of repeaters, depending on their latency characteristics.

- Class I repeaters are repeaters that have a latency of 0.7 μs or less.

- Class II repeaters are superior and have a delay time of 0.46 μs or less. (Class II repeaters are preferred because they provide more flexibility for building your network. With 10BASE-T latency was not an issue, but with 100BASE-T it becomes a major feature for a repeater. Expect all 100BASE-T repeaters to be classified as Class I or II, and pay careful attention to the actual latency specifications.)

Copper segments cannot exceed 100m in length (In accordance with the EIA 568 rule). The total network diameter for copper-only installations is limited to 205m.

- For a Class I repeater, only one single repeater hop is allowed. This means two links of 100m each are possible.

- For Class II repeaters, two repeater hops are possible. This means two links of 100m each are possible, and an interrepeater link of 5m.

- Half-duplex or full-duplex switch-switch segments linked via copper wire still have to adhere to the EIA 568 standard of 100m.

For fiber-only installations, the maximum segment length without repeaters is 412m, or 2,000m for full-duplex. (For single mode fiber connections operating in full-duplex even longer segments are possible.)

- For switch-switch or cross-over connections, the maximum length of 412m or 2,000m applies.

- Class I repeater installations permit two links, the sum of which cannot exceed 272m.

- Class II repeater installations permit two links, and one interrepeater link, the sum of which cannot exceed 228m.

For mixed copper-fiber installations, the picture gets even more complicated. Table 3.10 illustrates the different possibilities. Figure 3.10 represents a graphical depiction of Table 3.10.

Table 3.10

Fast Ethernet Collision Diameter Rules

CONNECTION	COPPER	COPPER/FIBER	FIBER
DTE-DTE (or switch-switch)	100m	N/A	412m
One Class I repeater	200m	260m	272m
One Class II repeater	200m	308m	320m
Two Class II repeaters	205m	216m	228m

As in 10-MHz Ethernet, the overriding design rule is that the round-trip collision delay may not exceed 512 bit-times. The numbers and diagrams above are just examples of what can be accomplished using standard equipment, as most hardware manufacturers do not specify latencies for their products. Technically it is possible to build a network with more than two repeaters

Figure 3.10

The network diameter for a 100BASE-T network can range from 205m to 320m, depending on cabling and type and number of repeaters used.

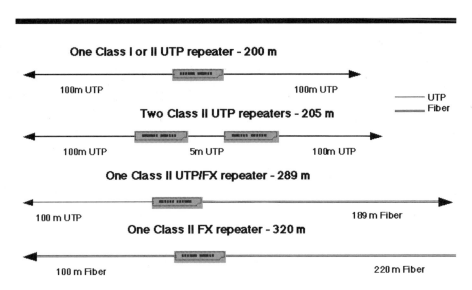

if the cable lengths are reduced substantially. Since network diameter is so tight in 100BASE-T, we have included a detailed table showing the actual bit budgets. Table 3.11 can be used to calculate the bit budget for an unusual esoteric network configuration, such as using three cascaded repeaters.

Use the Table 3.11 and the following guidelines to calculate your total network round-trip propagation delay and collision diameter.

- Note that the final numbers need to be multiplied by a factor of two to determine round-trip collision delay time.

- Obtain actual repeater and DTE (NIC or switch) specifications from the manufacturer. Use the numbers in the table if you cannot get data from the manufacturer.

- If you are using an MII cable, it needs to added to the cable segment length.

- Decide on an appropriate safety margin (we recommend 5 bit times).

- The sum of all delay times must not exceed 512 bit times or 5.12µs. If it does, remove a repeater or reduce the cable length.

For example, one could build a network with three class II TX repeaters, each having a latency of 0.4µs. Total repeater delay would be 3*0.4µs = 1.2µs. The two DTEs on either end would add another 0.5µs. This makes a total of 1.7µs one-way, or 3.4µs round-trip. This would leave 5.12 - 3.4 = 1.72 µs for cable. The cable length can be calculated by dividing 1.72 µs by 5.7ns/m, obtained from Table 3.11. This results in a 302m round-trip cable

Table 3.11

Individual Network
Component Delays Are
Shown to Calculate
Network Diameter.

COMPONENT	DELAY TIMES IN BIT TIMES PER METER	DELAY TIMES IN NS PER METER	MAXIMUM ROUND-TRIP DELAY IN BIT TIMES	MAXIMUM ONE-WAY DELAY TIMES IN MS
Two TX/FX DTEs			100	0.5
Two T4 DTEs			138	0.69
CAT3 cable segment	0.57	5.7	114	0.57
CAT4 cable segment	0.57	5.7	114	0.57
CAT5 cable segment	0.556	5.56	111.2	0.556
STP cable segment	0.556	5.56	111.2	0.556
Fiber optic cable segment	0.501	5.01	408	0.501
Class I TX repeater			140	0.7
Class II TX repeater			92	0.46
Class II repeater, any port T4			67	0.355

length or 150m one-way. This 150m length can be evenly divided up among the three segments, as long as no single segment exceeds 100m. If in doubt about any of this, please use the collision diameter Table 3.10. If your network exceeds the Fast Ethernet bit budget, it will result in late collisions, lost packets, and other strange, intermittent phenomena that will create havoc on your network.

Five years ago a network diameter of 205m combined with one repeater hop would have made 100BASE-T impractical if not altogether useless for most LAN managers. However, two technological developments have made it possible for 100BASE-T repeaters to work well even within these tight restrictions:

- Most 100BASE-T networks will be additions to an existing 10BASE-T network. Every new 100BASE-T segment that is added to a 10-Mbps network will require a switch to get from 10 Mbps to 100 Mbps. The 205m calculation is started at the switch, and 205m is sufficient to get to most nodes with one or two intermediate repeater hops. If the distance from switch to node is more than 205m, then another switch has to be added to further extend the network diameter. Alternatively, 100BASE-FX could be run to repeaters or nodes that are more than 205m away from the switch.

- Standalone, unmanaged 100BASE-T repeaters are going to be rare. Most 100BASE-T repeaters will be stackable, meaning that many repeaters can be physically placed on top of each other and connected via a fast backplane bus. The fast backplane bus does not count as a repeater hop, and makes the entire stack look like one larger repeater. In fact, most 100BASE-T stackables can be stacked four or more high. Electrically, the repeater stack appears as one larger repeater.

■ Ethernet Switching Standards

Ethernet switches have only recently appeared on the market, but they are not an entirely new invention. Conceptually, switches are multiport bridges, which have been around for many years. Technically, bridging is an OSI Layer 2 function, and all of today's common networking standards such as Ethernet, Token Ring, and FDDI can be bridged or switched. What is new are features and uses of these multiport bridges or switches. A few days ago two-port Ethernet bridges were used to connect two different LANs together. Then vendors started building intelligent multiport bridges, which are essentially a number of two-port bridges connected together. Today these multiport bridges have been enhanced and are called switches. These switches are now used within an existing network to disconnect or segment a larger LAN into many smaller ones.

Since bridging and therefore switching is an OSI model Layer 2 function, today's Ethernet switching is not a new IEEE standard at all, merely an application of existing standards. Since this book has *switching* in its title, we would like to provide you with some insights into the technology behind Ethernet switching.

The IEEE 802.1D spanning tree protocol is the only IEEE specification relevant to bridges and switches. This specification can provide for redundancy in mission-critical networks by offering a redundant bridging loop. This specification is discussed in more detail in Chapters 6 and 7.

Bridges Defined

A repeater is a network device that indiscriminately regenerates and forwards a received Ethernet packet, good or bad. Repeaters are known as passive, or shared, components of the network because they do not logically act upon incoming frames. Repeaters merely regenerate incoming signals, thus extending the diameter of the network. In this way, repeaters are invisible to network events such as collisions or errors, merely propagating them along. Hence, a repeater cannot extend the collision domain of a network. Repeaters are used for enlarging a network.

Bridges connect different Ethernet LANs. Bridges perform basic packet filtering functions before retransmitting the incoming packet. While repeaters forward all packets, a bridge forwards only those packets that are necessary. If a packet does not need to be forwarded, the bridge filters it out.

Ethernet LANs that use different physical layer technologies also need to be bridged together. For example, a 10BASE-T LAN can only be connected to a 10BASE2 LAN by a bridge. Bridges also do speed-matching—regular 10-Mbps Ethernet and 100-Mbps Fast Ethernet can only be connected by means of a bridge. See Table 3.12 for a comparison of Ethernet repeaters and bridges.

Table 3.12

Ethernet Repeaters and Bridges

	REPEATER	BRIDGE
OSI Layer	Layer 1/PHY	Layer 2/MAC
Number of hops	5	Unlimited
Look at packets?	No, only regenerates entire packet	Yes, looks at individual address
Invisible devices?	Yes	No
Port-port latency	< 3 µs	50–1,500 µs, depending on packet size
Propagate Errors?	Yes	No
Network design implications?	Extend diameter	Extend collision domain

Every Ethernet packet has a field defined as the *destination address,* which tells the packet which node it is ultimately destined for. Figure 3.11 below shows the structure of an Ethernet or Fast Ethernet frame and the location of the destination address.

Figure 3.11

Ethernet frame and bridge

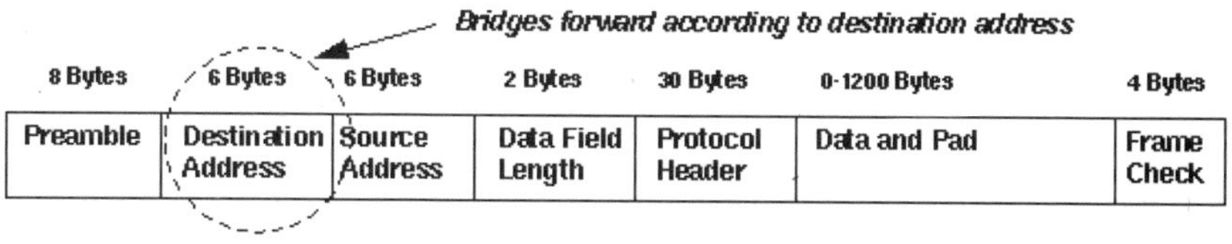

Bridges forward according to destination address

8 Bytes	6 Bytes	6 Bytes	2 Bytes	30 Bytes	0-1200 Bytes	4 Bytes
Preamble	Destination Address	Source Address	Data Field Length	Protocol Header	Data and Pad	Frame Check

Bridges look at an incoming Ethernet packet and analyze the destination address encapsulated in the packet's header. From this information, the bridge can check its "memory" of past frames and determine whether to forward the packet to another port or filter it out; that is, do nothing and discard the packet. In this way, bridges can isolate network traffic between network segments.

A bridge works like a good postal mail delivery system—a bridge knows exactly where everyone lives. A bridge delivers a piece of mail only to the recipient, looking at every address on the envelope and delivering the envelope to that particular address. If an envelope or packet is damaged—that is, if it contains an error—a bridge mail system would return the damaged mail to the sender, with a note saying "damaged." A repeater works very differently. A repeater mail system uses the brute force approach to mail delivery—a repeater would make photostats of a piece of mail it received and then deliver a copy to you and everyone in your neighborhood. You would get not only your mail but also copies of everyone else's mail. Damaged mail would be copied and distributed just like regular mail. Repeaters typically are cheaper to buy, because they don't need to be able to read, sort, or return damaged mail.

Switches Defined

In general, a *switch* is defined as a network component that receives incoming packets, stores them temporarily, and sends them back out to another port. Switches are very similar to multiport bridges in that switches transfer data between different ports based on the destination addresses of the individual packets. Switches can be used to segment LANs, connect different LANs, or extend the collision diameter of a LAN. Switches are crucial to Fast Ethernet deployment because of their ability to increase network diameter.

Virtual Connections and Address Tables

Switches use a concept called a *virtual connection* to temporarily connect source and destination. After the packet has been sent from source to destination, the virtual connection is terminated. An Ethernet switch maintains a two-way table that associates physical ports connected to it with the Ethernet MAC addresses attached to that port. In Figure 3.12, Ethernet node with address A sends a packet to the destination address D. The switch knows that address A is connected to its port 1, while node address D corresponds to port 4, and hence the switch is able to establish a virtual connection from port 1 to port 4 and transmit the data successfully.

Figure 3.12

This illustration shows how a four-port switch uses an address lookup table to forward traffic.

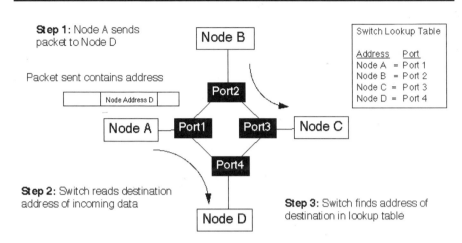

Step 1: Node A sends packet to Node D

Packet sent contains address

| Node Address D |

Step 2: Switch reads destination address of incoming data

Switch Lookup Table

Address   Port
Node A = Port 1
Node B = Port 2
Node C = Port 3
Node D = Port 4

Step 3: Switch finds address of destination in lookup table

Steps 4-6: Node B sends packet to Node C. This occurs in parallel to Steps 1-3.

Multiple Simultaneous Conversations

In an Ethernet switch, data transfers between different ports can occur in parallel. In our example shown above, node A is sending to D. At the same time, node B can be transmitting to node C.

Since each transmission occurs at 10 Mbps, the total switch throughput is actually 2*10=20 Mbps. If more port pairs are transferring data, throughput goes up accordingly. A switch's total bandwidth is determined by adding the bandwidth available for each connection. For instance, a 16-port 10 BASE-T switch has an aggregate throughput of 80 Mbps. The aggregate bandwidth of a switch or bridge can be calculated as follows:

$$\text{Theoretical aggregate forwarding rate} \quad \frac{\#\text{ of ports } * \text{ wire speed}}{2}$$

By comparison, a 16-port 10BASE-T repeater still only gives 10 Mbps of aggregate throughput. If 16 nodes are trying to contend for the available bandwidth, the average bandwidth per node becomes much smaller. Sometimes the maximum realizable forwarding rate of a switch is less than the theoretical aggregate forwarding rate because of internal design limitations. In that case internal blocking exists.

Although Ethernet switching uses Ethernet frames, the familiar Carrier Sense Multiple Access/Collision Detect (CSMA/CD) medium access scheme no longer applies when there is only one node connected per port. With a dedicated connection for each port, there is no contention for the wire, and therefore no need for a carrier. More importantly, there can be no source of collisions, either.

Differences between 10- and 100-Mbps Switches

Fundamentally, 10-Mbps classic Ethernet and 100-Mbps Fast Ethernet switches work the same way. The only difference is that a 100BASE-T switch designer needs to accommodate a data rate that is ten times as high, and this means that the internal design of the switch has to accommodate this. For example, switches contain a microprocessor and memory for storing and processing packets. With a 100-Mbps switch, these components have to be an order of magnitude faster or larger. This will often make 100-Mbps switches very expensive.

Switch Forwarding Mechanisms

Switches use three kinds of packet-forwarding techniques. Packet forwarding may be store-and-forward, cut-through, or modified cut-through. Each one has its own advantages and disadvantages; Chapter 6 will discuss switches in more detail.

Store and Forward   All conventional bridges use the store-and-forward method of forwarding packets. Store-and-forward bridges and switches completely store the incoming frame in internal buffers before sending it out on another port. In this case, there is a switch latency equal to an entire packet, which could turn into a performance issue if enough of these switches are cascaded in series.

Cut-Through   Cut-through switches only examine a packet up to the destination address. This allows the packet to be forwarded almost immediately, resulting in very low switch latencies. The drawback to cut-through switching is that bad packets will also be forwarded. In fact, any packet arriving with a valid destination address will be forwarded.

Modified Cut-Through   Modified cut-through switches attempt to offer the best of both worlds by holding an incoming Ethernet packet until the first 64 bytes have been received. If the packet is bad, it can almost always be detected within the first 64 bytes of a frame, so a tradeoff between switch latency and error checking is achieved. In effect, modified cut-through switches act like a store-and-forward switch for short frames, which usually are acknowledge frames and are very latency critical. For large frames, modified cut-through switches act like cut-though switches.

The three types of packet forwarding methods are illustrated in Figure 3.13. The point at which a frame is forwarded is shown for each type of forwarding mechanism.

Figure 3.13

Ethernet frame and the forwarding points for different switch types

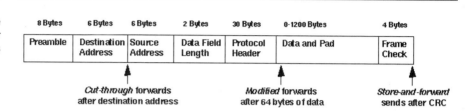

8 Bytes	6 Bytes	6 Bytes	2 Bytes	30 Bytes	0-1200 Bytes	4 Bytes
Preamble	Destination Address	Source Address	Data Field Length	Protocol Header	Data and Pad	Frame Check

Cut-through forwards
after destination address

Modified forwards
after 64 bytes of data

Store-and-forward
sends after CRC

Full-Duplex Switched 10 Mbps Ethernet

Regular Ethernet is a shared-media access method. All shared networks are half-duplex by definition, meaning that one station sends while all others have to listen. In other words, the channel is only carrying data in one direction at any time; it is either transmitting or receiving, but never both.

Full-duplex Ethernet was never part of any of the original PHY or MAC Ethernet specifications. A number of events occurred over the last few years that have made full-duplex Ethernet a reality (Figure 3.14).

- The introduction of 10BASE-T wiring offered the *capability* for separate transmit and receive data paths, something that coaxial cable physical layers didn't previously offer.

- The emergence of Ethernet Switching meant that the transmission channels were no longer being shared by multiple users, but were being used to connect two hubs or a hub and a NIC together in a point-point manner.

In 1992 Kalpana seized upon this opportunity and started working with several other industry vendors to establish a de facto industry standard for full-duplex Ethernet over UTP wire.

Kalpana proposed that the existing MAC specification be used, with two significant modifications:

- One pair of UTP wire (or one fiber strand) is exclusively used for transmission, and one for reception of data.

- No carrier-sense (CRS) is required, as the cable is dedicated to transmitting to receiving for one node only.

- Similarly, no collision-detection (CDT), jam, or exponential backoff is required as collisions only happen in a multiple-user segment.

All 10-Mbps full-duplex-capable equipment available today features the Kalpana method.

Figure 3.14

Full-duplex Ethernet requires a point-point connection.

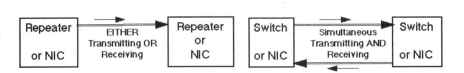

NOTE: *Switching is a prerequisite to full-duplex Ethernet, as full-duplex requires a point-point connection with only two stations present. Note also that Switched Ethernet does not automatically imply full-duplex operation.*

■ Future Ethernet Enhancements

The IEEE's 802.3 working group has finished the 802.3u Fast Ethernet/ 100BASE-T standard. However, the working group is still investigating some additional subjects. We will briefly discuss the two most relevant topics.

Fast Ethernet Full-Duplex/Flow Control—A Standard in the Making

10-Mbps full-duplex has become a defacto standard for 10-Mbps switches, and many 10-Mbps NICs have incorporated this feature as well. Some of the early 100BASE-TX hubs from Bay Networks and Grand Junction, as well as NICs from 3Com, Intel, and other vendors, feature a 100-Mbps full-duplex mode. However, these devices are not interoperable in full-duplex mode because no 100-Mbps full-duplex standard or de facto standard has yet emerged. An IEEE 802.3 committee is currently investigating different proposals on how to make full-duplex part of the 100BASE-T standard.

Switches are also used to speed-match 10-Mbps to 100-Mbps Ethernet networks. This poses an interesting challenge for switch design engineers. If the station transmitting on the 100-Mbps link puts out a continuous data stream that exceeds more than the 10-Mbps side can receive at any one time, the switch will store excess data internally as long as it has sufficient memory available. However, when the speed difference is 10:1, an overflow or congestion condition could occur relatively quickly. This condition can also occur when the two end-stations are connected at the same speed, but the receiving station is preoccupied doing other things. One way to overcome this congestion is for the switch to send a "slow down" or "stop" condition to the fast transmitter. This process is called *flow control* and is used in many of today's analog and digital modem technologies. The IEEE will likely standardize full-duplex and congestion/flow-control as an addendum to the Fast Ethernet standard by late 1995 or early 1996.

100BASE-T2—A New Physical Layer Being Considered by the IEEE

10BASE-T requires 2 pairs of Category 3 cable, whereas 100BASE-T either requires two pairs Category 5 or 4 pairs of Category 3. Having a two-pair Category 3 solution would make 100BASE-T truly backwards-compatible with 10BASE-T from a wiring perspective. The ANSI TP-PMD workgroup that developed the FDDI two-pair Category 5 solution (which was in turn used for 100BASE-TX) investigated 2-pair Category 3 support for many years and ultimately abandoned it. The IEEE has decided to reopen this subject of 100-MHz data transmission over 2 pairs of Category 3 and has chartered a task force to look into this, and various proposals have been made. Technically, it appears feasible to do 100BASE-T2, largely due to the advances in Digital Signal Processing techniques that semiconductor manufacturers have at their disposal. We think the IEEE will adopt 100BASE-T2 as the official fourth physical layer sometime in 1996. However, the market for T2 will be relatively small at that point, since the installed base of Category 5 wiring will have grown substantially by then.

■ Summary

In May 1995, the IEEE officially adopted the new IEEE 802.3μ specification for 100-Mbps Ethernet. The specification allows Ethernet's proven CSMA/CD protocol to be run at ten times its original speed. The IEEE also approved three physical layer standards. 100BASE-TX requires two pairs of Category 5 UTP wiring, 100BASE-T4 requires four pairs of Category 3 or better wiring. Both permit distances of 100m. 100BASE-FX is the third physical layer utilizing fiber cabling of 412m, or up to 2,000m once a full-duplex standard becomes a reality.

100BASE-T design rules differ significantly from 10BASE-T in that the maximum network diameter for UTP wiring is 205m. 802.3μ also specifies two types of repeaters, Class I or Class II. Class I repeaters allow for only one repeater hop, whereas Class II repeaters permit two hops. This compares to a network diameter of 2,500m and 5 repeater hops for 10BASE-T.

Ethernet switches are high-performance multiport bridges used within a LAN, whereas classical bridges are typically used to interconnect different LANs. 10/100 bridges and switches serve a critical need in a Switched and Fast Ethernet network. Switches perform speed-matching, allowing 10-Mbps Ethernet networks to be attached to 100-Mbps segments. Switches also extend the network diameter.

Full-duplex and an additional physical layer for 2-pair Category 3 wiring are currently under consideration by an IEEE 802.3u study group.

- *The EIA/TIA 568 Cabling Standard*
- *The 100BASE-T Cabling Standards*
- *Important Considerations for New and Existing Installations*
- *Catagory 5 Wiring Closets and Cross-Connection Considerations*
- *Test Equipment and Certification*
- *Cable Plant Certification*

C H A P T E R

Cabling

D<small>ID</small> <small>YOU KNOW THAT CABLING PROBLEMS ARE THE BIGGEST</small> single cause of network down time, causing more disruptions than anything else? It's too bad, then, that many people don't pay enough attention to their cabling infrastructure. We have discussed the importance of thinking strategically with respect to networking hardware. Paying attention to a few things up front with respect to network cabling will save you lots of trouble later on. In addition, while personal computers and networking hardware have a useful life of between three and five years, your building's cabling plant should outlast the network infrastructure itself by many years. Some cabling companies now offer 10-year warranties for their installation work, so planning ahead for the long term makes a lot of sense! Taking short cuts or trying to save money during the installation can have disastrous consequences in the long run, as troubleshooting cabling problems later on can be very time consuming, expensive, and disruptive.

Switched Ethernet has no special wiring requirements, as it runs on existing Ethernet coaxial, or fiber cabling. This chapter will focus on the installation and troubleshooting tips of a 100BASE-T cabling plant, as well as key differences between 10BASE-T and 10BASE-F cabling and the new 100BASE-TX, -FX and T-4 standards. This chapter assumes that you are already familiar with a lot of the basics on cabling. If you are not, we suggest that you buy one of the books on cabling listed in Appendix B.

The IEEE has attempted to make 100BASE-T run on existing cabling as much as possible, so we will start off by describing today's existing cabling standards first.

■ The EIA/TIA 568 Cabling Standard

There are many different wiring specifications in existence today. Over the years, companies such as AT&T, IBM, Northern Telecom, Digital Equipment, and Hewlett-Packard have each introduced their own structured cabling system specifications, called *premises distribution systems* (PDS). These PDS standards specify cabling properties as well as wiring closet equipment. The AT&T and IBM specifications have had the most impact on the networking industry over the years, and we will discuss certain aspects of their PDS standards.

In the early 1990s, Ethernet, Token Ring, and FDDI were modified to run over unshielded twisted pair, and today UTP represents the majority of the installed base and new shipments of cabling. As a result the IEEE chose to focus on UTP for 100BASE-T as much as possible. In addition, the IEEE wanted to use existing cabling standards wherever possible. In 1991 the Electronics Industry Association (EIA), in conjunction with the Telecommunications Industry Association (TIA), started publishing a series of specifications for unshielded twisted-pair wiring and installation, which has become the most widely accepted vendor-independent standard for UTP. The IEEE chose to use the EIA/TIA 568 specifications as a basis for the new IEEE 802.3u Fast Ethernet standard.

IBM Type 1 Wire and Connector

IBM's cabling system specifies many different types of cables, five of which are shielded twisted pair, one is fiber, and one is UTP cable. The most common and well-known IBM wire type is Type 1.

Type 1 wire has two shielded twisted pairs of 22 AWG (American Wire Gauge) solid wire, with an impedance of 150 ohms. Each pair is shielded, and the entire cable is shielded again, providing for 100-MHz bandwidth capability. IBM also specified a Type 1 data connector and a DB-9 network adapter connector. Originally, Type 1 STP was the only cabling type capable of running 4- and 16-Mbps Token Ring, so the installed base of Type 1 cabling is still relatively large, but is decreasing as Token Ring now runs over UTP and RJ-45 connectors as well. Because of this large installed base the IEEE also included support for IBM Type 1 wiring in its 100BASE-TX specification. The IBM Data Connector is not part of the IEEE specification, but the DB-9 connector can be used.

The EIA/TIA-568 Cabling and Connector Specifications

EIA/TIA wiring standards were first published in 1991 and have been evolving ever since. Organizationally the EIA and TIA are similar to the IEEE in that it publishes open standards that are based on the work of many different people and companies. The EIA/TIA-568 standard defines the specifications of the cable to be used as well as some installation rules. The latest version of the EIA/TIA standard is 568B, which contains some minor enhancements to the original 1991 standard. So far the EIA/TIA only accommodates UTP cabling. Instead of differentiating among different cable "Types" like IBM does, the EIA/TIA standard uses the term category. The EIA/TIA has specified five categories of UTP:

- Category 1 typically uses 22 or 24 AWG solid wire and can have a wide range of impedances. It is not recommended for data transmissions.

- Category 2, like Category 1, is loosely defined, and it also uses 22 or 24 AWG solid wire without a specific impedance range. It is often used for PBX and alarm systems, as well as AppleTalk or IBM 3270 data transmissions. It is tested to a maximum bandwidth of 1 MHz.

- Category 3 specifies 24 AWG solid wire and is the most widely installed twisted-pair wire today. Category 3 has a typical impedance of 100 Ohms and is tested to 16 MHz, making it suitable for 10BASE-T and 4-Mbps Token Ring installations, although it is technically capable of running 16-Mbps Token Ring as well. Category 3 represents over 50 percent of the installed base of UTP wiring today.

- Category 4 is identical to Category 3 except that it has been tested at 20 MHz, allowing it to run 16-Mbps Token Ring with a better safety margin.

- Category 5 is the highest-quality UTP cable available today. It is tested at 100 MHz, allowing it to run high-speed protocols such as 100-Mbps Ethernet and FDDI. Category 5 also uses 22 or 24 AWG unshielded twisted-pair wire with an impedance of 100 ohms. Category 5 has been available for a number of years. Most new installers are using Category 5 wiring. Category 4 cabling has essentially been made obsolete by Category 5. Category 3 wire is also known as voice grade, and Category 5 is often called data grade. The RJ-45 connector is the standard connector for UTP wiring. The older EIA/TIA-568A connector was different from the AT&T 258A RJ-45 connection, but the newer EIA/TIA-568B standard is the same as the AT&T 258A specification. Both the older EIA/TIA-568A and the newer EIA/TIA-568B connections are shown in Figure 4.1A and 4.1B, as well as the IEEE 10BASE=T connector in Figure 4.1C .

The EIA/TIA-568 standard also specifies exact cable lengths between the wiring closet hub and network node. This length of cable is also called the segment, link, or channel. For UTP, the wiring closet to node segment length is limited to 100m, the breakdown of which is shown in Table 4.1 and illustrated in Figure 4.2.

Figure 4.1A

The EIA/TIA-568A connector specification, introduced only a few years ago, is being phased out in favor of EIA/TIA-568B.

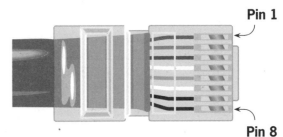

T3	White/Green	1
R3	Green/White	2
T2	White/Orange	3
R1	Blue/White	4
T1	White /Blue	5
R2	Orange/White	6
T4	White/Brown	7
R4	Brown/White	8

Pin 1

Pin 8

EIA/TIA-568A

Figure 4.1B

The EIA/TIA-568B and AT&T258A connectors use the same identical wiring pattern and have become the most commonly used configuration. This configuration is recommended by the IEEE for 100BASE-TX and T4 operation.

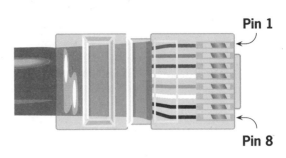

T2	White/Orange	1
R2	Orange/White	2
T3	White/Green	3
R1	Blue/White	4
T1	White /Blue	5
R3	Green/White	6
T4	White/Brown	7
R4	Brown/White	8

Pin 1

Pin 8

AT&T 258A and EIA/TIA-568B

Figure 4.1C

The IEEE 10BASE-T connector is similar to the EIA/TIA 568B and AT&T 258A standards, but only terminates conductors 1, 2, 3, and 6.

T2	White/Orange	1
R2	Orange/White	2
T3	White/Green	3
R1		4
T1		5
R3	Green/White	6
T4		7
R4		8

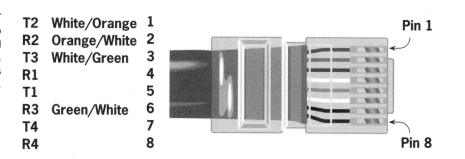

Pin 1

Pin 8

IEEE 10Base-T

Table 4.1

EIA 568 Link Segment Length

SOURCE	DESTINATION	MAXIMUM LENGTH	NAME OF CONNECTION
Network node	Wall plate	L1*	Equipment cord
Wall outlet	Cross connect	90m	Horizontal wiring
Cross connect	Cross connect	L2*	Cross-connect cable
Cross connect	Network hub	L3*	Equipment cord
Total segment length		**100 m**	**Segment or link**

* L1+L2+L3 <=10m

Figure 4.2

The EIA/TIA-568 UTP wiring standard specifies 100m from hub to node, with 90m of field wiring, and 10m for patch panel and equipment chord cabling.

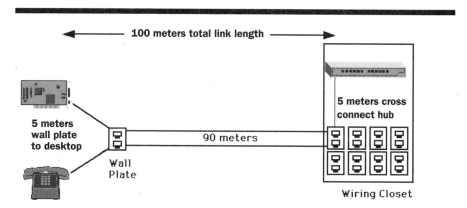

100 meters total link length

5 meters wall plate to desktop

5 meters cross connect hub

Wall Plate

90 meters

Wiring Closet

In addition, the EIA specifies maximum cable lengths between different wiring closets: 2,000m for a fiber optic and 800m for a UTP backbone or interrepeater link. Note that all these EIA numbers are technology independent, so all the IEEE limitations will still apply over and above the EIA guidelines. In the case of Fast Ethernet the maximum segment length for UTP is 100m, irrespective of whether the connection is between different hubs or a hub and a node. For Fast Ethernet fiber optic cabling, the link length can be a maximum of 2000m, but only in certain instances. This is further discussed in the 100BASE-FX section.

The EIA/TIA is currently investigating standards for fiber optic, shielded, and coaxial cabling and connectors. For the time being there is no EIA/TIA specification governing fiber cabling, but a few de facto standards have emerged over the last few years.

- IBM's Type 5 cable specification describes a 100 micrometer (μm) diameter fiber cable, but this cable is not very popular.

- The ANSI FDDI specification accommodates different fiber cables, among them the IBM Type 5 cable as well as other multimode and singlemode fiber cables. Singlemode fiber cabling is higher quality and more expensive, allowing for transmissions of many kilometers. Multimode cable, on the other hand, is cheaper, but can only carry the signals for a few kilometers. Multimode fiber with a diameter of 62.5/125μm has become the most widely used fiber cable. The actual fiber core has a diameter of 62.5μm, whereas the outside cladding has a diameter of 125μm, hence the designation 62.5/125μm.

■ The 100BASE-T Cabling Standards

The IEEE has defined three new physical layers for 100-Mbps Ethernet. The three standards are 100BASE-TX, which requires two pairs of Category 5 UTP or Type 1 STP cabling; 100BASE-FX, which uses two strands of fiber; and 100BASE-T4, which requires four pairs of Category 3 or better cabling. A fourth specification for two-pair Category 3 media support is under consideration by the IEEE. The following section provides an overview of the different 100BASE-T physical layers.

100BASE-TX: Fast Ethernet for Category 5 UTP

100BASE-TX is based on the ANSI-developed copper FDDI Physical Layer Dependent sublayer technology (TP-PMD), also known as CDDI . Its features are as follows:

- Segment length: 100BASE-TX has numerous similarities to 10BASE-T. It utilizes two pairs of unshielded twisted-pair cable with a maximum segment length of 100m. This complies with the EIA/TIA-568 UTP wiring standard that has become commonly accepted for office LANs. As in 10BASE-T, one pair of wiring is used to transmit data, the second pair is used to receive data.

- Cable type: 100BASE-TX uses Multi-Level Transmission-3 (MLT-3) waveshaping to reduce the signaling frequency from 125 MHz down to 41.6 MHz. The signaling frequency for 10BASE-T is 20 MHz, allowing transmission over Category 3. 100BASE-TX, on the other hand, requires Category 5 wiring due to the higher frequency.

- Connectors: Category 5-capable eight-pin RJ-45 connectors are required. In this way the same RJ-45 connector can be used for 100BASE-TX as well as 10BASE-T. The very same conductors are also used, making 100BASE-TX backwards-compatible with 10BASE-T. The 100BASE-TX connector is shown in Figure 4.3.

Figure 4.3

Both 100BASE-TX and 10BASE-T use the same conductors, making it possible to use the same cable for both.

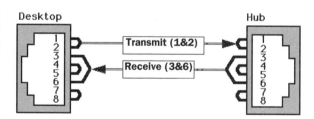

- IBM Type 1 STP wiring and DB-9 connectors, popular with Token Ring installations, may also be used.

100BASE-FX: Fast Ethernet for Fiber Optic Cabling

Here are the features of 100BASE-FX technology:

- 100BASE-FX (like 100BASE-TX) borrows its physical layer from the ANSI X3T9.5 FDDI Physical Layer Dependent (fiber PMD) standard. It utilizes two strands of multimode (62.5/125µm) fiber cabling, made popular by FDDI. (100BASE-FX can also be run on singlemode fiber cabling, but exact distance limitations are not specified). 100BASE-FX uses the same encoding method as 100BASE-TX—4B/5B.

- 100BASE-FX specifies three different connectors: SC, MIC (Figure 4.4), and ST. The ST connector (Figure 4.5) appears to be the most popular at this time because both 10BASE-F and FDDI use it extensively. The IEEE officially recommends the low-cost SC connector.

Figure 4.4

The MIC or FDDI connector is one of the "official" 100BASE-FX connectors.

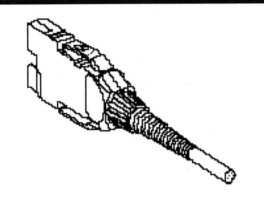

Figure 4.5

The ST connector is the de facto standard for 10BASE-F and FDDI, and now 100BASE-FX also.

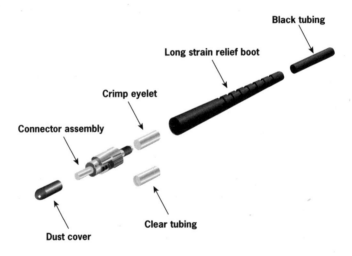

100BASE-FX is suitable for high-speed backbones, extended distance connections, or environments subject to electrical interference.

The maximum segment length for fiber optic connections varies. For two switches or a switch-adapter connection using multimode fiber, 412m is allowed. This number can be increased to 2,000m if the link is full-duplex. Single mode fiber, which is higher quality, will allow for full-duplex connections of 10,000m or more. 100BASE-FX repeater segment lengths can typically be 150m, but actually vary depending on the type and number of repeaters used. Table 4.2 illustrates the maximum link lengths for different fiber cabling installations.

Table 4.2

Fiber Optic Link Segment
Distance Limitations

DEVICES	CONNECTION TYPE	DISTANCE LIMITATION	FIBER TYPE
Switched	Full-duplex	10,000 m*	Single mode
Switched	Full-duplex	2,000m	Multimode
Switched	Half-duplex	412m	Multimode
Repeater connection**	Half-duplex	Max. network diameter 320m	Multimode

* Check with hub and cabling manufacturer for exact distance specification.

** Maximum distances for connections involving repeaters depend on the type and number of repeaters. 320m is the maximum network diameter of the repeated segment for one Class II repeater. This includes the repeater-node segment as well. For a Class I repeater or two Class II repeaters the network diameter has to be reduced substantially. Please refer to the repeater section in Chapter 3 for details on network diameters.

100BASE-T4: Fast Ethernet for CAT3 UTP

100BASE-T4 is the only completely new PHY standard, as both 100BASE-TX and 100BASE-FX were developed using the ANSI FDDI standards. 100BASE-T4 essentially caters to the huge installed base of Category 3 voice grade wiring.

*   100BASE-T4 utilizes four pairs of unshielded twisted-pair telephone cable. Since the signal frequency is only 25 MHz, Category 3 wiring can be used. Three of the four pairs are used to transmit data at one time, while the fourth pair is used for collision detection.

*   The same eight-pin RJ-45 connector used for 10BASE-T is also used for 100BASE-T4 (see Figure 4.6). Unlike 10BASE-T and 100BASE-TX, no separate, dedicated transmit and receive pairs are present, so full-duplex operation is not possible.

Figure 4.6

100BASE-T4 RJ-45
connector and pair
arrangement. Note that
100BASE-T4 requires all
4 pairs of Category 3
cabling.

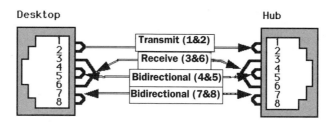

- The maximum segment length for 100BASE-T4 is 100m. This again complies with the EIA 568 wiring standard.

- 100BASE-T4 uses an encoding scheme called 8B/6T, which is more efficient than the 10BASE-T Manchester encoding or the 4B/5B that 100BASE-TX uses.

■ Important Considerations for New and Existing Installations

The next section will contain some practical tips for you to consider when wiring a building for the first time, as well as some discussion on running 100BASE-T over your existing cabling plant.

New Installations

Your cabling plant is supposed to last you quite a number of years, so if you want to make sure that your cabling plant is state of the art, Category 3 should not be an option. The choice, then, is between fiber and Category 5 UTP—and that can be a tough choice.

Fiber optic cabling used to be expensive to buy and install, but over the last few years the cost of fiber has declined to the point where it is becoming a very attractive option. You may be tempted to install fiber because it provides the capability to transmit data at speeds in excess of 1 gigabit per second, which will provide you with lots of room to grow in the future. In addition, Category 5 installation and certification issues have prompted a lot of people to look at fiber very closely. Unfortunately, all 100BASE-FX-based networking hardware is considerably more expensive than comparable TX- or T4-based equipment. Table 4.3 contrasts the costs of fiber to that of UTP Category 3 and 5 installations. Note that in a new installation the cost of the cabling accounts for a third or less of the total cost.

As you can see in Table 4.3, the cost of fiber cabling is only about $100 more than the cost of UTP cabling. Unfortunately fiber-based network hardware equipment is significantly more expensive than UTP counterparts. As a result, a fiber connection costs almost $1,200, or twice as much today as a Category 5 connection.

Table 4.4 compares Category 5 to fiber wiring using a number of different criteria. While fiber has a lot of advantages, it's not worth running fiber to everyone's desktop before the price of FX-based equipment approaches TX levels. Our recommendation is that you install Category 5 to all desktop outlets for the time being. Use fiber for backbones, distances that exceed 100m, EMI noise-prone environments, conduits where space is limited, or any other place where you might be running high-speed networks a few

Table 4.3

Comparing Installation
Costs for a 100m of
Category 3, 5 UTP, and
Fiber Segment

100M SEGMENT	UTP CAT 3	UTP CAT 5	62.5/125 UM FIBER
Installation Cost*	$0.60/m	$0.60/m	$0.80/m
	$60	$60	$80
Cabling/material cost**	$0.30/m	$1.20/m***	$1.90/m
	$30	$120	$190
Cross-connect device	$4/connection	$6/connection	$15/connection
SUBTOTAL CABLING	*$94*	*$186*	*$285*
100BASE-T NIC	$200	$200	$400
NIC installation cost	$50	$50	$50
100BASE-T hub	$200	$200	$400
hub installation cost	$50	$50	$50
SUBTOTAL H/W	*$500*	*$500*	*$900*
TOTAL SEGMENT	*$594*	*$686*	*$1,185*

* Based on a labor charge of $45/hour

** Includes connectors and cable

*** This cost applies to plemum cable, which is currently three times as expensive as PVC cable due to a temporary
shortage. PVC Category 5 sells for about $0.40/meter.

years from now. When installing multimode or singlemode fiber make sure
you run bundles with lots of spare strands. The cost of the cable will be
cheap; you will always be able to terminate and use the spare fibers later on.
When FX-based products become more widely available and cheaper, you
should consider running fiber to the desktop as well.

Existing Installations

If you are upgrading an existing network from 10BASE-T or Token Ring to
Fast Ethernet, there are some things you ought to know before choosing one
Fast Ethernet physical layer technology over another.

If You Have Category 3 or 4

While Category 5 wiring has been available for about five years, it has only
been used in significant volumes since about 1993. As a result, Category 3
and 4 wiring still dominate, accounting for over 50 percent of the installed
base. If your cabling system is more than two years old, it is likely that your

Table 4.4

Comparing Different
Features and Benefits of
Fiber and Category 5 UTP
Cabling

	UTP CATEGORY 5	MULTIMODE FIBER
Segment cost (NIC, hub, cable, from Table 4.3)	$686	$1,185
Capacity for higher speeds	No, limited to 100 Mbps	Yes, 1 Gbps plus
Bundles available for conduits & easy installation	No*	2,4,6,8,12,24,48 bundles
Distance limitation	100m	Many km
Affected by EMI	Yes	No
Certifiable today	Not yet**	Yes
Temperature range	-5 C to +50 C	-20 C to +70 C
Reliability	Excellent	Excellent
Availability of hardware equipment	Excellent	Low
Availability of skilled installers	Good	OK

* AT&T and other manufacturers have recently started selling 25-pair Category 5 bundles and Amphenol or TELCO connectors as well. These products are too new to tell if they are truly Category 5 capable.

••The EIA=TIA is working on certification guidelines, which are expected to be complete by late 1995.

cabling is Category 3 or 4. This is illustrated in Figure 4.7. In this case you can only use 100BASE-T4 products. Note that 100BASE-T4 requires all four pairs of UTP wire, whereas both 10BASE-T and Token Ring only require two pairs. The PDS specifications from AT&T and the EIA have always required the use of four pairs of cable for data and a separate telephone or modem line, so you should have two free pairs available on your data cabling. However, some people may have used the two spare lines for a phone or modem connection, so make sure that the two spares are indeed available. One or both of the spare pairs may also be damaged (four pairs were originally specified to provide for spare pairs).

If You Have IBM Type 1 Cabling

If your cable plant uses IBM Type 1 STP, you will be able to convert to 100BASE-TX with some work. STP Token Ring NICs use a DB-9 connector and not the common RJ-45, so you will have to change connectors. Make sure you use Category 5-capable RJ-45 connectors and cross-connect equipment! (We know of one 100BASE-T equipment vendor that includes a DB-9

Figure 4.7

By late 1994, Category 5 was already outselling Category 3/4 wiring. However, it will take years before the installed base of UTP becomes predominantly Category 5 also.

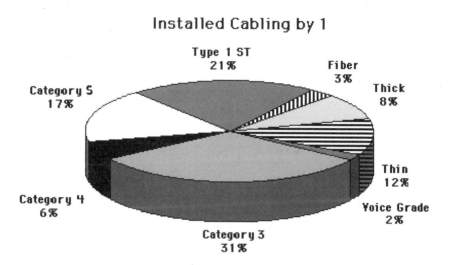

Installed Cabling by 1

Type 1 ST 21%

Fiber 3%

Thick 8%

Thin 12%

Voice Grade 2%

Category 3 31%

Category 4 6%

Category 5 17%

connector on their 100BASE-TX NICs.) Most new Token Ring installations use UTP, and probably have Category 5 wiring and RJ-45 connectors installed.

If You Have Category 5 Cabling

Most new installations use Category 5 wiring these days. A minimum of four pairs of Category 5 wiring is specified for EIA/TIA-compliant cable and connectors, so you have a choice of running either 100BASE-TX or 100BASE-T4 over the same Category 5 wiring plant. Which one is preferable? A comparison of 100BASE-T4 and 100BASE-TX follows below:

- 100BASE-T4 operates at a much lower frequency than 100BASE-TX. This makes 100BASE-T4 a superior solution in certain situations. 100BASE-T4 will work better in inferior cabling installations. Often the actual cable will meet Category 5 requirements, but other parts of the wiring system may not. For example, connectors or cross-connect devices such as punch-down blocks or patch panels may not meet Category 5 standards. In such instances 100BASE-T4 will work fine, but 100BASE-TX will encounter problems.

- The major disadvantage of 100BASE-T4 is that it requires all four pairs of wiring. Theoretically most Category 5 installations should have all four pairs of wiring available, but often cabling installers only terminated two pairs, or two pairs are used for something else, or a pair may be damaged.

- 100BASE-TX will soon be capable of full-duplex, but 100BASE-T4 by design is not capable of full-duplex operation. Remember that full-duplex requires a full-duplex capable switch at the other end, so if you are going to use repeating hubs, full-duplex is not an option.

Which one is for you? The 100BASE-TX technology was borrowed from the ANSI CDDI standard, whereas T4 was newly invented. As a result, many different 100BASE-TX products are already available, whereas T4 products only started shipping in mid-1995, over a year after 100BASE-TX products became available. Since all new wiring is going to be Category 5, it is unclear at this point whether or not the robustness of 100BASE-T4 will be sufficient to catch up with the market momentum that 100BASE-TX has gathered. It is likely that both physical layers will coexist for many years to come.

Our conclusion is that 100BASE-T4 is the safer choice, whereas 100BASE-TX offers higher performance. We recommend that if you have any doubts about the quality of your wiring plant, go with T4. Table 4.5 compares 100BASE-TX with 100BASE-T4.

Table 4.5

Comparing 100BASE-TX and 100BASE-T4 shows no clear advantage for either UTP physical layer technology. Both are likely to coexist.

	100BASE-T4	100BASE-TX
Number of pairs required		2
Cable Category required	CAT 3/4/5	CAT 5 or STP Type 1
Connectors required	CAT 3/4/5	CAT 5
Lower cost	✓	
Proven		✓
Full-duplex capable		✓
Broader product support		✓
Better noise margins	✓	

■ Category 5 Wiring Closets and Cross-Connection Considerations

We mentioned before that a network system is always as weak as its weakest link. The same concept applies to wiring, especially Category 5 cabling plant installations. When you are installing or using Category 5 cable, you need to make sure that your entire cabling system is truly Category 5-capable. A Category 5 system consists of many different elements:

• Wall plates (the data or information outlet close to the node)

- Station cables (the cable that runs from node to wall plate)
- Category 5-capable shielded RJ-45 connectors everywhere
- The actual horizontal Category 5 cabling connection nodes
- Wiring closet patch panels

Cross-Connect Devices

The wiring closet is the center of the network, and the importance of quality work in the wiring closet is often overlooked. Figure 4.8 shows a typical wiring closet layout.

Figure 4.8

A wiring closet includes many different components, all of which need to be Category-5 capable.

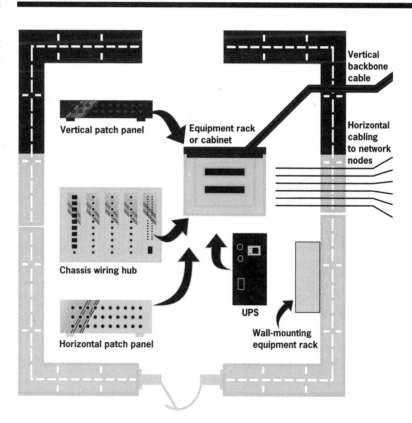

Wiring closet cross-connect devices are needed in order to expand or re-configure your network. Punch-down blocks were first used in the telephone industry to facilitate changing connections, and have been used for data connections over the last few years. Older punch-down blocks are not Category-5 capable, but the newer 110-style products are (the older type was known as the

66-style punch-down block, the new one is called the 110-style, and is manufactured by AT&T, Siemens, and others). Over the last few years, many customers have a new type of cross-connect device called the patch panel, which is easily reconfigurable because the connection is made via a patch cable that uses RJ-45 connectors. These devices can be mounted in distribution cabinets or racks, and the newer types of patch panels are Category 5 quality (Figure 4.9).

Figure 4.9

A patch panel connects the hub with the network node cabling. Category 5 patch cables terminated with Category 5 RJ-45 connectors are used to cross-connect.

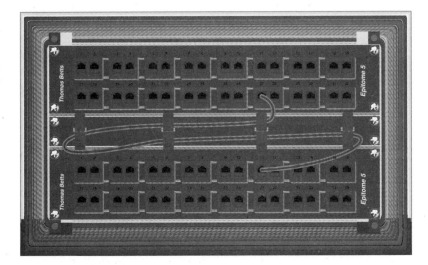

Frequently, 25-pair bundle cabling is used for interconnects between panels and networking hubs. 25-pair bundle cable is always Category 3. Some 100BASE-T4 equipment may work on 25-pair bundles, but you need to check with the network hub and NIC manufacturer to see if this is the case. Category 5-capable 25-pair bundles are also becoming available, but this type of cable still needs to be proven.

■ Test Equipment and Certification

This section will discuss the subject of cable testers. In addition, we will discuss how to certify cable plants with these cable testers, as this is a very current topic that has undergone some changes recently.

Twisted Pair Testers

Today a hand-held cable tester to troubleshoot wiring problems is part of every LAN administrator's tool kit. Until recently, these hand-held twisted-pair cable testing devices were only capable of testing cables up to a frequency of 20 MHz, limiting these devices to testing 16-Mbps Token Ring or 10-Mbps Ethernet cables. However, 100BASE-T4 operates at a signal frequency of 25 MHz, slightly higher than what current testers analyze, so it may be okay to use existing test equipment. Since 100BASE-TX transmits a 41.6-MHz signal, you definitely cannot test your cabling plant with one of the older testers.

Fortunately, a number of 100-MHz-capable cable testers have emerged over the last two years. That means you can now reliably test, certify, and troubleshoot both four-pair Category 3 cable for 100BASE-T4 capability and four-pair Category 5 UTP or two-pair Type 1 STP cable for 100BASE-TX installations.

Many companies now offer Category 5-capable testers. We like the Pentascanner from Microtest, the LANCAT V from Datacom Technologies, the WireScope 100 from Scope Communications, and the Fluke DSP-100. New models are being introduced all the time, so check the trade press for reviews on the latest and greatest testers.

These hand-held testers are quite an engineering feat. Although they look like Nintendo Gameboys, they are rather impressive measurement devices. All of them offer the same basic wire test functionality plus features to spare. The testers feature a single-button autotest function that will analyze the cable link completely. Some sort of loopback or injector module has to be plugged into the other end of the wire before starting the test. The testers initially check the wiring map, which includes wiring faults such as basic continuity and miswired, split, reversed, open, or shorted pairs. Then a complete cable link analysis follows that includes the cable's electrical properties such as attenuation, internally generated noise (NEXT or near-end cross-talk), external noise, length, resistance, and characteristic impedance. All of this happens in a matter of seconds. The tests can be run individually as well, and the results can be displayed, printed, archived, or transmitted via a serial link to a PC.

What Is NEXT?

NEXT is the coupling of signals from one twisted pair to another twisted pair. NEXT is undesirable because it represents unwanted spillover from one pair to the other. The term *near-end* means that the coupling takes place on the end of the cable where the transmission originates. If NEXT becomes too large, data transmissions could be corrupted. The UTP cable itself causes near-end cross-talk, but male and female RJ-45 connectors, patch panels, and wall plates can also contribute a significant amount of NEXT. Major contributors to NEXT are Category 3 connectors, crossed or split pairs, untwisted cables or patch panels, and cables that are damaged by being pulled so tightly that the pairs change position inside the jacket.

Attenuation Loss

Cable resistance, inductance, and capacitance reduce the signal strength of a transmission from one end of the cable to the other. As UTP cable transmission needs to meet EMI emission standards, the original transmitted signal is relatively weak to begin with. If the attenuation of the signal is too large, the receiving end will not be able to distinguish a signal from noise, and data errors will occur. Both NEXT and attenuation are measured on a relative logarithmic decibel (dB) scale.

Attenuation and near-end cross-talk are the most difficult to measure accurately. Professional network cable testers made by Hewlett-Packard, for example, cost tens of thousands of dollars. Manufacturers are differentiating their products through ease of use, test time, software upgradeability, and additional features, such as data test result management software. Others, such as the LANCAT V, even offer network utilization and collision readings that also make them useful as traffic analysis tools.

■ Cable Plant Certification

Certification means comparing your cabling plant's performance to a predetermined set of values. Certification is important so that you know that your installer has done a quality job. In the old days of Category 3 cabling, certification of a cabling plant was not a big issue. That was because a correctly wired installation was very forgiving and likely to pass all certification tests because the requirements were relatively easy. With Category 5 installations, all that has changed. Quality of workmanship, cross-connect equipment, connectors, and so forth now can make or break a Category 5 installation. To address this need for certification, the EIA/TIA is publishing a new standard for certification testing.

To date there has been a lot of confusion about Category 5 certification. In the past, an appendix to the original EIA/TIA 568 specification and a Technical Service Bulletin (TSB) was used to determine pass/fail guidelines for installed cable systems. However this Appendix E and TSB-36 were intended for laboratory testing only and proved insufficient for certification purposes. For example, impedance of a cable varies significantly with temperature, and the original standards only allowed for measurements at a specific temperature. This is of course impossible when testing is done in the field. Then, there were no clear certification rules—what to test, what the acceptable test values were, and how accurate the test equipment itself was. Subsequently, an EIA/TIA task force (called the Link Performance Task Group) started investigating the subject of field testing of cabling systems in order to come up with a clear set of certification standards. This task force has almost completed its work, and the upcoming EIA/TIA 568 *TSB-67 Link Performance Test Standard* will likely define a complete standard for test equipment, test methods, and guidelines for interpreting the results.

1. Two different types of test configurations are defined, called Channel Link and Basic Link. The Basic Link only includes the actual horizontal cabling, and is also known as the contractors link. The Channel or users link defines the entire network connection from network node to hub, and includes the actual cable as well as equipment and patch cables, connectors, cross-connects, and so on. Neither link includes the RJ-45 connectors that are used to connect to the NIC or to the hub.

2. TSB-67 will specify exact NEXT, attenuation, and other values that will form the pass/fail limits. Hand-held scanners will then certify cabling by comparing test results against predetermined values (Figure 4.10).

Figure 4.10

The Fluke DSP-100 cable tester is a Level II cable tester that can certify Category 5 links in accordance with the upcoming EIA/TIA TSB-67 standard.

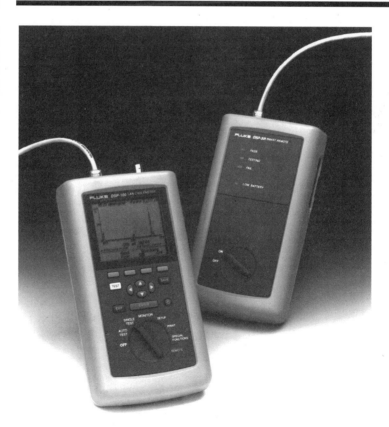

3. The specification will also define the accuracy levels required for field test equipment. Actual measurement error has been an issue with some of today's hand-held testers, and hence the quality of hand-held testers will be specified also. There are two levels under consideration, with Level II being the more stringent one. A Level II instrument would be accurate enough to perform certification work and would have an accuracy of +- 2dB. A Level I type instrument would have a much-reduced accuracy sufficient for troubleshooting only.

The EIA/TIA expects to complete TSB-67 by the end of 1995.

Fiber Optic Cable Testers

Fiber test equipment for the FDDI market has been available for a number of years (Figure 4.11). As both FDDI and 100BASE-T use the same physical layer interface, the same fiber cabling and the same ST connector, FDDI testers can be used for testing 100BASE-TX cabling as well. Fiber testers are much simpler than UTP testers because they need to measure only two things: continuity and attenuation loss. Hand-held testers are available from many different companies and consist of two pieces of equipment. A fiber test source connected to one end of the fiber sends a test signal that is then measured by a fiber optic power meter connected to the other end of the fiber cable. In this way continuity and attenuation loss can be measured in a matter of seconds.

Most of the problems in fiber networks involve faulty connections. Connectors in particular require careful assembly and testing, but modern technology and suitably trained installers can now install a fiber connector in a matter of minutes. Troubleshooting is also relatively easy, and can be done by injecting a bright visible light into the fiber and then finding the fault through visual inspection.

If the cable cannot be visibly inspected, a more expensive optical time domain reflectometer (OTDR) may be required. Reflectometers are expensive, so we suggest that you hire a company if you need to do this kind of troubleshooting.

The Importance of Professional Work

People often take shortcuts when installing cabling hoping that just installing the right cable will be sufficient. Shoddy work during the installation process can impact the overall quality of your cabling plant. For example, Category 5 cable needs to have the proper twisting retained right up to the RJ-45 connector (13mm). Bending or pulling Category 5 UTP wire too much will change the carefully controlled twists and impact its performance. Fiber connectors, on the other hand, are difficult to install without proper training and

Figure 4.11

The Fotec Fiber Optic Test kit contains a fiber optic light source, a FO power meter, and accessories. With fiber, many UTP issues such as NEXT and miswired pairs do not exist, making certification and troubleshooting of fiber cabling easier.

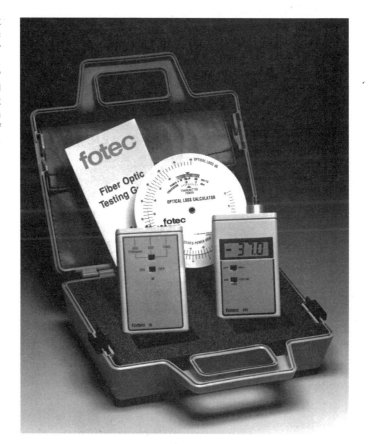

equipment. We recommend that you hire only reputable, quality contractors to install all your cabling for you. Make sure that your cabling plant is properly labeled and documented. Neatness is important. Also, hire only contractors that can have received the proper training for doing optical fiber or Category 5 installations.

■ Summary

This chapter discussed the different cabling requirements for 100BASE-T. You can run 100BASE-TX on either IBM STP Type 1 cable, or two-pair Category 5 UTP. 100BASE-T requires four pairs of Category 3/4/5 wire. Multimode or singlemode optical fiber will support 100BASE-FX for extended distances. We recommend that you use 100BASE-FX equipment for backbones and areas where you might upgrade to ATM at some point in the future. Otherwise we recommend 100BASE-T4 unless your connections are full-duplex.

A reputable, well-trained contractor that can certify your wiring plant is important. Don't take shortcuts when installing new cable or equipment—make sure your cabling plant will outlast your networking hardware!

- *Objectives of This Chapter*
- *How to Tell If Your Network Is Overloaded*
- *Why Ethernet Is Running Out of Bandwidth*
- *Conclusion*
- *Recommendations*

5

Bandwidth: How Much Is Enough?

TEN YEARS AGO, WE INSTALLED OUR FIRST PC LAN. WE DECIDED TO *go for 10-Mbps Ethernet, although the StarLAN and Arcnet sales people told us we would never need more than 1 or 2 Mbps. Over the years we kept adding more users and servers and bought laser printers, and as a result, network traffic grew. Fortunately our Ethernet network had plenty of capacity left, so bandwidth never became an issue. Then, about five years ago, everyone wanted e-mail and network traffic started growing more rapidly. Bandwidth still wasn't a problem—if a network became too heavily loaded we would segment it into smaller LANs, and that would do the job. So today my users are complaining again about how slow the network is. I have decided to do something about it and upgrade my network. That's why I bought this book.*

This story probably sounds familiar to many of you. This chapter will talk a lot about networking bandwidth. Bandwidth is like CPU MIPS or memory on your PC—you can never have enough of it. Remember those days when we thought that 64KB of RAM or a 10MB hard disk was a lot? Remember the days when nobody was ever going to need the power of a 386? If nothing else, two things have become predictable in the personal computer industry. First, you can never have enough of anything—RAM, CPU MIPS, hard-disk space, or bandwidth. Second, the stuff you buy today will automatically become obsolete a few years from now. Remember the last point when planning your network for future growth.

■ Objectives of This Chapter

Before you spend all this money on new networking hardware, you need to figure out if it's really the hardware that's not keeping up or if other bottle-necks are slowing down your network. The first objective of this chapter is to help you understand the bandwidth capability of your existing network—in other words, to help you find out if your network is overloaded, and if so, by how much.

What is really driving this need for more speed on our networks? Some may say that the answer is to be found on our desks—Ethernet can no longer keep up with clients and servers that now regularly feature Pentium micro-processors with 100 or more MIPS of computing power, 16MB of RAM, and hard disks that exceed one gigabyte (GB). The answer lies not just in the in-creased computing power available today. These high-performance personal computers that are available now will only impact your network if they are actually using the network. In this chapter we will examine some of the trends in networked computing, and how these trends are using up band-width at a rapid pace. We will discuss the very familiar reasons behind the ever-increasing levels of network traffic, such as more users, larger files, and so on. We will also talk about the new types of networked applications such as client-server, multimedia, and the Internet, and how they use increasingly more bandwidth.

Last, this chapter will provide some guidelines on how to manage your network's growth over the next few years to accommodate these emerging applications.

A Reality Check

A lot of the current hype surrounding high-speed networking equipment is being generated by a self-serving hardware industry trying to enlarge the market for its own products. The industry as a whole is trying to convince you, the potential buyer of networking equipment, that your LAN is running out of bandwidth fast. The motivation is clear—vendors want to sell you new, faster, more expensive and more profitable equipment. So how overloaded are today's networks? Is 10-Mbps Ethernet really at the end of its life?

Are Today's Ethernet Networks Overcrowded?

Do all of today's Ethernet networks resemble a Los Angeles freeway? Probably not. There are literally millions of different Ethernet networks out there, and many of them are doing fine as they are. After all, the average Ethernet network has only 21 users on it, with network utilization in the single digits. Networks with such a small number of nodes are unlikely to saturate a 10-Mbps Ethernet network any time soon. However, 21 users per network is a statistical average, which means that there are quite a few networks out there that have significantly more than 21 users on them. These networks can and do experience gridlock during peak hours. Larger networks account for a significant amount of nodes and traffic out there, and here overloading has become an issue. That's why concepts such as segmenting, moving users around, and using backbones and server farms have all become very popular tools for dividing up a large LAN into many smaller LANs and thereby reducing traffic levels.

Has the Network Infrastructure Become the Weakest Link?

When we speak of a *network* we need to be more precise, because today's network is a complex assembly of many different building blocks that interact with each other to form what we refer to as "the network." This network *system* consists of NICs, hubs, and physical cabling, as well as clients, file/print servers, application servers, network operating systems, applications, and other components.

In order to improve the overall *system* performance, it may not be enough to just upgrade one part of it. There is always at least one critical path item that is slowing the entire system down, but replacing only this one critical component may immediately reveal another performance-limiting piece that was invisible before.

The reality of today's client-server system is that you are probably using or buying other system elements that can outperform your network hardware infrastructure. For example, when you buy a Pentium processor-based server and install Microsoft Windows NT 3.5, you automatically get a server that delivers orders of magnitude more performance than a 386-based server running LAN Manager did five years ago. It makes sense, then, that you should take a good look at your 10-Mbps LAN to determine whether it is still capable of providing your system with enough performance capabilities or whether your network has or will become the next critical path item. One word of caution: Don't just automatically assume that your networking hardware has become the bottleneck. Author Martin Nemzow, in his book *LAN Performance Optimization,* claims that the LAN transmission speed is the bottleneck in only 10 percent of all networks. Installation errors, specification violations, less-than-perfect configurations, poor node performance, poor placement of firebreaks, and overloaded file servers account for most of the bottlenecks in today's networks. The bottom line is that you shouldn't just look at upgrading your physical hardware infrastructure alone.

■ How to Tell If Your Network Is Overloaded

The easy part of the diagnosis is determining whether or not the network is overloaded. The difficult part is determining what to do about it. The following section will help you figure out if your network is overloaded. Chapters 6 through 8 will then tell you what to do about it.

There are two ways to tell if your network is running out of steam. The first way is to listen to your customers, the network users. Unfortunately, this is also the reactive way, because your customers are unlikely to notice that your network is overloaded until it is too late. At that point they will be calling you and complaining about the speed of the network.

The second way to tell if your network is overloaded is the proactive way—measuring what's going in your network. We recommend that you do a regular check-up on your network even when it is working fine, because—as the doctor says—prevention is better than cure.

The Customer Way: Unhappy Users

If you are a network manager, it will eventually become very obvious to you when your network has become saturated. In this connection, Ethernet and your network operating system will still make sure the data gets delivered—it could just take a very long time. However, your users will be calling frequently to complain about sluggishness in loading networked applications, long waiting periods for transferring files, or the infamous *NETWORK ERROR* Windows message that typically indicates a lost or missing server connection. Look for signs of trouble especially during rush hour on the network, which is typically between the hours of 8 and 10 a.m., when everyone arrives at work and logs on to the network simultaneously. Obviously you don't ever want to get to this stage, because at this point your patient, the network, will be ill and exhibiting signs of severe overloading.

The Technical Way: Measuring Utilization

This section will first discuss the capacity limits of Ethernet networks. You may be surprised to learn that although Ethernet is a 10Mbps LAN technology, its actual data throughput is limited to less than half of that. We will also discuss ways of measuring your LAN's actual data throughput in order to determine if your network is indeed overloaded.

Some Background on the Theory of Ethernet

Before discussing how to analyze your network bandwidth utilization, we need to discuss some basics of Ethernet transmission theory.

Shared Ethernet networks use the CSMA/CD protocol, which exhibits certain characteristics that make it unsuitable for high network utilization. The CSMA/CD protocol was discussed in detail in Chapter 3, but here is a recap of how it operates: A station wanting to transmit has to ensure that no other nodes are currently using the shared media wire, so a station listens to the cable first to make sure it is free. If the channel is free, the station will start transmitting. A collision may occur if two or more stations listen while waiting to transmit, then simultaneously determine that the wire is free and begin transmitting at almost the same time. This event would lead to a collision and destroy the data.

Imagine multiple stations going through this process at the same time. Collisions are an indication of a resource conflict and increase exponentially as the number of stations and traffic load increase. A collision causes the network to reset, which forces the relevant nodes to retransmit some time later. Ethernet has no built-in overload protection, and adding more traffic to the network increases collisions even more. At some point the entire available bandwidth becomes used up by collisions and subsequent jam signals and stations waiting for another chance to retransmit after a collision. This condition is called network saturation.

Definitions

Before we tell you what the capacity limits of an Ethernet network are, we need to define and explain some terms that are used to describe LAN traffic. This list is not complete; we have described only the most commonly used terms that are relevant to our discussion.

Wire speed is measured in Mbps. Ethernet wire speed is 10 Mbps, Fast Ethernet wire speed is 100 Mbps. Wire speed defines the actual speed of the data transmission along the cable once a transmission has started, not the actual capacity or throughput that the LAN is capable of. Sometimes the term *bandwidth* is used as a synonym for wire speed.

Please note that 10-Mbps "classic" Ethernet and the new Fast Ethernet operate in exactly the same way. The only difference is that the wire speed for Fast Ethernet is ten times that of regular Ethernet. All other concepts and properties are the same, except that absolute numbers are ten times as large. For example, Fast Ethernet still saturates at the same percentage point as regular Ethernet, but the throughput in Mbps is ten times as large.

The following pages discuss 10-Mbps Ethernet networks and its real-world throughput capability; keep in mind that everything would scale by a factor of 10 if we were discussing Fast Ethernet instead.

Every Ethernet packet includes data, as well as a preamble, source, and destination address, length field, and error checking. In addition, every packet or frame is separated from the next one by the minimum interframe gap (IFG). The preamble, address, length of field, and IFG make up a significant amount of the total Ethernet frame length. We have lumped the bits and length field, and IFG makeup together and called them *overhead*. We chose this name because these bits do not represent actual data transmission. For the maximum packet of 1,518 bytes, this overhead takes up 2.5 percent of the total transmission time. This gives Ethernet a best-case efficiency of 97.5 percent. For a packet size of 500 bytes, overhead increases to 7.4 percent, reducing the efficiency to 92.6 percent. Table 5.1 below illustrates how Ethernet efficiency varies as a function of packet size.

Table 5.1

Ethernet Efficiency Ratings Vary Depending on Packet Size.

DATA SIZE	PACKET SIZE	OVERHEAD	MAXIMUM EFFICIENCY
1,492 bytes	1,518 bytes (maximum)	2.5%	97.5%
974	1,000 bytes	3.8%	96.2%
474 bytes	500	7.4%	92.6%
38 bytes (no PAD)	64 bytes (minimum)	50.0%	50.0%
1 byte (plus 27 bytes PAD)	64 bytes (minimum)	98.7%	1.3%

Utilization means that there is some sort of activity on the wire. This can be an actual packet that gets received, a packet that later collides with another packet, an acknowledgment signal, or a jam signal. Also included in this number is the interframe gap (IFG) time. If the wire is not being utilized it would be idle. Utilization is measured in percent of time. For example, if there is activity on an Ethernet wire one third of the time, the utilization is 33 percent.

Peak utilization is the maximum utilization that has occurred within a given time period. When the actual Ethernet transmission is occurring, data is being transmitted at a wire rate of 10 or 100 Mbps. We have so far been discussing average utilization only, but most Ethernet test equipment can measure both average and peak utilization.

We define *throughput* as measures the actual data rate that is successfully transmitted across the wire. Throughput is also measured in Mbps and excludes all overhead bits, as well as bad frames and jam signals. Note that most traffic analyzer tools report only actual frames transmitted, not data throughput. In order to record data rates, the analyzer would have to deduct the overhead.

Traffic in our case means utilization.

Efficiency of a network is a measurement of how much effort is required to produce a certain amount of data throughput.

$$\text{Efficiency} = \frac{\text{Results}}{\text{Effort}} = \frac{\text{Data throughput}}{\text{Utilization} \times \text{wire speed}}$$

If, for example, the data throughput rate is 2 Mbps on a 10-Mbps Ethernet network with a wire utilization of 30 percent, then the efficiency is $2 / (30\% \times 10) = 67\%$.

Saturation describes the point at which an Ethernet network has reached its practical limits. In terms of throughput, the CSMA/CD protocol makes Ethernet a very cost-effective and high-performance network for light to medium loads or a small number of stations. When the network utilization increases beyond a certain point, collisions will start increasing until they overwhelm all actual data throughput. When adding nodes or traffic to a network that is in saturation, throughput will no longer increase. Once a network is deeply saturated, adding more load will cause throughput to decline.

Next we will discuss the actual throughput capabilities of Ethernet. Let's take a look at how collisions change our theoretical throughput and efficiency numbers by looking at two real-world networks. Figure 5.1 shows a network that has only two nodes, which is similar to a switched environment; and a network that has 200 nodes connected, representing a fully loaded large corporate network. We have also plotted the theoretical 1,000-byte/96-percent line for reference purposes.

The line labeled *2 nodes with collisions* shows what kind of real-world data throughput can be achieved with a network consisting of only two nodes. A two-node network will exhibit a limited number of collisions, as there are only two stations competing for the wire, so collision degradation is not significant. The maximum throughput is achieved when the utilization reaches 100 percent and is a respectable 7 Mbps. This means that collisions only account for $(9.6–7.0) = 2.6$ Mbps, or about 25 percent of the available bandwidth. The efficiency at this point would be $7 \text{ Mbps}/(10\text{Mbps} \times 100\%) = 70\%$.

Figure 5.1

This graph shows actual Erthernet throughput with collisions. Ethernet has no built-in overload mechanism; therefore, real-world throughput is significantly lower than wire speed.

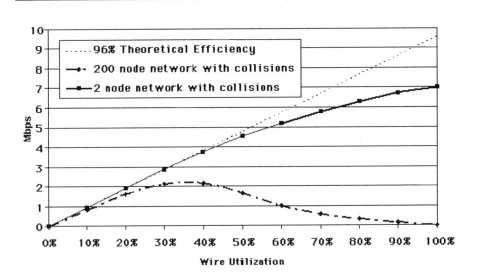

The line labeled *200 nodes with collisions* illustrates another real-world network with 200 nodes contending for the same wire. The *maximum* throughput on this kind of network amounts to about 2.5 Mbps and corresponds to 40 percent utilization. If the wire utilization exceeds 40 percent, saturation occurs and throughput actually declines to the point where no data can be delivered across the wire because collisions dominate.

Switched Ethernet

A Switched Ethernet connection operates like a two-node network and does not exhibit the same saturation characteristics as a large shared network and operates extremely well even beyond the 40 percent utilization level. Note that the maximum throughput rate is achieved at 100 percent utilization, although some saturation takes place beyond 80 percent utilization. However, the data throughput does not decrease, as it does in shared Ethernet networks. Switched Ethernet connections can, in fact, be operated at utilization rates of up to 100 percent!

Full-Duplex Switched Ethernet

Full-duplex Ethernet provides performance capabilities that exceed those of Switched Ethernet. Full-duplex Ethernet requires a switched two-node connection and allows for simultaneous transmission and reception on two pairs of cable. Full-duplex under ideal circumstances can therefore sustain *100 percent utilization on each channel*, which means a theoretical utilization limit of 200 percent. This number can be reached only if other parts of the network are also full-duplex capable, which is often not the case. For example, switch-switch connections will often see utilization rates that exceed 100 percent, but any connections involving clients or servers will be limited to 100 percent because today's network operating systems and protocol stacks do not yet support full-duplex properly. Please refer to the full-duplex discussion in Chapter 3 for more details.

Figure 5.2 plots the throughput for the same identical 200-node network, but on a smaller and more legible scale (area plot, right scale). The network efficiency (line plot, use the left scale) is superimposed on the same graph. Please note that for a network utilization below 40 percent, the efficiency remains high, above 50 percent. When the utilization reaches 30 percent, the throughput has almost reached its peak at about 2.2 Mbps. The maximum throughput of 2.5 Mbps is reached at a utilization of 37 percent. Once utilization starts exceeding 40 percent, the efficiency drops below 50 percent very rapidly, approaching almost zero percent. This means that the wire is saturated and that throughput has declined to zero! You want your network to stay below the 40 percent average utilization line, which corresponds to a data throughput rate of about 2.5 Mbps and an 8 percent collision rate.

Figure 5.2

Ethernet efficiency and throughput are plotted for a large 200-node network. Note that throughput and efficiency decline rapidly beyond 37 percent utilization.

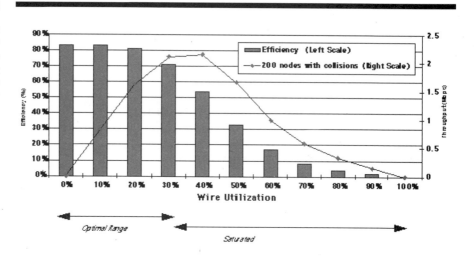

Note also that the throughput line can be approximated by a straight line if the utilization does not exceed 35 percent. This means that we can use the variable utilization to infer throughput capabilities. This fact can be used to estimate the available remaining throughput that your Ethernet network is capable of. If, for example, your utilization is 17 percent, then your network is running at approximately 50 percent of total capacity.

Conclusion

Utilization is a very reliable way of measuring the loading of an Ethernet LAN. Due to the nature of the CSMA/CD protocol, shared Ethernet networks cannot operate at high utilization rates. Peaks above 37 percent can be tolerated for short periods, but loading your shared network with more than 37 percent for extended periods of time will not be productive. We recommend that you use 37 percent average utilization as the maximum value for your shared Ethernet network. This corresponds to actual data throughput of about 2.5 Mbps for 10-Mbps Ethernet or 25 Mbps for a Fast Ethernet network. Attempting to load your Ethernet network beyond this point will result in unsatisfactory response times and possible errors. This should serve as your guideline for determining if a shared Ethernet network is overloaded.

Switched Ethernet connections have two major advantages in that the available bandwidth does not have to be time-shared with numerous other stations. The connection can also operate at up to 100 percent utilization if required, which translates to a data throughput of 7.0 Mbps. Full-duplex Ethernet provides even more performance allowing for simultaneous transmission and reception. Under ideal circumstances, 100 percent utilization on each cable pair can be achieved, which increases the theoretical utilization limit to 200 percent. Table 5.2 summarizes the real-world throughput capabilities of 10-Mbps, 100-Mbps shared, Switched, and Switched full-duplex Ethernet.

Next, we will look at the many tools that are available for measuring network utilization.

Tools to Measure Loading

The nice thing about a shared media network is that all the traffic is transmitted to all points on the network simultaneously. That means you can "tune in" or listen for traffic at any point on the LAN and find out what the utilization is like. For switched or segmented networks, the procedure becomes much more cumbersome—you may have to physically measure each segment or connection in order to get an accurate reading of the traffic on that segment.

There are many kinds of tools available for analyzing the loading of Ethernet networks. We have mentioned a wide variety of products here that allow you to measure utilization levels, in the hope that you will have at least one of them around to get the job done. The most common tools available for network analysis are software-based traffic analyzers. Protocol analyzers will also do the job, although they are somewhat of an overkill for the task of measuring network utilization. Last, there is a new breed of hand-held diagnostics tools that may be the best choice for measuring utilization.

Table 5.2

Real-World Data
Throughput for 10- and
100-Mbps Ethernet
Networks

CORRECTION TYPE	WIRE SPEED	UTILIZATION LIMIT	BITS ON WIRE	ACTUAL DATA THROUGHPUT LIMIT
Shared Ethernet	10 Mbps	37%	3.7 Mbps	2.5 Mbps
Switched Ethernet	10 Mbps	Up to 100%	8.3 Mbps	7.0 Mbps
Switched Full-Duplex Ethernet	10 Mbps	Up to 200% *	20 Mbps	14 Mbps *
Shared Fast Ethernet	100 Mbps	37% (same as regular Ethernet)	37 Mbps	25 Mbps (10X of regular Ethernet)
Switched Fast Ethernet	100 Mbps	Up to 100% (same as regular Ethernet)	83 Mbps	70 Mbps (10X of regular Ethernet)
Switched Full-Duplex Fast Ethernet	100 Mbps	Up to 200% *	164 Mbps	140 Mbps *

* These are approximations and can only be achieved in ideal circumstances, such as switch-switch.

Protocol Analyzers

Protocol analyzers are expert tools used for analyzing and troubleshooting networks. Protocol analyzers typically consist of a dedicated PC, combined with networking hardware and software. Probably the best-known protocol analyzer is the Sniffer, made by Network General. The Sniffer protocol analyzer does exactly what its name implies—it analyzes data down to the protocol level, looking "inside" the actual data packet to capture information such as protocol type (IPX, TCP/IP, and so on). Protocol analyzers also allow you to figure out exactly where specific packets of data are coming from and going to. Protocol analyzers are very sophisticated tools, primarily used for troubleshooting networks. (see Chapter 10 for more details). They can, however, be used to measure network utilization as well.

For larger switched or routed environments, Network General also makes a version of the Sniffer called Distributed Sniffer that allows you to monitor remote sites either in-band with the aid of RMON or through an out-of-band telephone link. (The RMON protocol is part of the SNMP specification and allows for remote network segment monitoring. It is discussed in detail in Chapter 9.)

Software-Based Protocol Analyzers

These analyzers are software applications that run on a standard PC or work-station. They provide almost the same functionality as a protocol analyzer, with less detail. For our job here they still work fine. The most common one is probably Novell's LANAlyzer for Windows product. Most of today's network and desktop management suites also contain a traffic analyzer of some sort. Figure 5.3 below shows Intel's LANDesk Traffic Analyst, which is part of LANDesk Manager Suite 2.0.

Figure 5.3

Many desktop and network management packages, such as Intel's LANDesk Manager, feature built-in traffic monitoring capabilities.

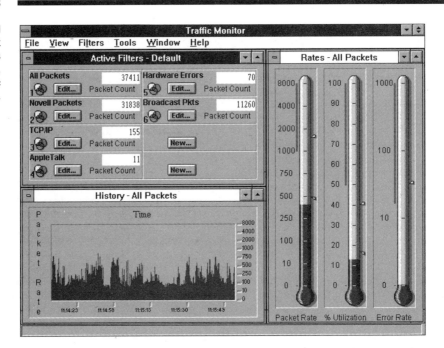

Don't go and buy a protocol analyzer just to measure traffic—other tools can do the same task for significantly less money. For switched or routed segments, a product from Triticom called RMONster may do the job—it's a PC-based software package that is cheap and will allow you to monitor traffic levels and many other functions in switched segments.

Network Management Software

Most managable hubs collect statistics that include traffic data as well. This data can usually be viewed from any SNMP network management platform, such as Bay Networks Optivity. Some, but not all, switching hubs also provide this capability. In this case the management software allows you to look at the traffic of each switched port. The SNMP remote monitoring function, called RMON, is often used to achieve this. Please refer to Chapter 9 for more on this.

Hand-Held Diagnostics Tools

Some of the newer hand-held cable testers incorporate a network utilization function. To date, there have been two very different kinds of testers available, either protocol analyzers or hand-held cable testers. Conceptually, both have been around for a while, but recently the lines between cable and protocol testers have begun to blur as a new class of hand-held diagnostics tool has emerged that can test a variety of network functions. These new hand-held testers do a little bit of everything, including some protocol, MAC, physical layer, and wiring analysis; you can think of them as universal testers. These new testers are primarily targeted at quick network troubleshooting. Examples are the Compas from Microtest and the FrameScope 802 from Scope Communications. These new Ethernet "handypeople" include a variety of features, such as cable testing, protocol and frame analysis, server monitoring, file server diagnostics, and general traffic measurements. It's the last function that we are interested in—you can use these diagnostics tools to measure utilization and collision rates. While these diagnostics tools do not provide the level of functionality that a dedicated protocol or cable tester does, they are very useful portable tools. Unfortunately, 100BASE-T versions are not available yet, but are in the works according to the manufacturers. Figure 5.4 illustrates what kinds of functions these different hand-held devices perform.

Figure 5.4

Several types of hand-held testers have emerged over the last few years.

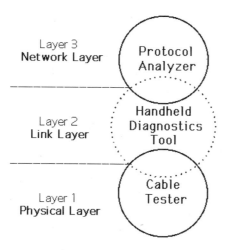

The three types of testers are shown in relation to the OSI model. Conventional cable testers were discussed further in Chapter 4, and classical protocol analyzers are covered in Chapter 10.

The PsiberNET Tool

Recently we came across a brand-new product that deserves special mention in this chapter. The problem with *all* the analyzers that we discussed so far is that they need to be connected to the network that you are testing. While that's relatively easy with today's 10BASE-T networks, it still means that you need to physically connect to the network or segment that you are trying to measure. If you are trying to measure traffic on a switched or point-point connection, you may have to add another repeater in order to plug in the monitoring station. Connecting the analyzer is a hassle at best and may require taking down the network.

The PsiberNET tester is unique because of its ease of use and price. The PsiberNET allows you to measure utilization in a matter of seconds anywhere on your network without having to physically connect the network. It looks like a hand-held cable tester or a multimeter, but it actually measures traffic without having to establish an electrical connection to the network. It simply latches on to the cable to be tested and uses magnetics to listen to the traffic on the network. The PsiberNET's functionality is limited to measuring utilization, but it does that particular job very well. The PsiberNET features an LCD display that shows current, average, and peak bandwidth utilization. The product can be programmed to beep when thresholds are exceeded. The currently shipping version supports 10-Mbps Ethernet over UTP, STP, and coax, as well as Token Ring. Since you are going to monitor 10-Mbps LANs for signs of overloading, not having 100-Mbps capability will work for the time being. According to the manufacturer, a 100-Mbps Ethernet version is planned for late 1995. This tool is especially useful for testing switched and segmented LANs where you can quickly check one segment at a time without having to interrupt the network connection. The best thing about the PsiberNET is its price—$695!

Which Nodes Are Generating the Most Traffic?

You have now determined the overall traffic or utilization level in your network. The next step is to figure out which individual nodes are responsible for creating all this traffic, or if all of them are equally responsible for the traffic level in your network. A perfect switched environment would allow you to measure the actual traffic going to every node, but in a shared network it is, of course, very difficult to figure out exactly where your bottlenecks are coming from, since all servers and clients share the same wire.

A protocol analyzer or some of the newer hand-held diagnostics tools we just discussed can help you to figure out which nodes are creating the traffic. Protocol analyzers will display and group traffic for you in terms of source and destination address, quickly allowing you to figure out which nodes are creating the most traffic. Gathering this information will be most useful when you move on to Chapters 6 through 8, which discuss the upgrade options. Use Table 5.3 as an example of how to record individual traffic patterns.

Table 5.3

Recording Individual
Traffic Patterns

10-MBPS NODE	ETHERNET ADDRESS	AVERAGE TRAFFIC	TYPE OF STATION
Node 1	OOAAXXXX	10MB/hour	Normal user
Node 2	OOEAXXXX	50MB/hour	Power user
Node 3	OOCDXXXX	2MB/hour	Low
Node 4	OOAAXXXX	500MB/hour	Server

What to Do When Your Network Is Overloaded

Next, we will describe briefly the steps necessary to get your network utilization down to a satisfactory loading level. The detailed "How To" follows in Chapters 6 through 8, but these points will provide you with a quick rule of thumb on what to do.

- Note average and peak utilization rates over at least a 24-hour period. Take readings on all segments in your network, if you have more than one.

- Determine target utilization rates for the users in these segments. For example, you may want to provide the engineering segment with a little more bandwidth because you expect the company to hire additional engineers over the next year. You may also want to provide the advertising department with a lower peak rate because of the large desktop publishing files the group transfers across the network.

- Compare actual numbers with targets so you know where you need to start working on your infrastructure.

- Chapter 7 details a series of steps that provide you incremental bandwidth for overloaded networks. Start implementing step 1 from Chapter 7.

- After performing the upgrade, measure your utilization rate again and compare it with your targets. If the rates are still too high, you haven't done enough. If the rate has dropped below your target rate, then you have excess capacity, which is perfectly acceptable. This means that you have room to grow in the future.

Use Table 5.4 to guide you in your analysis.

Table 5.4

Use a Table Like This One to Record Traffic Patterns Before and After Your Upgrade

SEGMENT NUMBER	NAME	CURRENT PEAK UTILIZATION	CURRENT AVERAGE UTILIZATION	TARGET PEAK UTILIZATION	TARGET AVERAGE UTILIZATION	COMMENT
Segment 1	Finance	70%	30%	< 50%	15–25%	Peak too high
Segment 2	Engineer-ing	50%	40%	< 60%	10–20%	Need room for more users to be added
Segment 3	Advertis-ing	80%	20%	< 50%	15–25%	Need more peak room

■ Why Ethernet Is Running Out of Bandwidth

Is Ethernet getting old? Ethernet as we know it is over 20 years old. When Bob Metcalfe developed Ethernet at PARC in the early 1970s, it ran at 2.94 Mbps. Later the speed was increased to 10 Mbps, which seemed much faster than any computer network at the time could require. Metcalfe's intentions were to create a technology that would last about 30 years: ten years to standardize and bring products to market, followed by ten years of growth, and then ten years of decline and obsolescence. That model has worked relatively well, and now—22 years after its invention—shared Ethernet is running out of steam. What Metcalfe did not envision in his 30-year plan were life-extending technologies such as Switched and Fast Ethernet, which gives Ethernet at least another ten years of existence.

Moore's and Amdahl's Law

In the early 1970s Ethernet networks were used primarily to connect mini-computers, where one MIPS represented a lot of computing power. 10-Mbps

Ethernet was more than adequate to connect these types of computing devices. The PC revolution, driven by the microprocessor, also started during this time, when Intel invented the first microprocessor—the 4004—in 1971. Almost ten years later, the IBM PC AT, powered by an Intel 80286 microprocessor, surpassed the 1-MIPS barrier. At about this time, Gordon Moore, cofounder and chairman of Intel, observed an empirical law describing semiconductor design and manufacturing capabilities. Moore's Law states that the number of transistors that can be integrated into a semiconductor chip doubles every 18 months. For almost 20 years this rule has been accurate, and as a result today's personal computers based on the Intel Pentium processor feature 100 MIPS of processing power, a phenomenal hundredfold increase in about ten years During this time the speed of Ethernet has remained constant at 10 Mbps. The exponential growth of PC MIPS and Ethernet bandwidth is graphed in Figure 5.5.

Figure 5.5

Ethernet has remained a 10-Mbps LAN for 20 years, while PC performance has grown exponentially.

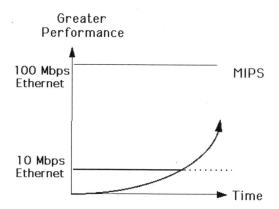

During this time, Amdahl, founder of the mainframe computer manufacturer of the same name, came up with what is now known as Amdahl's Law. It states that 1 MIPS of networked computing power requires 1 Mbps of bandwidth. Since Ethernet started off at 10 Mbps, it had sufficient headroom growth capabilities built-in to last two decades. However, microprocessors crossed the 10-MIPS barrier about five years ago when 486-based machines were first introduced. It has taken about five years for most of us to purchase 486-class machines, and many older machines are still in existence. In addition, most of these networked personal computers cannot really be called networked computing power because they represent standalone machines that are merely hooked up to a network cable for file and print sharing. However, recent developments in the software industry are making PCs act more like real distributed computing devices (client-server, and so on) connected via a network. The conclusion is that personal computers featuring 100-plus MIPS performance will enable true distributed personal computing applications, and 10-Mbps Ethernet networks will no longer be sufficient.

So much for the theory. Now that we have all these high-performance PCs scattered around the office, what are we actually doing with them? After all, the real question is not what our PCs are capable of, but what we do with them. The next section of this chapter will examine some of the applications that are going to drive Ethernet traffic through the roof.

Practical Reasons Why You Are Running Out of Bandwidth

Corporate networks have been hit by a double whammy of growth over the last few years. First of all, personal computer sales have been booming, with year-to-year growth exceeding 20 percent for the last five years. As a result, over 50 million personal computers will be sold worldwide in 1995, up from just 20 million as recently as five years ago. A large percentage of these 50 million computers will end up being networked. As the number of PCs sold increases, the load on networks will increase accordingly.

In addition, an ever-increasing share of personal computers sold end up being connected to LANs. According to industry analysts, close to 70 percent of personal computers sold to companies end up being networked today, as opposed to less than 50 percent just two years ago. The bottom line is that the number of LAN connections and associated traffic levels have grown exponentially. Network adapter sales, a good indication of network nodes, have been growing at 50 percent per annum for the last few years, a result of surging PC sales and higher network connectivity rates.

What has been the driving force behind this phenomenal growth in networks? A few years ago the word processor and the spreadsheet were motivating people to purchase personal computers. These applications (known in industry jargon as "killer applications"—programs that every PC needed to have) were primarily responsible for the growth in personal computers and, to a lesser degree, company networks. Networks became useful for word processor or spreadsheet users to share files or print to the common laser printer, but networks were by no means a must. As a result, most of today's personal computer networks still act as file and print networks only. However, over the last five years a third killer application has emerged that requires a network—electronic mail. Only in the last few years have applications emerged that really use a network more intelligently. These applications do a lot more than just file and print sharing; they share data and sometimes even computing power. Today, after years of hype, the first true client-server application has appeared—shared databases have now become an important application for corporate networks. So what lies ahead? Let's talk about the applications that will continue to drive network traffic through the roof.

More Users

By now we have become familiar with the reality of the explosive growth in network nodes. That's bound to continue, as every new employee automatically gets a PC these days. Soon after the PC arrives, it gets connected to the LAN. Bingo—more traffic for everyone! Look for the number of PCs in your company to continue increasing at about 20 percent per year, and look for the percentage of PCs to be connected to reach 95 percent by the end of the decade.

Networking Branch Offices

Only recently has networking "infiltrated" branch offices as well. Today most branch offices have only a local LAN to share printers and files, so their traffic doesn't impact your main office LAN traffic. As the push toward enterprisewide connectivity continues, these remote offices are bound to get a router/WAN connection in order to connect to the main corporate network. Look for the routed traffic from these remote sites to start loading up your main network also. The bottom line will be more nodes and more traffic. Here driving applications are going to be primarily e-mail and database access.

More File and Print Servers

Of course, all the new users means more traffic, but you will also need more servers and printers in order to service the growing client base.

Application Servers

As we know, file, print, and now e-mail servers are just the beginning. Networked fax servers, centrally accessible CD-ROM drives, and other application servers are going to continue growing. These types of servers often transfer large files, not just ASCII text, across the network. For example, an incoming fax being sent across the LAN to the recipient can often be a few hundred kiloBytes in size, two orders of magnitude larger than a regular e-mail message.

For most networks, 10-Mbps Ethernet was enough for existing applications. There are, however, many applications in use already that have definitely pushed 10-Mbps Ethernet LANs to the limit, and beyond. For example, very large corporate PC networks just cannot cope any more with the amount traffic generated through the sheer number of users. Design artists using their Macintosh computers for desktop publishing or prepress work need more than 10-Mbps throughput rates if they hope to accomplish their work without too much delay. Engineers running computer-aided simulations on their workstations already run them at night when the network is empty. Stock traders doing time-critical financial analyses have already replaced their Ethernet equipment with higher-speed networking hardware. These applications are however not going to make it onto everyone's LAN, so let's look at some of the applications that are going to be running on everyone's network a few years from now.

Client-Server Computing

The office LAN as we know it is currently undergoing some radical transitions that are going to use up bandwidth at an ever-increasing rate. Despite predictions of gloom and doom, mainframe and minicomputer sales have not declined substantially over the last ten years. That's because networked PCs have not yet managed to replace more expensive mainframe and minicomputers as mission-critical data centers. The concept of client-server computing has been an elusive buzzword for the last ten years because most of today's personal computer networks act as file and print networks only.

Over the next few years we will finally see applications being taken off the mainframe and minicomputers and being run on PC-based application servers instead. That's because PC servers and operating systems have finally become a stable and robust enough platform to allow company-critical applications to be moved from the mainframe to a server. As a result, all the major database vendors such as Sybase, Oracle, and Informix are offering their products for PC servers. This means no mainframe application is safe anymore—everything can and will run on a PC LAN. Emerging applications such as SAP's R13 business process package are just examples of an accelerating trend to move from big, expensive computing platforms to inexpensive, distributed PC LANs. These kinds of applications are going to require large amounts of network bandwidth because the client and server actually interact over the network. Data is continuously sent back and forth, as opposed to a short one-way burst of traffic for most of today's prevailing network applications. Figure 5.6 illustrates how the computing world has evolved from the old mainframe-centric environment to the chaotic world of standalone personal computers only to be eclipsed by client-server networks.

More Electronic Mail

Electronic mail has become the latest killer application, and will become as pervasive as a telephone connection for office and home PC owners. In addition, we will no longer just be sending 3K ASCII files, but instead we'll be transmitting 3K ASCII files with 3MB Powerpoint attachments—a thousandfold increase! An Internet e-mail address is already becoming a must-have on the company business card. Intercompany mail will continue to fuel the growth in e-mail traffic, expected to be 50 percent per year for the next few years.

Figure 5.6

The computing world has almost come full circle. Twenty years ago the mainframe-terminal model dominated, then minicomputers and standalone PCs became popular, now client-server is becoming dominant.

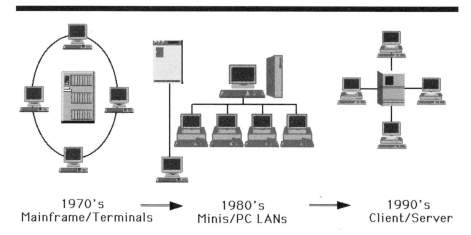

1970's
Mainframe/Terminals

1980's
Minis/PC LANs

1990's
Client/Server

Messaging

PC-LAN-based e-mail as an application has been in existence for a number of years. Some newer applications such as Lotus Notes are an interesting mix of e-mail, scheduling software, and distributed databases. This mix of applications is commonly called messaging, also known as groupware. Unfortunately, *groupware* is a misleading term because both IBM and Novell use this term in their product names. Just like e-mail made many of us buy or install our first PC LAN, messaging may well become the preeminent application driving networking in the 1990s. *Messaging* consists of a central database server and networked client platforms that communicate with the central server. Messaging combines different applications such as electronic mail, scheduling, and discussion forums to enable richer, more interactive communication. Just like client-server databases, messaging applications make extensive use of the network—in fact, they exist only because of the network.

Backing Up Data

As the network becomes a much larger and more important company asset, it makes good business sense to protect and insure those assets. Smart LAN managers are already backing up servers. Today's network backup and storage products provide the programmability and flexibility to do this at night, but at a speed of 10-Mbps you will soon run out of nighttime hours to do a backup job. For example, a server with 1 gigabyte of data takes about 30 minutes to back up, assuming there's no other load on the network. If you have the network available from 7 p.m. to 7 a.m. for backup purposes, you can back up 24 servers in that time, that's it. It's easy to see how you can run out of backup time: If, for example, your servers are significantly larger than

1 gigabyte, or if there is other traffic on the LAN at night, or if you have more than 24 servers, or if choose to back up clients as well, you will soon discover that 10-Mbps Ethernet just doesn't cope any more.

The "Discovery" of the Internet

The Internet is essentially a huge WAN, but we wanted to describe this phenomenon briefly, as it is going to account for substantial growth in traffic on your LAN as well. A few years ago private enterprise "discovered" the Internet. While the Internet has been in existence for about 30 years, recently traffic on the Internet has been virtually exploding, growing at 25 percent *per month.* Much of this growth can be attributed to home users, but a large percentage of the growth in traffic is coming from businesses. Many computer companies have had FTP file servers connected to the Internet for a while, mainly as a customer support/software distribution tool, similar to a CompuServe Forum or BBS for downloading files. However, within the last year, virtually every major company has started up a World Wide Web server. WWW servers are more sophisticated than FTP servers because they provide a much richer, GUI-based environment. WWW servers typically feature company and product information. WWW servers have become online infomercials: The golden rule of a good Web server is to make it as entertaining as possible to keep people in your area as long as you can. Good Web servers feature color graphics, photos, video clips, sound bites, animation—all the stuff that takes up huge amounts of data to transmit (Figure 5.7). Web browsers are becoming one of the fastest-selling applications around. So where does this Internet add traffic to your self-contained LAN? Internet traffic will impact your LAN traffic for two reasons. First, your employees are accessing the Internet from your network. The traffic goes from your LAN to your WAN connection, and then onto the Internet. Second, if your company puts up an FTP or WWW server of its own, remote Internet users may have to access your WWW server across the LAN.

Multimedia

We are discussing multimedia in this book because it is going to require great amounts of bandwidth. Like client-server applications, multimedia has been another one of those elusive buzzwords that has finally become a reality. For home PCs, multimedia has become synonymous with a PC that features a CD-ROM drive as well as a sound card to play games or to access interactive encyclopedias. The word *multimedia* refers to a variety of media—sound, video, and animation. For corporate computer networks, multimedia is still ill-defined. That's changing because the personal computer is fast becoming a personal communicator. As such, multimedia is becoming an ingredient for most applications that we have discussed so far. That's because richer, natural

Figure 5.7

A home page is like the cover page of a magazine. Home pages are supposed to be eye-catching, so you strart browsing through them.

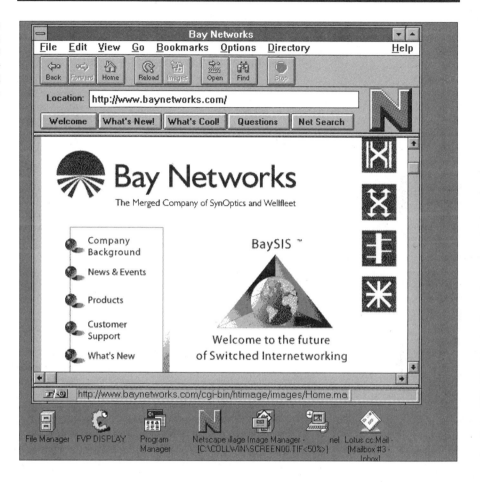

data types such as voice and video make our personal communicator much more effective. There are other applications beyond better communication that multimedia is good for, such as training, but essentially the concept of multimedia is used in these applications to improve communication between machine and user.

Multimedia relates more to contents and the type of data that is being transferred across the network, as opposed to what we do with the data, which are applications. Multimedia uses bandwidth unlike anything else we know. To many people the phrase, "A picture is worth a thousand words" captures the essence of multimedia very well. "Multimedia takes up 1,000 times the bandwidth" is what it should mean to you as a LAN manager.

In order to show you how real multimedia-based applications already are in use today we will discuss two applications that use multimedia very effectively.

Video-Conferencing Just as e-mail has replaced the office memo, video-conferencing is predicted to become a mainstream, multi-billion-dollar indus-try in just five years (Figure 5.8). PC-based video-conferencing comes in vari-ous shapes and sizes, depending on the number of participants and the type of data connection.

- Two-way, or point-to-point, conferencing uses regular telephone or ISDN lines. It is the most popular type because it spans large distances, possibly avoiding time-consuming and expensive travel.

- Point-to-point conferencing can also operate over in-house LANs. It re-quires that both users be on the same LAN. Since the availability of high-speed ISDN WAN lines is still a major issue, LAN-based systems can uti-lize the existing high-speed WAN routing connectivity infrastructure such as a T1 or frame relay link. This allows two LAN-based systems to be connected over extended distances.

Figure 5.8

Over the next few years video-conferencing is likely to become as pervasive as electronic mail and the telephone system are today.

- A multipoint video-conference system is similar to a teleconference bridge call, in that multiple users can all see and talk to each other at the same time. LAN and/or WAN connections are utilized for this type of video-conferencing.

Many types of PC-based video-conferencing systems are sold today. Key differences are the number of users that can participate and the type of data connection required.

There are numerous barriers to widespread video-conferencing, but they are expected to dissolve in a few years:

- The price of equipment is still too high (equipment today typically consists of a small video camera, a video capture board, and an ISDN card, and it sells for $2,500).

- Users need to become familiar and comfortable with the concept of video-conferencing.

- The availability of high-speed WAN lines is a major barrier to adoption, but telephone companies around the world are starting to adopt ISDN at a rapid rate.

Once you have the appropriate video-conferencing hardware, you can also send video attachments, embed videos into presentations, and so on. While video-conferencing is great technology that could become as popular as e-mail is today, it does have significant repercussions for your network infrastructure. Video in general takes incredible amounts of data to store. Using state-of-the-art compression, full-motion 30-frame-per-second, full-screen video requires about 2 to 4 Mbps of network bandwidth. That's almost 100 percent of the usable bandwidth of a 10-Mbps shared Ethernet LAN. Video can be transmitted over ISDN links, but only if the size, resolution, and frame rate are reduced significantly. Unfortunately, the loss of image quality is not acceptable to many users. More LAN and WAN bandwidth appear to be the only solutions.

Real-Time Network Video Transmission Another popular use of multimedia is going to be in the training and information distribution area. The corporate network can be used to transmit video and audio to users on the network, much like an intercom broadcast message or an e-mail to everyone on the network. Intel is selling a product called CNN at Work that can turn every networked PC into a TV showing CNN (Figure 5.9). A small window displays the CNN TV channel live, while the user can go about their regular business. The possibilities of this technology are mind-boggling: in-house video broadcasts, training classes, and so on will all be accessible from your local PC.

As usual, this kind of application uses up a lot of bandwidth. For example, Intel's CNN at Work application supposedly uses only 5 percent of the

Figure 5.9

Intel's CNN at Work allows network users to view the TV channel CNN live in a small window on their PC

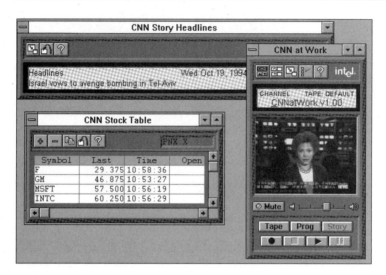

total Ethernet bandwidth, which sounds like relatively little. However, Ethernet only has a practical capacity of 37 percent in the first place, so the 5 percent that this product uses actually becomes 13 percent of the total bandwidth available, a significant amount.

■ Conclusion

This chapter discussed why some of today's networks are running out of bandwidth, and what the reasons behind this trend were. Your network traffic will continue to grow, as mail, backup, and so on continue to create more traffic. In addition, newer applications such as real client-server applications or multimedia data are going to require significantly more bandwidth than is available today. We also discussed various methods to measure the utilization of your network so that you can be prepared to implement suitable upgrade options that will be discussed in the second half of this book.

■ Recommendations

We have some simple recommendations that you should keep in mind at all times when thinking about bandwidth.

Plan for lots of future growth: It is part of your job as a network manager or an IT professional to think short-term as well as long-term. Make sure that you buy new equipment that allows for lots of future traffic growth.

Don't waste your time and the company's money on upgrades that give you a year before you find yourself in the same situation.

Buy scalable products and technologies: Remember to buy products or technologies that you can grow with. Buying things that are at or close to the end of their life cycle means that you will need to change products or technologies soon, always a painful experience.

Be proactive, not reactive: Don't let your network get overloaded. Measure your network utilization regularly, and take the appropriate steps before you run out of bandwidth. Once your network is approaching saturation you will be in a fire-fighting mode that is going to make your life and the life of your network users a misery.

Test new applications extensively: Many of the new applications we discussed such as video-conferencing, distributed or client-server databases are going to consume a lot of your bandwidth. It will be difficult to tell exactly what the impact on your network will be without appropriate testing. We recommend that you run a "beta program" for new applications to study the compatibility of these new apps with existing applications, the impact these new apps have on your utilization, and if your users will be happy with the new applications.

- *Building Blocks Defined*
- *Network Interface Cards*
- *Workgroup Components*
- *Interconnect Components*

C H A P T E R

The Building Blocks:
Switched and Fast Ethernet

THIS CHAPTER BEGINS BY DISCUSSING THE BASIC BUILDING BLOCKS
of a Switched and Fast Ethernet network. These building blocks,
or components, define how a network is connected. A description
of each component is included, along with some of the more common features for that particular device. The chapter also discusses
why some features may be more desirable than others. An understanding of this chapter is necessary before reading about
Switched and Fast Ethernet deployment in Chapters 7 and 8.

■ Building Blocks Defined

As in any hierarchical communications scheme, several distinct components make up most of today's networks. Network administrators use these components to effectively deploy Local Area Networking to their customers. These components fall into three broad categories: *Network Interface Cards (NICs)*, *workgroup hub components*, and *interconnect* components. Each group has its own distinct set of features and functions that make it critical to LAN operations. This chapter attempts to break down each category into its fundamental defining properties, organizing each by its feature set and performance characteristics.

A *Network Interface Card* (*NIC*) is broadly defined as the *node,* or *server/client* piece of the network. The network symbol for a NIC is shown in Figure 6.1. Every client, workstation, and server system must have a NIC to connect to the network. Because of this, NICs are crucial to LAN deployment, illustrated by the 24.5 million NICs sold in 1994 alone. Many view the NIC as the least important piece of the network puzzle; however, a good network administrator will weigh the NIC purchasing decision just as heavily as a workgroup hub or interconnect decision. This chapter will consider various trade-offs in the evaluation of a desktop and server NIC; and how the correct choice of a 10/100-Mbps NIC can make Fast Ethernet deployment easier.

Figure 6.1

Network Interface Card
(NIC)

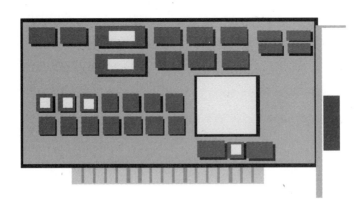

This chapter also introduces the workgroup hub. A *workgroup hub* is commonly thought of as a central point where several users tap into the network. Some examples of workgroup hubs are standalone repeating hubs, stackable hubs, workgroup switching hubs, and chassis hubs. Throughout the rest of this book, we will refer to these components by their network symbols, shown in Figure 6.2. This chapter explains how correct workgroup hub selection can greatly increase network performance and decrease installation cost.

Figure 6.2

Workgroup hubs include standalone repeaters, stackable hubs, workgroup switches, and chassis hubs.

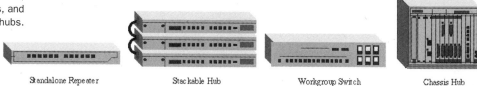

Standalone Repeater   Stackable Hub   Workgroup Switch   Chassis Hub

Interconnect network components are typically used to connect several workgroup hubs in the network architecture. Interconnect components break down larger networks into manageable subnetworks and route traffic from one place to the next. Examples of interconnect devices include bridges, routers, and backbone switches. Their network symbols are shown in Figure 6.3. Most network administrators will agree that interconnect devices are expensive and that proper selection is very important to network performance. The performance trade-offs and other relevant features of interconnect devices are discussed later in this chapter.

Figure 6.3

Interconnect components include bridges, routers, and backbone switches.

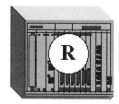
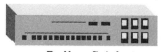

Bridge   Router   Backbone Switch

■ Network Interface Cards

There are many different NICs, each suited for a particular type of installation or application (see Figure 6.4). Consequently, when looking at a NIC, there are several factors to consider. With the availability of affordable 10/100 Fast Ethernet NICs, network professionals will have to make conscious choices about the NICs installed in their networks. To make a well-informed decision, they will have to consider not only wire speed, but bus type, performance, driver support, technical support, Macintosh, PC and workstation connectivity, and the differences between server and client NICs.

Figure 6.4

Intel's EtherExpress™
PRO/100 NIC runs at
either 10 Mbps or
100 Mbps

NIC Wire Speed

With the broad availability of Switched Ethernet and Fast Ethernet, wire speed and its associated cost will be on the mind of everyone who recommends LAN Equipment. A NIC's wire speed indicates how fast the physical signaling can take place—for instance, 10 Mbps or 100 Mbps. Nobody wants to make the mistake of buying something today that can't grow to meet the needs of an expanding network infrastructure. By the same token, no one wants to pay for something they don't need and will never use. A good compromise for these two seemingly opposed criteria is 10/100-Mbps NICs. 10/100-Mbps NICs are the newest addition to the Ethernet NIC family, competing with 10-Mbps-only and 100-Mbps-only NICs. The 10-, 100-, and 10/100-Mbps NICs also may include full-duplex modes or multiple ports per NIC, both of which will be discussed later.

NIC Price Trends

The prices of 10/100 NICs are decreasing steadily; they will soon cost little more than a 10-only NIC. Consider the Token Ring market of a few years ago. When 4/16-Mbps Token Ring cards were introduced they overtook the 4-Mbps-only market very quickly. The primary reason for this immediate shift was that 4/16 prices were very similar to those of 4-only cards. The same reasoning can be applied to 10/100 Mbps NICs. If everything else were equal, including price, it would be difficult to justify a 10-only purchase over a 10/100 purchase. A 10/100 NIC is a universal solution, no matter what type of network you plan to invest in, 10 or 100 Mbps, shared or switched. Therefore, it is highly recommended that you purchase 10/100 NICs instead of 10-only or 100-only NICs whenever the budget allows. This ensures a network designed to meet future needs.

NIC Bus Type

When looking at today's installed base of 10-Mbps Ethernet NICs, the predominant bus architecture is still the Industry Standard Architecture (ISA). However, when examining the ISA bus as a vehicle for delivering 10-Mbps dedicated bandwidth (in the case of 10-Mbps switching) or 100-Mbps bandwidth, there are definite performance issues:

- The ISA bus is only 16 bits wide.

- The ISA bus runs at a clock rate of only 8 MHz.

- The ISA bus doesn't allow burst data transfers.

- Most ISA bus adapters are I/O mapped, causing data transfers to be slower.

These factors produce a theoretical ISA bus bandwidth of 5.33MB per second (MB/s), or 42.67 Mbps. A more realistic ISA bus bandwidth is determined by actual measurements of many different NICs in various ISA systems. The real-world ISA bus bandwidth available to the NIC is only about one-fourth of the theoretical amount, or 11 Mbps—barely enough to fill a 10-Mbps pipe, and definitely not enough for multiple 10- or 100-Mbps NICs.

In most newer desktop systems, however, Extended Industry Standard Architecture (EISA), Peripheral Component Interconnect (PCI), Micro Channel Architecture (MCA), S-Bus (Sparc Workstations), and NuBus (Apple Macintosh) adapters are starting to ship in larger numbers. For instance, of all Pentium processor class systems shipped in 1995, over 90 percent had PCI slots. PCI delivers a theoretical bandwidth of 132 MB/sec and true plug-n-play features, much like Sun's S-Bus. In the future, high-speed buses like PCI and S-Bus will be the logical home for high-performance network adapters. Table 6.1 compares ISA, EISA, MCA, PCI, NuBus, S-Bus, and PCMCIA adapters. Note that the PCI bus is high performance, processor independent, and widely supported by computer manufacturers. Even Apple and Sun, two of the biggest non-PC-compatible computer manufacturers, have announced plans to use the PCI bus in upcoming products.

Table 6.1

Comparison of Bus Types

FEATURE	ISA	PCMCIA	EISA	MCA	NuBus	S-Bus	PCI
Supported architecture	PC	PC	PC	PC	Apple	Sun	All
Bus speed (MHz)	8	8	8	8	8	33	16-33
Theoretical bus bandwidth (MB/s)	5.33	5.33	32	40	5.33	132	132
Practical bus bandwidth for an NIC (MB/s)**	1.4	1.4	8	10	1.4	30-100	30-100
Bus width (bits)	16	16	32	32	16	32	32-64
Burst mode data transfer?	No	No	Yes	Yes	Yes	Yes	Yes
Processor independent?	Yes	Yes	Yes	Yes	No	No	Yes
Widely accepted by major computer manufacturers?	Yes	Yes (in laptops)	Yes	No	No	No	Yes
Set-up utilities	Manual or Plug and Play* BIOS	Card & Socket Services	EISA Config. Utility	POR Register Config. Utility	True Plug and Play	True Plug and Play	True Plug and Play BIOS

* Plug and Play BIOS refers to ISA Plug and Play specification.

** Includes measurements in buses with multiple adapters such as SCSI, IDE, and VGA.

Don't throw away all those old ISA cards yet. Most new PCs support a combination of bus types, like PCI-ISA, or PCI-EISA, which allows customers to get additional use from their legacy adapters. Since most computer manufacturers are making combination systems, one can experiment with PCI without much risk, since the ISA or EISA bus is there as a backup. However, as shown in Table 6.1 above, PCI NICs have the potential to perform far better than ISA NICs in these systems, both in throughput and in

CPU/Bus utilization. Therefore, a PCI NIC is recommended for any new PCI/EISA or PCI/ISA system added to the network.

Performance isn't the only reason to move your desktops and servers away from the ISA architecture. ISA has also been traditionally difficult to configure with multiple adapters. Recently, tools designed to make ISA configuration easier, such as ISA Plug and Play BIOS, have helped in this area, but the move is too late.

ISA Plug and Play is a standard driven by Microsoft and Intel that attempts to take the guesswork out of assigning interrupts, memory mapping, I/O mapping, DMA channel assignment, and other system resources. Each Plug and Play-compatible adapter in the ISA system asks for resources at boot time. The ISA Plug-n-Play BIOS then looks at all the requests and grants resources accordingly, thus avoiding conflicts. Unfortunately, ISA Plug and Play is too late to save the ISA bus from being displaced by PCI, which supports this type of configuration in a native fashion. All PCI-compliant adapters are, by default, auto-configuring. With ISA, you will have some Plug and Play adapters and some older, non-Plug and Play adapters, which will most likely confuse your system. Unless you buy all Plug and Play-compatible ISA adapters, you will still have to fiddle with interrupts and I/O mapping. In the PC world, true auto-configuration comes with a migration to PCI. Of course, if you use Macintoshes or Sun Sparc workstations, you have been enjoying the concept of Plug and Play for years now. In this respect, the PC is really only now catching up with Apple.

NICs in Laptops

A LAN administrator also has to plan for users who frequently travel away from the office. Typically, these people require laptop computers. Laptops on desktops are becoming increasingly common, and connecting laptops to the LAN is somewhat of a challenge. There are a variety of options to consider when connecting laptops to the LAN. One option is to invest in docking stations, which provide a special connector in the back of the laptop. The second option is to rely on NIC vendors to develop PCMCIA LAN adapters that work in your laptop systems (shown in Figure 6.5).

If your laptop strategy includes docking stations, make sure they support all types of LANs (Ethernet, Token Ring, Fast Ethernet, and so on) in your current network. Ask the laptop and docking station vendors how they plan to migrate their LAN support to Fast Ethernet and other high-bandwidth LAN options. The answers you get may help narrow your choices.

If your strategy involves using external PCMCIA adapters, ask your laptop vendor about the upcoming CardBus specification. The PCMCIA bus has come a long way in compatibility and availability, but PCMCIA cannot support high-speed LAN connections as CardBus can. CardBus defines a

Figure 6.5

PCMCIA NICs in Laptops provide portable connectivity. Fast Ethernet laptop NICs will most likely be CardBus instead of PCMCIA.

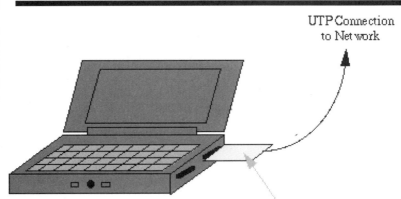

UTP Connection to Network

PCMCIA LAN Adapter

new, higher-speed PCMCIA bus that is 32 bits wide and operates at 33 MHz, much like the PCI bus. A PC vendor that is serious about his or her laptop product line will have plans to implement CardBus. Don't look to implement Fast Ethernet in laptops until CardBus sockets are available.

LAN on Motherboard

Another interesting point is the concept of *LAN on motherboard*, or *LOM*. LOM is defined as a desktop, workstation, or server that has networking silicon right on the motherboard, obviating the need for an add-in NIC. Apple and Sun pioneered this concept, which was later implemented by Compaq, IBM, Hewlett-Packard, and other high-end workstation vendors. The LOM idea hasn't really made its way into the volume PC desktop market, with the notable exception of the Compaq DeskPro™, mostly because there are too many different networking solutions to justify locking in one design. However, as Ethernet and Fast Ethernet grow to larger and larger market shares, more PC vendors may start shipping products with this silicon on the motherboard. Depending on your network, you may want to consider LOM in your purchasing decision.

What a Brand-Name NIC Buys You

Many experts recommend brand-name NICs such as 3Com, Intel, and SMC. Arguments for buying a name brand are definitely valid: A brand-name vendor typically has more to offer than a no-name vendor. Brand-name NICs usually excel in four areas: driver support, driver certification, technical support, and warranty/reliability.

Driver Support

Brand-name NIC vendors typically develop much of their driver suite internally. This is important because if a driver wasn't developed in-house, then it is likely the vendor will not be able to support it very well. A good example of this is the NE3200 NIC clones such as Eagle's NE3200. The drivers for these NICs were developed by Novell, so any problems that arise have to be jointly handled by Novell and the respective NIC vendor. Many vendors strike a successful compromise with the NOS vendors, enlisting them to write a driver for that particular NOS. Although support for this kind of driver won't be the same as for one developed by the NIC vendor itself, it is still better than a complete third-party driver. For instance, if 3Com and a third-tier NIC vendor like D-Link both ask SCO to develop drivers, it is likely that SCO will focus their efforts on 3Com. When using a nonbrand name NIC vendor, ask where the driver was developed and where the supported driver will come from.

Another point to consider when questioning driver support is hardware and software compatibility. Any brand name vendor should be able to provide a list of compatible software, such as memory managers and DOS versions tested. Likewise, any vendor that cannot produce a list of systems tested compatible with the NIC should be scrutinized.

Driver Certification

Brand-name NIC vendors typically won't ship a NIC unless it has passed all major certifications. These include certification tests with NOS vendors like Novell, Microsoft, and SCO. Third-party NIC vendors sometimes bypass this expensive and time-consuming task. Without a certified NIC and driver, you have no way of confirming the NIC vendor has tested the NIC and driver in a variety of configurations. Other tests that major NIC vendors perform are FCC emissions testing and environmental testing (temperature and mechanical stress tests).

Technical Support

A thorough review of a NIC vendor's technical support model should be as critical a factor in your NIC purchase decision as price or performance. If problems arise, you will be spending time with technical support long after the salespeople have disappeared. Brand name vendors have better technical support because they have more people, better training, and more money to dedicate to this function. Name brands have their reputation at stake when you encounter a problem with one of their products, so they are very responsive.

Warranty/Reliability

Regarding product quality, there are several key factors to consider when selecting a NIC. Brand-name NICs by vendors such as 3Com, Intel, and SMC all support lifetime warranties as well as 90-day money-back guarantees. Reliability is also a concern for mission-critical client/sever applications. NIC reliability is sometimes measured in Mean Time Between Failures (MTBF). Although this usually doesn't give you much information, you should be suspicious of any value below 180,000 hours. This indicates that a failure may occur, on average, every 180,000 hours, or 20 years. Most brand-name NIC vendors meet this level of reliability.

NIC Network Management

In a switched environment, it is even more critical to have a standards-based node management scheme on each NIC. Intel's FlashWorks software was a step in that direction, but the approach was new and it ended up as a proprietary method. Although extra management features are a definite plus, there are really only two requirements for network management: SNMP and DMI.

Simple Network Management Protocol (*SNMP*) is a well defined network management protocol that garners information from various SNMP agents. An SNMP agent can reside internally in a hub or router, or even as a software liaison to an NIC. An SNMP management console can be configured to specifically ask all SNMP agents on the network for statistical information. While this proves useful for network traffic management, it doesn't do much for node (desktop and server) management.

This fallacy of SNMP is why the Desktop Management Task Force (DMTF) was formed and the *Desktop Management Interface* (DMI) specification was developed. DMI requires all DMI-compliant NICs to keep information about network traffic and the system in a particular way. Network management software packages can then query NICs from multiple vendors to obtain information needed to effectively manage the traffic *and* the nodes on the network.

SNMP is currently the de facto standard for network management. For instance, Windows NT 3.5 and Windows 95 have built-in SNMP management applications, and most major NIC vendors will support built-in SNMP or a software SNMP agent. When purchasing a NIC, make sure it has SNMP support. DMI is not as well established or as robust as SNMP, but it shows promise of similar industrywide acceptance. DMI support should be considered as a bonus, not a requirement, in a NIC purchasing decision.

Server NICs

A *server* is broadly defined as a specific kind of system, built to be powerful, upgradeable, and dependable. These qualities are also important in a good server NIC. One server may support hundreds of clients, which can put an enormous stress on the server NIC. Unlike the desktop, where the CPU spends most of its time idle, the server is constantly working, trying to use every ounce of CPU power available. How hard a server CPU works is typically referred to as *CPU utilization*. Imagine a server that spends 60 percent of its time, or bandwidth, providing data to a server NIC. That server only has 40 percent of its cycles left to perform other activities. This is why the CPU utilization of a server NIC is very important. The less time the server CPU has to spend providing for the NIC, the more time it has to run applications, perform file transfers, and run NOS software. Servers also typically support more expansion slots than do desktops, which allow a wider variety of configurations, including additional hard drives and network adapters. In addition, many high-end servers offer fault-tolerant features such as redundant power supplies and hot-swappable hard drives.

Server NICs vary widely in features, function, and price. Some key questions to consider when selecting a server NIC are

- What wire type (CAT 3 UTP, CAT 5 UTP, Fiber) and speed (10 Mbps, 100 Mbps, 10/100) does the server NIC support?

- What bus type (PCI, EISA, ISA) does the server NIC support?

- What is the performance of the server NIC and how can it be measured?

- What NOS server drivers does the server NIC vendor support and is the server NIC optimized for a particular NOS?

Each of these NIC features is discussed later in the chapter.

Server NIC Bus Type

With Fast Ethernet now widely available, NICs come in different speeds: 10, 100, and 10/100 Mbps. As in desktops, servers are liable to move around the network over the course of their lifetimes, so an investment now in 10/100-Mbps server NICs will increase the flexibility and mobility of your servers. Also, an investment in a high-speed expansion bus will help prepare your server for high-speed networking. As discussed previously, ISA servers just won't support Fast Ethernet data rates. EISA, the current server expansion bus of choice, will support Fast Ethernet data rates, but does not do so efficiently, both in terms of CPU utilization and in price. PCI offers higher bandwidth, lower CPU utilization, and prices similar to ISA. When considering upgrades to current EISA servers, choose 10/100 NICs that offer lower CPU utilization, even at the expense of throughput. When considering new PC server purchases, you can choose from any number of PCI server NICs.

Server NIC 100BASE-T Flexibility

There are other choices to be made when considering a 100BASE-T server NIC. For instance, should you install 100BASE-TX or 100BASE-T4? Typically networks install servers in one of two locations—in the wiring closet or in the local workgroup. In the closet, the selection between 100BASE-TX and 100BASE-T4 is less critical because the closet wiring infrastructure is very tightly controlled and can be upgraded more easily. In a workgroup server, however, 100BASE-TX or 100BASE-T4 must be chosen depending on the type of wiring found in that workgroup. Some workgroups will have only Category 3 UTP and will require 100BASE-T4 workgroup hubs and server connections. Some will be Category 5 UTP and can be either 100BASE-TX or 100BASE-T4. Chapter 7 discusses these options in more detail.

With communications options such as 100BASE-TX, 100BASE-T4, and 10BASE-T all sharing a common twisted pair medium, a smart method of automatic configuration is need. In 1995, the IEEE 802.3 committee will finalize an autonegotiation scheme nicknamed *NWAY*. NWAY allows a NIC and a hub port to signal the communications speeds they are capable of and auto-configure to the highest common speed, much like modems do today. NWAY will be a 10/100 NIC necessity by 1996, but beware of early implementations that are not IEEE specification-complaint. (Technical details about NWAY are discussed in Chapter 3.)

Server NIC Performance

Understanding how to properly measure performance is a critical portion of a server NIC evaluation process. Certain types of tests will give different information about the server NIC. For instance, Novell's *Perform3* or Ziff-Davis's *NetBench 3.0* tests will determine the absolute maximum throughput a NIC can achieve and at what CPU utilization, but they will not give a very accurate view of real-world server NIC performance. NSTL's test suite offers a much better evaluation of real-world performance because it incorporates other aspects of the server, including hard disk speed, file transfer overhead, variable file sizes, and bursty (erratic) client traffic. NSTL tests will show that even the fastest server with the fastest Fast Ethernet NIC will only transfer files as fast as its hard disk will allow. Perform3 and NetBench operate out of cachable main memory and do not use the hard disk, so hard disk performance will not affect test results. In all three examples, test setups should use multiple clients (six or more) and one server to properly test the server NIC. Table 6.2 compares these three popular test suites and how they measure server NIC performance.

Table 6.2

Three Popular Server NIC
Performance Tests

TEST SUITE	HOW DOES IT WORK?	WHAT DOES IT MEASURE?	WHAT ARE ITS DRAWBACKS?
Perform3 (Novell Labs)	Copies variable file sizes from client cache memory to server	Isolates the NIC. Shows peak throughput of a NIC. Results are readily quantifiable.	Doesn't involve other server components like the hard drive. Doesn't model real-life traffic very well.
NetBench 3.0 (Ziff-Davis Labs)	Copies variable file sizes from client cache memory to server. Also performs read/write tests.	Isolates the NIC. Shows peak throughput of a NIC. Results are readily quantifiable. Other options allow for hard disk interaction.	Doesn't model real-life traffic very well.
NSTL (McGraw Hill Labs)	Simulates repetition of several accesses from multiple clients. Simulates random-length accesses.	Represents real world performance.	Doesn't isolate the NIC very well. Results will only be as good as the slowest test component.

Other aspects of server NIC architecture also contribute to performance. Some of these aspects should be considered when evaluating server NIC performance; these are detailed below.

Master versus Slave   *Bus-mastering* NICs access host memory directly and do not rely on the CPU to directly transfer data to them. Thus, in servers, bus-mastering NICs are ideal because of the low CPU overhead required to operate them. Bus master NICs typically have fast internal FIFOs with sizes ranging from a few bytes to 3- or 4K. *Buffered slave* NICs rely on the CPU to copy data to and from buffers on the NIC itself. The buffers on slave NICs are usually large external DRAM banks. Since DRAM is slower than a FIFO, the DRAM buffer sizes are usually much larger—4K to 64K. Any server NIC that is based on a slave architecture is bound to show higher (worse) server CPU utilization.

Buffering   Server NIC buffering is less critical than client NIC buffering because servers typically have high speed expansion buses capable of supporting Fast Ethernet throughput rates. When using a bus master in a newer Pentium processor PCI server, 1.5/1.5K of transmit/receive FIFO should be adequate. If the NIC is slated for an older 486-based EISA system, then more FIFO will help performance. With a slave architecture, more buffering is always better, although testing shows there is usually no discernable performance gain for buffer sizes over 32K.

Full-Duplex   In servers, full-duplex may give an NIC an extra 5- to 25-percent performance increase, but this increase is highly dependent on what the server is doing. Many protocols, such as IPX, aren't structured to take advantage of full-duplex. Also, full-duplex NICs require full-duplex switched ports to connect to at the hub. If all the correct pieces are in place, full-duplex may provide some incremental performance gains. Another important note is that 10-Mbps full-duplex has lost much of its early market momentum in light of the faster 100-Mbps full-duplex standards efforts. Don't get caught paying extra for 10-Mbps full-duplex.

Intelligent NICs   Intelligent server NICs are defined as having a local CPU on the NIC itself. For instance, the NE3200 designs all have an 80186 on board. The advantage of an intelligent NIC is that it can offload the host CPU of many networking tasks, allowing it to focus on running applications and NOS software. Intelligent NICs are typically very expensive and should only be considered for a specific server application where they provide a real benefit. Some examples are application servers and servers with multiple NICs. Fast Ethernet intelligent NICs will also be popular in servers where the host CPU would otherwise be spending 100 percent of its time providing data for the 100-Mbps wire.

Multiport NICs   Many PCI servers are shipping with only two or three PCI expansion slots. In a modern 10-Mbps network, where many servers have more than one NIC, this can be a restriction. Some NIC vendors, such as IBM and Cogent Data Technologies, have recognized this fact and have designed multiport server NICs. These NICs provide two or more network connections on a single card. As with intelligent NICs, multiport NICs will be useful in specific applications where server slots are at a premium.

Client NICs

Desktops, or clients, pose different challenges for NICs than servers do. Clients are often lower-performance systems and typically run different software than servers do. For instance, DOS and Windows 3.1 operating systems are predominant on clients today, whereas NetWare 3.11, 3.12, and 4.02 and Windows NT 3.5 are common on servers. Client trends indicate that 1995 will be a year of transition from single-tasking operating systems like DOS and Windows 3.1 to multitasking operating systems such as Windows 95 and UNIX (in fact, Apple Macintoshes have been shipping with multitasking operating systems for years). This type of OS will require a much different NIC than that of a DOS system in that the NIC driver will have to be cognizant of how it uses the host CPU. This is referred to as *client CPU utilization* and will prove to be one of the differentiating factors of 1995 in a commodity client NIC market.

Client NIC Bus Type

As in servers, 10/100-Mbps NICs provide an affordable upgrade path from 10-only, but how much should you be willing to pay for that upgradability? Currently, 10/100 PCI NICs cost about twice as much as 10-only ISA. By the end of 1995, 10/100 PCI will only be about 10 percent more expensive than 10-only ISA. With this information in mind, it is a good idea to start planning *when* to purchase 10/100 Mbps client NICs, rather than evaluating *if* you should.

10-Mbps Ethernet NICs are commonly available in ISA, PCMCIA, PCI, MCA, EISA, S-Bus and NuBus flavors. Fast Ethernet NICs are available in PCI, EISA and S-Bus flavors, but as discussed previously, ISA and Fast Ethernet do not mix very well. The future of the desktop is PCI, even for Macintoshes and workstations. With more demanding peripherals being added to desktops every day, the bandwidth of PCI is needed to deliver data to all these devices. Network cards are no exception. If you are not already doing so, look for PCI in your desktop systems and select PCI 10/100 LAN adapters to connect those systems. What do you do with all those old ISA systems? Continue to use them as an important part of your client base, but network them with 10-Mbps switching hubs as discussed in Chapter 7.

Client NIC Configurability

After making the decision to purchase 10/100, the next choice is between 100BASE-TX or 100BASE-T4. As in the case of a workgroup server, 100BASE-TX or 100BASE-T4 client NICs must be chosen depending on the type of wiring found in that workgroup. Some workgroups will have only Category 3 UTP and will require 100BASE-T4 clients. Some will have Category 5 UTP and can support either 100BASE-TX or 100BASE-T4 clients. As with server NICs, the best solution is to determine ahead of time which 100BASE-T specification matches your wiring infrastructure and purchase those types of NICs.

Another factor in selecting client NICs will be NWAY, or auto-negotiation support. An NWAY client NIC will negotiate the transmission scheme (100BASE-TX, 10BASE-T, and so on) with the hub, thereby making hub connections automatic and painless. Unfortunately, NWAY will not be fully implemented until late 1995, so proper selection of a 100BASE-TX or 100BASE-T4 NIC as soon as possible is essential to successful Fast Ethernet desktop deployment.

Client NIC Performance

The performance of a client NIC is measured in a slightly different way than is that of a server NIC. Where server benchmarks use multiple clients to maximize the traffic on the server NIC, client benchmarks use a one client/one server test setup. Maximum client performance is measured by using an ultrafast server, attaching the one client to be measured and running benchmark tests. The same server benchmark test suites apply, but the parameters are different for client NIC testing. For instance, in the server test, the clients should remain constant while the server parameters are varied. In the client test, the server should be the system to remain constant. Variable test parameters in client NIC tests include file size, test duration, and NOS-specific parameters like packet burst size.

One fallacy of client testing is the concept of *matched pair* testing. Some vendors claim higher performance with the same card in the server and the client, but a matched pair test does not represent real life. The best test methodology is to put a high performance server NIC in place and keep it constant for all client NICs tested. Table 6.3 re-examines the three top test suites, looking specifically at client performance aspects.

Table 6.3

Three Popular Client NIC Performance Tests

TEST	HOW DOES IT WORK?	WHAT DOES IT MEASURE?	WHAT ARE ITS DRAWBACKS?
Perform3 (Novell Labs)	Copies variable file sizes from client cache memory to server	Isolates the client NIC. Shows peak throughput from the client. Results are readily quantifiable.	Doesn't involve other server components like the hard drive. Doesn't model real-life traffic very well. Doesn't measure client CPU utilization.
NetBench 3.0 (Ziff-Davis Labs)	Copies variable file sizes from client cache memory to server. Also performs read/write tests.	Isolates the client NIC. Shows peak throughput from the client. Results are readily quantifiable. Other options allow for hard disk interaction.	Doesn't model real-life traffic very well. Doesn't measure client CPU utilization.
NSTL (McGraw Hill Labs)	Simulates repetition of several accesses from multiple clients. Simulates random-length accesses.	Represents real world performance, but doesn't indicate how good the client NIC is.	Doesn't isolate the NIC very well. Results are only as good as the slowest test component. Doesn't measure client CPU utilization.

Buffering plays an important role in client performance because client systems do not always have high-speed buses like PCI. Client NIC buffering will help, especially at 100-Mbps wire speeds, by storing incoming data temporarily while a slower I/O bus can read it from the card. In a bus master client NIC, buffering is usually of the FIFO SRAM type and 3K is considered large. In a buffered slave client NIC, buffering is usually external DRAM and sizes can vary from 4K to 32K. Since every network is different, there is no one buffer size that is best for a client NIC. A simple way to determine if a particular client NIC does not have enough buffering is to look at how many overruns (loss of data due to the NIC buffers being full) occur on the client in a performance test. If more than a few occur, then the client NIC buffer size is not adequate.

Full-duplex does not typically enhance client performance more than 10 percent at 10- or 100-Mbps data rates, so it should not be considered as a criterion when buying the client NIC. Do not pay extra for 10- or 100-Mbps full-duplex support on a client NIC.

With a thorough understanding of NIC tradeoffs and a solid grasp of the desktop and client piece of the network puzzle, you are now ready to delve into the next layer of network components, the workgroup hubs.

■ Workgroup Components

As stated, a workgroup hub is the center of the star-configuration network. Workgroup hubs allow multiple clients and local servers to connect to the network in one central location. Workgroup hubs fall into four broad categrories:

- Standalone repeating hubs

- Stackable hubs

- Workgroup switching hubs

- Chassis hubs

Buying criteria for workgroup hubs often include price per port, ease of installation, ease of management, scalability, and upgradability. This section starts by describing the most basic of workgroup hubs—the standalone repeater.

Standalone Repeaters

A *repeater*, also known as a concentrator (see Figure 6.6), is a device that was first introduced into LANs via Thin Ethernet. Network architects needed a way to extend the reach of Thin Ethernet past a single cable. To do this, they first employed simple, two-port repeaters to receive weak signals in one port, regenerate them internally, and send them out the other port.

When 10BASE-T came along, repeaters changed slightly to accommodate the new signaling scheme, but retained their basic purpose of regenerating signals. Figure 6.7 shows a basic repeater receiving an Ethernet frame on port A. It locks on to the incoming signal and recreates the data stream, passing it to the other seven ports. All other connected nodes, B for example, will see this frame and will defer their own transmittal according to the rules of CSMA/CD. In this way, the total bandwidth of the wire, either 10 or 100 Mbps, is shared between all ports on the repeater. This is how the term *shared network* came to be associated with repeaters.

Figure 6.6

Grand Junction Networks has a full line of standalone 100BASE-T repeaters.

Figure 6.7

A repeater works by forwarding an incoming packet to all ports on the repeater.

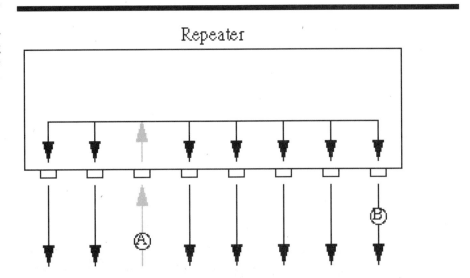

Repeaters are known as passive, or shared, components of the network because they do not logically act upon incoming frames. Their only function is to regenerate weak incoming signals, thus extending the diameter of the network. In this way, repeaters are invisible to network events such as collisions, merely propagating them. Hence, a repeater cannot extend the collision domain of a network. Standalone repeaters are limited in their ability to extend network diameters, but their low cost makes them an excellent choice for small workgroups.

Below are descriptions of the features of standalone repeaters.

Limits to Network Diameter

When a signal is sent down UTP wiring, it suffers losses for many different reasons. A signal that initially started out as a square wave, 5-volt peak-to-peak will lose amplitude and become somewhat spread out over the course of the 100 meters of wire.

A repeater will recognize the weak incoming signal, re-create it in its original form and retransmit it to all other ports. In this way, repeaters are useful in overcoming the distance limitations impose by the 100-meter distance restrictions of UTP cable. However, since a repeater is a shared media device and propagates all traffic, including collisions, it will not extend the collision domain of a network (remember, the collision domain is determined by the round-trip propagation delay of a packet, not the attenuation of the signal). A more powerful device such as a bridge, router, or switch is needed for this purpose.

Limits to Number of Users

In 10BASE-T, standalone repeaters could be cascaded together with standard 100-meter UTP connections as long as the collision domain was not overrun. This could result in a network three to five repeaters deep. In 100BASE-T, however, the speed of the network signal has been sped up by a factor of ten, so the collision domain must be shrunk by the same factor. This corresponds to a maximum of two Fast Ethernet standalone repeaters cascaded together. Since most standalone repeaters are 16 or 32 ports, a Fast Ethernet network made up of standalone repeaters would have a limited number of users. This fact should emphasize the importance of stackable hubs and switching hubs to the wide deployment of Fast Ethernet. We learned in Chapter 3 that the 802.3 specification allows only two Fast Ethernet repeaters to be cascaded together, therefore it is much more critical that each repeater provide the maximum number of ports possible (as stackable hubs do). Switches can be used to interconnect groups of stackable hubs in such a way that the collision domain is never overrun. This is explained more fully in Chapter 7.

Performance

Standalone repeaters will give good performance based on the amount of traffic and collisions that are propagated through them. Standalone and stackable repeaters are good for bursty, workgroup traffic where one node may have a short burst of activity, followed closely by another node. If too many nodes are put on the same repeater, or segment, collisions will start to occur. Too many collisions will invariably choke a shared media network. Repeater performance is typically measured in esoteric terms of throughput latency, jitter tolerance, and packet forwarding rates. In reality, most standalone repeaters, either 10 Mbps or 100 Mbps, display similar performance.

Class I versus Class II

One difference among Fast Ethernet repeaters involves how they are designed. Some Fast Ethernet repeaters are *Class I*, meaning that they fully decode incoming analog data into digital form before passing it to other ports. Class I Fast Ethernet repeaters may have all 100BASE-T4 ports, all 100BASE-TX ports, or some combination of the two. This latter version is referred to as a translational repeater. *Class II* repeaters take the analog input signal from one port and forward it directly to all other ports. Class II Fast Ethernet repeaters are restricted to ports of only one type (either 100BASE-TX or 100BASE-T4). Class II repeaters will exhibit lower port latencies than Class I repeaters because there is less overhead in forwarding a packet from one port to the next. Figure 6.8 below illustrates the architectural differences between Class I and Class II Fast Ethernet repeaters.

Figure 6.8

The architecture of Class I and Class II repeaters differs by the way incoming data is forwarded to other ports.

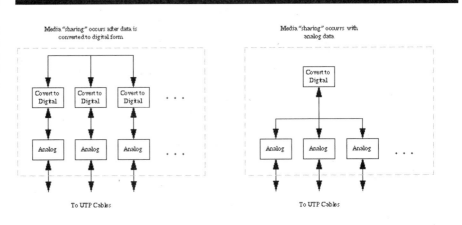

Class I Repeater   Class II Repeater

Low Price

Standalone repeaters are sold at very low prices. A typical managed 10-Mbps repeater port is around $50 to $60 today, while a managed 100-Mbps repeater port goes for about $200. Since Fast Ethernet repeater technology is very similar to Classic Ethernet, it is valid to assume that prices will decline in a similar fashion. Expect 100-Mbps standalone repeater prices to drop to under $50 per port by 1996.

Ease of Troubleshooting

Another positive aspect of standalone repeaters is their ability to "sniff," or listen to, the network from any port. Since repeaters merely propagate signals to all existing ports, a signal that exists on port A will also exist on port B or C. Network analyzers and sniffers, made popular by Hewlett-Packard and Network General, are designed to plug into an empty repeater port and give a complete view of the network traffic at any given instant. With switches, however, this is not so easily done. This is one reason why many LAN administrators stick with their shared media LANs—they are simply easier to fix when problems arise. The same rules apply for Fast Ethernet repeaters. There are several 100BASE-TX sniffers that use the same software as similar 10BASE-T versions.

Network Management

Because standalone repeaters are used primarily in smaller workgroups, management may not be an essential feature. Many shared networks are managed "outside" the repeater. The management tools are run independent of the repeater used. However, depending on the application, management options inside the repeater may be beneficial. Most standalone repeaters allow for a management module, which can be added at any time. Therefore, it is recommended to buy either managed standalone repeaters or unmanaged standalone repeaters with a management upgrade path.

Stackable Hubs

A stackable hub can be thought of as a repeater with an upgrade option. A stackable hub consists of several independent units, each with a given number of ports. Each unit acts as a standalone repeater in its own right, but also has an external connection for adding additional units exactly like itself. Since stackable hubs are shared media devices, the effective bandwidth for a stackable hub is always the same. The more ports that are added, the less average bandwidth available to any given port. Figure 6.9 shows an example of a stackable hub stacked six units high.

Figure 6.9

Bay Networks Fast
Ethernet Stackable hub.

The stackable hub's upgradability and inexpensive cost per port combine to make it the fastest growing segment of the entire hub market. Stackable hubs allow LAN administrators to purchase a single management unit to manage the whole stack, thereby distributing the management costs over many ports. Stackable hubs are also extremely useful in connecting many nodes on a Fast Ethernet network due to the associated network diameter restrictions.

Next we'll discuss the features of stackable hubs.

Similarities to Repeaters

A stackable hub is a special version of a standalone repeater. Stackable hubs are analogous to multiple standalone repeaters linked together with a high-speed bus or backplane, yet sharing the same collision domain. This makes them essentially look to the rest of the network like one large repeater. Stackable hubs are currently quite popular, both in 10BASE-T and 100BASE-T versions.

Stackable hubs are popular because they offer multiple connections at a low cost per port, they are manageable and easy to upgrade, and they fit well within the typical hierarchial network structure of large LANs. The architecture of a stackable hub is shown in Figure 6.10. At Port A, an incoming frame enters the bottom unit of the stack. As in a regular standalone repeater, the frame is forwarded to all ports in that unit, but is also forwarded to the stackable hub backplane bus (B), where it is forwarded to the next unit in the stack (C). The process repeats until all units in the stack are forwarding the same frame. This is how a set of stackable units can share the same collision domain, thus acting like one large, expandable repeater.

Figure 6.10

Stackable hub architecture. Incoming packets are forwarded through the backplane bus to other hub units.

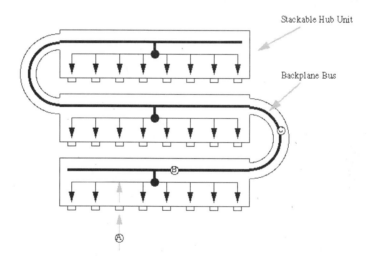

Limits to Network Diameter

Although stackable hubs are built for upgradability, they are not infinitely upgradable. There are limits to the number of units that can be added; this is often referred to as how high they can be stacked. The stacking height has to do with how the hub propagates the signal across its backplane, and since these backplane buses are usually proprietary to the hub vendor, stacking height can vary. Most 10BASE-T and 100BASE-T stackable hubs can be stacked about eight units high. Stacking height depends on design, but in general, each unit adds about ten meters of effective network diameter. So an eight-unit stack corresponds to about 80 meters of UTP in network diameter calculations.

Performance

Performance criteria for stackable hubs are very similar to those of stand-alone repeaters. Latency and forwarding rates are key things to look for; however, neither will affect performance drastically. Stackable hubs will excel in bursty traffic scenarios like you would find in a workgroup or server cluster. However, stackable hubs will not make good backbone hubs, even at 100 Mbps, because of their inability to filter unwanted packets and dedicate bandwidth to a specific port.

Price

Stackable hub prices are what really makes stacking attractive. A single stackable unit is more expensive than a standalone repeater. This is mainly because the first unit of any stack incurs the setup costs and the cost of the management unit, and it doesn't offer as high a port density. But as you add more units to the stack, the price per port goes down because additional stackable units are cheaper than additional standalone repeaters. Overall, the cost curves will drop in such a way that soon there will be no real price difference between 10- and 100-Mbps stackable hubs.

Management

Most stackable hubs offer a configurable management module that is capable of managing the entire stack. Therefore it is only essential to purchase this management module for one unit in any given stack. The best approach to stackable hub management is to buy the management module and associated software up front, thereby making it easier to add units to the stack later on. If you have ever tried to add management to an existing network, you know the effort involved. A few extra dollars up front will prevent headaches down the road. Also, considering the fact that stackables are shared media devices, a multitude of PC-based shared LAN management software can be used to manage the traffic on the stack. Before purchasing a stackable hub, make sure it supports SNMP or your current network management scheme.

Fast Ethernet Stackable Hubs

Fast Ethernet stackables are currently widely available in many shapes and sizes, but a few features will separate a good Fast Ethernet stackable hub from an average one. First, because of restrictions in the IEEE 802.3u specification, stackable units are either 100BASE-T4 or 100BASE-TX, but not both. Therefore, if you plan to deploy both in your network, carefully select a vendor that can stack 100BASE-TX and 100BASE-T4 units together. A good example of this is 3Com's Linkbuilder Stackable hubs. Another feature to look for is how stackable vendors plan to integrate stackable Fast Ethernet hubs with 10BASE-T. 3Com promotes doing this with an inexpensive, external 10/100 2-port bridge. There are other ways to do this, with special 10BASE-T downlink ports on the stackable hub (effectively integrating the 10/100 bridge inside the stackable).

Other Stackable Hub Features

Some stackable hubs may offer additional features, like redundant power supplies and hot upgradability (adding units without turning off power to the stack). Redundant power supplies are a plus because if any one unit in the stack has a power failure, the others can compensate. Hot upgradability is useful because you don't have to power down the stack to add another unit.

Workgroup Switches

Kalpana made the concept of LAN switching a household term, though all they really did was redesign and remarket a multiport Ethernet bridge. Not to take anything away from the brilliant EtherSwitch product, but the concept of switching is nothing new. The concept of marketing hubs as "switches" is what is new. The term *switching* is used by different vendors to mean different things. For instance, Bay Networks sometimes uses switching to mean routing, whereas Grand Junction Networks always uses switching to mean bridging.

In general, a switch is defined as a network component that receives incoming packets, stores them temporarily, and sends them back out on another port. Since a switch buffers incoming frames, it acts like an end node, or NIC. In this way, a switch can be used like a bridge or router to extend the collision domain of a network indefinitely. Switches are crucial to Fast Ethernet deployment because of their ability to increase network diameter (see Figure 6.11).

A switch's total bandwidth is determined by adding the bandwidth available to each port. For instance, a 16-port 100-Mbps Fast Ethernet switch gives an aggregate throughput of 1.6 Gbps (if you consider both incoming and outgoing traffic), whereas a 16-port 100-Mbps repeater still only gives 100 Mbps of throughput. A switch can be receiving frames on any number of ports while at the same time be forwarding frames to many other ports. This is shown in Figure 6.12, where incoming frames of ports A, B, and C are routed simultaneously to ports D, E, and F. Although the collisions found in a repeater are avoided in a switch, contention can still occur when two incoming ports want to forward data to the same outgoing port.

Switches can be very useful in constructing large, robust local area networks because they provide one of the lowest prices per megabit of bandwidth of any network component available today. Ethernet and Fast Ethernet switches are also especially useful when sending steady-stream traffic, such as

Figure 6.11

Kaplana's EPS-15 workgroup switch provides dedicated 10-Mbps connections to 16 parts. The model shown here also has a 100BASE-TX switched port.

Figure 6.12

How switching works: Multiple data streams can pass through a switch without affecting each other.

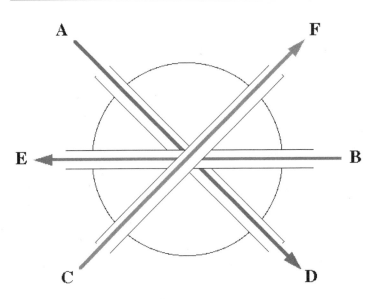

video, over the LAN because they provide dedicated bandwidth. In a switched architecture, traffic levels depend on network architecture and switch forwarding rates as well as the number of users on the network.

Another thing to consider with a switch is that the familiar Carrier Sense Multiple Access/Collision Detect (CSMA/CD) medium access scheme no longer applies. With a dedicated connection for each port, there is no contention for the wire, and therefore no need for a carrier and no source of collisions.

Four basic components make up a switch. These are ports, buffer size, the packet forwarding mechanism, and backplane architecture. These areas are highlighted in Figure 6.13. Note that a switch allows port D to send to port A, port B to F, and port E to C, all simultaneously. In a repeater, only one port is allowed to receive at any given instant. In addition, 10BASE-T and 100BASE-TX switches can incorporate full-duplex ports that can be used for higher-speed links.

Figure 6.13

Basic switch architecture

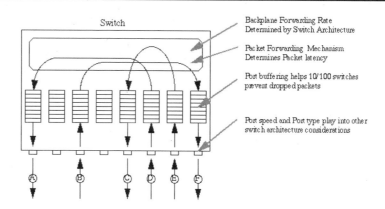

Port Speed and Type

Although FDDI and Token Ring switching products are shipping today, the immediate opportunity for network architects is in 10BASE-T and 100BASE-T switches. Switches with 10- and 100-Mbps Ethernet ports allow for a seamless migration from existing 10-Mbps Ethernet networks to 100-Mbps Fast Ethernet networks. In addition to being 10 or 100 Mbps, switch ports can also be 100BASE-TX, 100BASE-T4, or 100BASE-FX depending on the switch design.

Buffering and Congestion Control

Buffering can play a large role in 10/100 switching, especially with Novell VLMs and other sliding windows protocols. Sliding windows works with protocol stacks such as IPX, allowing for many back-to-back packets at 100 Mbps. For instance, consider the above switch, with port B connected to a 100-Mbps server and port F to a 10-Mbps client. With some of today's network protocols, up to 16 frames can be sent back-to-back from the server to the client, which amounts to roughly 24K of data. Each 1.5K frame takes 122 microseconds to transfer at 100 Mbps and 1,220 microseconds to transfer at 10 Mbps, which means that ten frames can be received on port B before one is completely sent out on port F. In the case of 16 back-to-back 100-Mbps frames, port B will be deluged with 24K of incoming data before port F can send it all out at 10 Mbps. If port B's buffer size is not 24K or greater, the incoming data will overrun the buffer.

A logical deduction of the above scenario is that larger buffers mean better performance. This assumption is basically true, but large buffers are inherently expensive. Therefore, many switch vendors have opted for a congestion control mechanism to prevent an underrun case of this type. The congestion control concept involves sending a "fake" collision back to the high-speed port, forcing it to back off. In our example, port B would recognize when its buffer is almost full and send a jam pattern back to the transmitting node. The transmitting node interprets this jam pattern as a collision so it enters the standard backoff state. The switch can keep the transmitting node in this state until it has emptied its internal buffers. This type of congestion control is specific to half-duplex switch ports and will be implemented as a feature in certain switching hubs. Beware of claims of full-duplex congestion control, as this implementation is likely to be proprietary.

Forwarding Mechanism

The forwarding mechanism in a switch is defined by two factors. First of all, the switch must know if it is performing a bridging or routing function. Secondly, if configured as a bridge, the switch must know what type of packet forwarding to use. Packet forwarding may be store-and-forward, cut-through, or modified cut-through. Some high-end switches may be configured as a router, which means that it must completely store each incoming frame, analyze it, and forward it to the appropriate port based on protocol header information. Other switches, such as the Kalpana ES-15, are configured as bridges and need only analyze the destination address of a given frame before switching it to another port. If a switch with routing capabilities is desired, make sure it supports the protocol stacks used in your network. Commonly, IPX/SPX and TCP/IP protocol stacks are supported.

In a bridge-configured switch, packet-forwarding mechanisms will make a tradeoff between packet latency and error-checking robustness. Let's look at the three types of switch-forwarding mechanisms more closely.

Store-and-forward switches completely store the incoming frame in internal buffers before sending it out on another port. In this case, the switch latency is equal to an entire packet, which could turn into a performance issue if enough of these switches are cascaded in series. However, store-and-forward switches provide excellent packet error checking in the form of CRC-checks, runt packet filters, and collided packet filters. A store-and-forward switch may be a good investment for critical points in the network, but not necessarily for the workgroup.

Cut-through switches only examine a packet up to the destination address, much like a bridge. This allows the packet to be forwarded almost immediately, resulting in very low switch latencies. The drawback to cut-through switching is that runt packets, collision packets, and packets with CRC errors will also be forwarded. In fact, any packet arriving with a valid destination address will be forwarded. Proponents of cut-through switching point out that end nodes are, by default, set up to do this level of error checking so a switch doesn't have to. This tends to be more true in workgroups than on the backbone, so if your workgroups do not encounter many errors, a cut-through switch may be a good choice.

Modified cut-through switches attempt to offer the best of both worlds by holding an incoming Ethernet packet until the first 64 bytes have been received. If a collision or runt packet occurs, it is very likely that it will occur in the first 64 bytes of a frame, so a tradeoff between switch latency and error checking is achieved. However, modified cut-through switches act like store-and-forward switches for short frames, which are typically control frames and like cut-through switches for large frames, which are usually made up of data. This is a shortcoming of modified-cut-through switches because control frames require low switch latencies and data frames require good error checking. This may be a moot point, however, in many networks because CRC errors are usually measured in parts per billion (a few errors in a billion packets).

The type of forwarding mechanism you use should depend on your network criteria. If your network needs speed and low latency, then cut-through switches are the best choice. If your network needs efficiency and stability, then store-and-forward switching may be the way to go. To get a better understanding of the three types of packet forwarding, consider Figure 6.14. The point at which a frame is forwarded is shown for each type of forwarding mechanism.

Backplane Architecture

A switch's backplane architecture defines how packets are forwarded from one port to the other through the internal electronics of the switch. The backplane architecture of a switch is important because vendors may claim

Figure 6.14

The three types of Packet-forwarding mechanisms

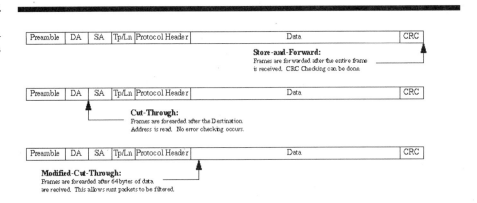

forwarding rates of 1 or 2 Gbps, but this forwarding rate may be very dependent on traffic patterns. For instance, a switch with very little buffering can achieve its maximum forwarding rate only if all ports are the same speed and the traffic is equally loaded between the ports. In addition, workgroup switches are a lot like PC Interrupt Controllers in that they can be designed for round-robin or priority port service.

A *round-robin*, or first come, first serve, switch architecture services ports one at a time. If a port has no activity, then it is skipped. This architecture plays well into a heavily utilized switch where the traffic on each port is basically equal (as in a backbone switch). A *priority* port scheme introduces the concept of active ports competing with each other for the backplane. This type of architecture lends itself to 10/100 switches with bursty traffic (as in a workgroup) and is generally more flexible than a round-robin architecture. The top switch vendors offer switches that can be configured to either type of architecture.

Other Workgroup Switch Features

Workgroup switches may be defined by other characteristics besides the four basic features of a switch. Some of these commonly overlooked features are discussed below.

Number of Addresses per Port   A differentiating feature of many workgroup switches is how many network addresses they support per port. Since each port acts as a forwarding bridge, a list must be kept of what node addresses lie beyond that port. These lists can be long and use costly amounts of memory, so many switch vendors allow for only a small number of addresses per port. A good example of two totally different schemes is Grand Junction's FastSwitch 100 and Bay Network's 28115. The FastSwitch 100 supports only one address per port because the design assumes that only nodes will be connected to a port. The Bay Networks 28115 and the Cisco Catalyst, on the other hand, supports 1,024 addresses per port, which allows it to be used as a workgroup switch or a backbone switch. The tradeoff is that the 28115 is more costly than the FastSwitch 100.

100BASE-T Flexibility   With many switches today, configurability is a key factor. As networks become increasingly dependent on high bandwidth, network architects are going to look for switches that can be upgraded or modified to suit the needs of the growing network. For instance, buying 100BASE-TX switches will allow you to deploy Fast Ethernet into workgroups with Category 5 UTP, but you will need 100BASE-T4 for workgroups with CAT 3 UTP only. By purchasing a switch that has some ports that can be configured to either 100BASE-T4, 100BASE-TX, or 100BASE-FX, you will be covering many of your potential installations. This can be accomplished by switches with Media Independent Interface (MII) ports. External transceivers can be connected to MII ports to allow connectivity to any type of Ethernet or Fast Ethernet transmission protocol.

Network Management   Switch management is a dilemma facing many switch vendors and LAN administrators today. With a shared media network, the management was straightforward because all ports on a segment saw all the traffic on that segment. Since switches actually filter traffic, they must have some other means of collecting vital network management statistics. So far, two methods have been developed for doing this. One method incorporates management into the backplane architecture of the switch. Statistics are collected on each packet that is forwarded on the switch backplane and stored in a management unit with its own unique Ethernet address. This management unit may be polled from any station on the LAN. The only problem with this method is that each switch vendor has implemented its own scheme for doing this; so compatibility is at a minimum, usually limited to SNMP statistics. The second method is called port aliasing, which allows the switch to "mirror" any given port to a dedicated management port. The management port is fed into a specific management terminal or PC, which looks at overall switch statistics and individual port information. Once again, no specific standard exists for this type of switch management.

Some switch vendors have incorporated the new Remote Monitor (RMON) MIB, which allows SNMP based port-by-port management of a switch. Chapter 5 delves into more detail on RMON and the management problems associated with switching.

High Price Tag   So are you convinced that switching is the answer to your network bottlenecks? Well, get out your checkbook. Switches can cost anywhere from two to five times as much as repeaters with a similar number of ports. Although pricing will fall in the next few years, standalone repeaters and stackable hubs will always be less expensive than similar workgroup switches.

Chassis Hubs

A chassis hub generally refers to a chassis-based box that can accept modules based on repeaters, bridges, routers, or switches (see Figure 6.15). In this way, a chassis hub is simply a collection of the other components in this chapter. A chassis hub can be thought of as a "hub of hubs" in that it primarily provides a socket for individual modules. When a customer buys a chassis hub from a vendor, he or she is buying into a specific architecture and expecting to purchase additional modules for that hub over time. Therefore, chassis hubs like The Bay Networks Series 5000 have also become popular for their fault tolerance, expandability, and upgradability. Chassis hubs, like routers, usually have optional high-end features such as uninterruptible power supplies, diagnostic ports, and hardware and software tools for advanced hub management.

Figure 6.15

Bay Networks Series 5000 chassis hub. 100BASE-T modules will be available for the 5000 near the end of 1995.

The following sections outline the key features of chassis hubs.

Wide Assortment of Networking Modules

Chassis hubs are sometimes thought of as a convenient place to collect individual networking modules, providing a common power supply and chassis.

Chassis hubs do not necessarily interconnect all the modules that are plugged into them, but chassis hubs do offer the promise of upgradability with the simple addition of a new module. Chassis hubs commonly support Token Ring, FDDI, 10BASE-T, Thin Ethernet, ATM, and Fast Ethernet. Most high-end chassis hubs also offer switching, bridging, or routing through a high-speed backplane.

A chassis hub should offer some type of backplane interconnectivity between modules. If it doesn't, then external routing or bridging may be necessary, which can complicate network designs. Also, make sure the chassis hub supports various modules that perform switched and shared Ethernet and Fast Ethernet. If a chassis hub does not have a module under development for both Fast Ethernet and ATM, then it is a good bet that the hub cannot support high amounts of traffic.

Cost and Extra Features

Chassis hubs usually cost much more per port than do stackable hubs, and they often don't offer much better performance. The real benefit of installing a chassis hub comes from the extra features that usually accompany them. These include hot-swappable, redundant power supplies, hot-swappable modules, advanced network management modules, and a chassis designed specifically for rack mounting. If these features match your workgroup hub requirements, then chassis hubs may be the best type of workgroup hub for your network.

The combination of standalone repeaters, stackable hubs, workgroup switches, and chassis hubs makes for a wide array of products for the workgroup. The features of these products are summarized in Table 6.4.

Table 6.4

Comparison of Workgroup Hubs

FEATURE	STANDALONE REPEATER	STACKABLE HUB	WORKGROUP SWITCHING HUB	CHASSIS HUB
Port density	Low	High	High	High
Is performance scalable?	No	No	Yes	Yes
Manageable?	Yes	Yes	Yes	Yes
Cost per port	Low	Low	High	High
Allows for 10BASE-T and 100BASE-T	No	Yes	Yes	Yes
Allows large network diameters	No	No	Yes	Yes

If your network is small (fewer than 20 users) you will probably never need to consider any network components beyond workgroup hubs. If your network is large, however, more powerful network devices are needed to separate and distribute network traffic. These devices, called interconnect components, are discussed in the next section.

■ Interconnect Components

In a network, interconnect devices can number anywhere from none to several hundred. The components themselves fall into three broad categories: bridges, routers, and backbone switches. Their function is to provide fast, robust, and efficient connections for a variety of different subnetworks. This function typically requires very fast silicon and is available only at a high price: It is not uncommon for a high-end router to cost tens of thousands of dollars. Though the interconnect function may seem to be required only in large, multinode networks, routers are also quite common in smaller networks. For instance, a branch office with 20 users, a few servers, and a connection to headquarters through a wide area network (WAN) can employ a low-end router to route traffic from the branch office LAN to the WAN. When describing interconnect components it is common to start with the most basic of these devices—bridges.

Bridges

A bridge is a network device that not only regenerates an incoming signal like a repeater, but also can perform basic packet filtering functions. Every Ethernet packet has a field defined as the *destination address,* which tells the packet which node it is ultimately destined for.

A bridge can look at an incoming Ethernet packet and analyze the destination address encapsulated in its header. From this information, the bridge can check its "memory" of past frames and determine whether to forward the packet to another port or do nothing. In this way, bridges can isolate network traffic between network segments. Figure 6.16 shows the general structure of an Ethernet or Fast Ethernet frame and the location of the destination address.

Figure 6.16

A bridge looks for the destination address of an Ethernet frame

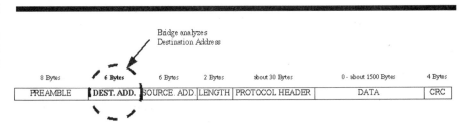

Bridges come in all sizes and shapes, with a wide variety of price tags. Many people feel bridges are a dying breed, soon to be replaced with switches. This may prove to be true, with the exception of 10/100 speed matching bridges (10BASE-T to 100BASE-T). 10/100 Speed matching bridges will be a cost-effective way to connect existing 10-Mbps networks to new Fast Ethernet networks.

Increasing Bandwidth with Bridges

Standalone bridges are popular because they can separate network traffic without changing the overall look of the network.

Bridges are basically invisible to all network software since they perform their functions at the bit level on the wire. A bridge will look at a network address, analyze it, compare it to an internal list of addresses, and send the packet to one port. When a bridge first powers up, it doesn't know anything about the network around it, but as it starts receiving packets, it can develop a list of which addresses are coming from which port. In Figure 6.17, we examine a three-port bridge at three distinct points in time. In example A, we look at a packet coming in on port A, with a destination address (DA) of 00AA00001111 and a source address (SA) of 00AA00003333. The bridge has just been powered up so it doesn't know where this packet is supposed to go and it has no choice but to forward it to all ports, hoping the right party eventually receives it. The bridge also remembers that it received a packet on port A from SA=00AA00003333. Later, in example B, the bridge receives a packet on port B with a DA of 00AA00003333. It remembers that this address lies beyond port A, so it forwards the packet only to Port A. Now, assume in example C that the bridge has received traffic from many different nodes and the structure of its address table is as shown. A packet comes in on port C with a DA of 00AA00006666. Since the bridge sees that that address lies beyond port C, it assumes the packet is already on the right segment and does not forward the packet to ports A or B.

Today, simple bridges match 10BASE-5 Coaxial Ethernet to 10BASE-T UTP. In 1995, simple bridges will match 100BASE-T to 10BASE-T and will be very inexpensive. Bridges are one of many possible ways to connect 10- and 100-Mbps networks. As seen earlier in this chapter, another way is by using a switch to perform a bridging function. Bridges are at the lowest level of functionality of the Interconnect components. Routers, which take bridging one step further, are discussed next.

Routers

A router (Figure 6.18) can perform all the functions of a bridge and more, which allows it to be used in many different applications. A router differs from a bridge in its ability to examine the protocol header of a packet. This

Figure 6.17

How a bridge works (A) after initial power-up, (B) forwarding a packet through the bridge, and (C) not forwarding a packet

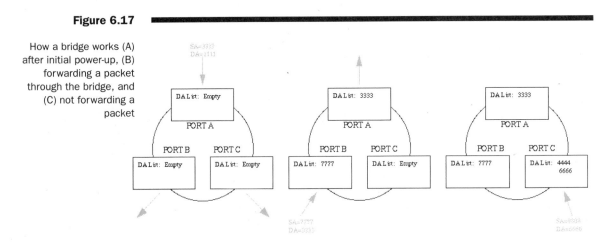

allows the router to break LANs into subnetworks based on Internet Protocol (IP) or IPX Network number *and* destination address. This basic feature allows a router to be used in three distinct manners:

- Improved network segmentation
- Routing between dissimilar LANs
- Routing to the WAN

These applications are discussed in more detail in the sections to follow.

Better Network Segmentation

According to the Ethernet specification, the protocol header is merely part of the data field. A bridge only understands the Ethernet specification, but a router can look at the data field, interpret it as a frame originated by a certain protocol stack, and act upon it accordingly (see Figure 6.19). Bridges automatically learn how to forward packets, whereas routers must be configured for this task. For instance, a router that understands NetWare's IPX/SPX protocol stack can tell the difference between a packet originated on IP network 00000001 and IP network 00000002, but only if it knows to look for this. In this way a router can route not only between network segments, but also across different types of networks.

Routing Dissimilar LANs

Another beneficial feature of a router is its built-in ability to communicate between dissimilar packet-based networks. Routers are commonly employed to allow Token Ring and Ethernet users to communicate. A router will take an incoming frame and store it in memory. Once the frame is stored, the

Figure 6.18

The Cisco 5000 Router features slots that can be filled by modules. 100BASE-T modules will be available at the end of 1995.

Figure 6.19

A router examines the entire Ethernet frame, including the protocol header and data fields.

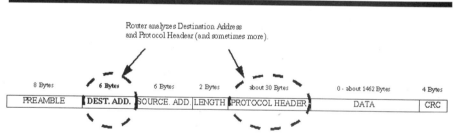

router software will strip off the data and protocol header fields, reform a new frame based on the type of network it is destined for, and send the frame out on the correct port. In this application, routers are not invisible to the network as are bridges, but must be directly addressed at specific destination addresses. Therefore, if an Ethernet user wants to send information to a user on a Token Ring, the information will first be addressed to the router, which interconnects the two LANs. An example of a router in this application is shown in Figure 6.20.

Figure 6.20

Routers are often used to route between dissimilar LANs.

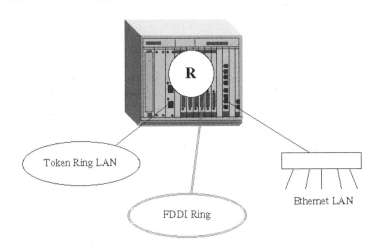

Routing to the WAN

Routers also play an important role in WAN connectivity. WANs are typically much lower-speed (T1, T3) connections than LANs because the signals travel such great distances over marginal mediums. Since routers provide the highest level of packet screening, both at the destination address and IP level, they make good gates for outgoing traffic. Sometimes routers in this configuration are referred to as *gateways*. The branch office discussed previously is a good example of this type of router application. When users in a sales office send information to each other, the LAN-to-WAN router does not forward this information to the WAN. However, when those same users want to access information at company headquarters, the router allows LAN-to-WAN access.

Other Router Features

Routers typically support multiple network types and have broader variations in functionality than other interconnect components. For this reason, a router may have other features that could be desirable to a network administrator. Some of these features are discussed below.

100 Mbps Routing Modules   Some of the leading routers today are the Cisco 7000, Bay Network's AS400, and Cabletron's MMAC Plus. Most router vendors provide chassis-based routing systems that allow Fast Ethernet modules to be added after the point of purchase. Fast Ethernet modules for these product lines provide the same type of service as their Ethernet counterparts—except, of course, at ten times the speed. Since routers are commonly found at critical junctures of the network, their modules are usually hot-swappable and highly manageable. A router chassis will typically provide other features such as redundant power supplies and dedicated management modules.

Servers Acting as Routers   A less expensive way to achieve routing is through PC or workstation-based software products such as Novell's Multi-Protocol Router or by using Novell Netware's standard routing services to route within IPX. This will cost you far less than any of the dedicated routers discussed previously, but network architects tend to shy away from software-based routing because of its unreliability and low performance. As an example of the performance limitations of PC based routing, most MPR servers cannot route frames at full Fast Ethernet wire speed without the help of an intelligent server card.

Backbone Switches

The concept of switching was introduced and defined in the Workgroup Switches section earlier in this chapter. Backbone switches (Figure 6.21) are similar to workgroup switches in many ways; however, there are a few notable differences. Backbone switches typically provide many more high-speed ports than do workgroup switches. Backbone Ethernet and Fast Ethernet switches many times employ full duplex connections on some ports in order to double bandwidth between switches. Some backbone switches also provide extra network management features such as *Virtual LANs* and advanced packet filtering. In general, a backbone switch is much more expensive and much higher performance than its workgroup cousin.

Figure 6.21

Bay Networks LattisSwitch 28115 backbone switch. The 28115 allows for 10 or 100 Mbps on each port.

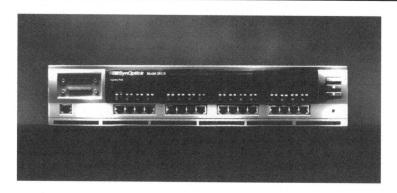

Port Type and Speed

Many backbone switches provide multiple ports for Fast Ethernet, FDDI, ATM, and other high-speed protocols. This allows the switch to be employed in a *collapsed backbone* configuration. A switch configured in this way will provide dedicated bandwidth to a network segment connected to each port. This is more fully explored in Chapter 7. Typically, a switch is considered a backbone switch if over half of its ports are high-speed capable. Also, many backbone switches allow for speed selection on a port-by-port basis. Bay Network's 28115 offers this feature by allowing 10BASE-T or 100BASE-TX configurability on each and every port.

Backbone Switches and Full-Duplex

Backbone switches are put under enormous traffic loads, which can lead to all sorts of bottlenecks between switches. If each switch port is a dedicated 100-Mbps connection and the switch-to-switch connection is also 100 Mbps, then traffic forwarded from switch to switch may encounter extra delays. One way to overcome this effect is to provide full-duplex connections in between switches. In fact, switch-to-switch connections are the only place full-duplex really lives up to its bandwidth-doubling potential. Both the Grand Junction FastSwitch 100 Collision Free™ and the Bay Networks 28115 support ports of these types. When implementing 100BASE-TX full-duplex switch-to-switch connections, be sure to use the same kind of switch on each side, as most vendors have their own proprietary 100-Mbps full-duplex implementation.

Other Backbone Switch Features

Backbone switches are usually much more expensive than workgroup switches because of the high-speed silicon and buffers required to support the packet-forwarding rates of 100-Mbps backbones. Since price is not much of a differentiating factor for backbone switches, many vendors have implemented other features. Two features of note are Virtual LANs and advanced packet filtering. *Virtual LAN* refers to switches that can be configured as routers and can separate traffic not only according to Ethernet address but also according to IP network number. Switches like this are even more expensive, but they provide on-the-fly configurability that is second to none. *Advanced packet filtering* is used in backbone switches to filter out all error, runt, and misaligned packets, and requires that the switch be of the store-and-forward variety.

■ Summary

Table 6.5 summarizes many of the important features of each type of network component, with examples and features of each.

Table 6.5

Summary of Network
Components

TYPE OF COMPONENT	EXAMPLES	BASIC FEATURES TO CONSIDER
Network Interface Cards	Server NICs Client NICs	Wire speed: 10 or 10/100 Bus type: PCI, ISA Brand name: 3Com, Intel Performance: buffering, full-duplex Management: SNMP, DMI
Workgroup Hub	Standalone repeaters Stackable hubs Workgroup switches Chassis hubs	Port density (number of users supported) Performance or bandwidth Upgradability Network diameter allowed Management Switch forwarding mechanism Switch backplane architecture
Interconnect components	Bridges Routers Backbone switches	LAN segmentation Advanced packet filtering Packet error detection Routing between dissimilar LANs Routing from LAN to WAN Full-duplex switching

With a thorough understanding of the basic network components, you are ready to tackle the job of deploying Switched and Fast Ethernet. The next chapter discusses the issues involved with implementing these components in the most important network of all—yours.

7

Deploying Switched and Fast Ethernet

IN CHAPTER 2 WE SAW THAT SWITCHED ETHERNET AND FASt Ethernet solve many of the bandwidth problems facing today's local area networks. In Chapter 3, we discussed the various standards involved in ensuring that Switched and Fast Ethernet are widely interoperable technologies. In Chapter 6, we delved into the basic building blocks of a network, and now, in Chapter 7, we will apply what we have learned. This chapter is all about deploying Switched and Fast Ethernet in today's Ethernet networks. The chapter's focus is on how to seamlessly migrate your existing 10-Mbps shared Ethernet networks to Switched and Fast Ethernet without a major cabling overhaul or a costly change in LAN architecture.

Switching and Fast Ethernet go hand in hand because each needs the other for widespread deployment. Switched Ethernet is usually not of great benefit without a high-speed link, or fat pipe, to collect the various 10-Mbps data streams. Fast Ethernet needs switching to overcome basic diameter restrictions that would otherwise prevent it from being installed in all but the smallest of networks. Switching and Fast Ethernet also combine well because switching is often thought of as a tops-down technology, required in high-end solutions. Fast Ethernet, on the other hand, is thought of as a bottoms-up technology—a logical extension to the 10-Mbps desktop of today. (A *tops-down* technology is one that is implemented first in the backbone, whereas a bottoms-up technology finds its way first into desktops and workgroups.) When used together properly, Switched and Fast Ethernet can increase performance in the desktop, the server, the backbone, and the network as a whole.

■ How to Use This Chapter

The chapter begins by discussing some basic rules of deployment and installation for both switched and shared 10BASE-T and 100BASE-T. Many references are made to Chapter 3 and Chapter 4, so it is assumed the reader has a good understanding of prior topics. After discussing the general rules, we'll categorize the actual deployment of Switched and Fast Ethernet into five sections, or steps. Each step has a specific role in the overall conversion from shared 10BASE-T to Switched 10BASE-T and 100BASE-T. Depending on how large or overloaded your network is, you may only want to implement some of the steps. For instance, if you implement 10-Mbps switches, as discussed in step 1, and you find network performance acceptable, then there may be no need to progress to the following steps. However, the steps are structured in such a way that they can be implemented slowly, even over the course of a few years. The five steps to a Switched and Fast Ethernet network are outlined below.

Step 1:   Adding 10-Mbps switches to your current network (where they help)

Step 2:   First deployment of Fast Ethernet (10/100 cards into new clients and servers)

Step 3:   Convert workgroups to Fast Ethernet

Step 4:   Convert backbone (including server farms) to Switched and Fast Ethernet

Step 5:   Completing the Switched and Fast Ethernet Environment (100BASE-T routing)

We'll break these steps down into deployment examples later in the chapter. (Note that many of the deployment options reference Chapter 6, where each network component and its associated features are more fully explained.) Deployment examples from actual networks are discussed in Chapter 8.

As a refresher, this chapter begins by covering the general rules of 10BASE-T and 100BASE-T.

■ General Rules of Deployment

As we saw in Chapter 4, the EIA/TIA 568 cabling standard recommends 100 meters from hub to desktop in all UTP cabling infrastructures. This specification is mirrored in the international standard, ISO 88023. The 100 meters is further broken down into the following distances:

- 5 meters from hub to patch panel

- 90 meters from patch panel to office punch-down block

- 5 meters from punch-down block to desktop connection

Most UTP installations conform to the *100 meter rule*, as it is commonly called. This makes it very easy to install 100BASE-T.

Most cable installers also recommend that hub-to-hub UTP connections be made with 5 meters of cable or less. Short cables in a noisy wiring closet translate to less induced noise on the wire and less crosstalk in large multiple-cable bundles. However, short cables may restrict hub location in large wiring closets, so this guideline is often overlooked. In 10BASE-T networks, this rarely causes a problem, but when installing Fast Ethernet *shared* workgroups, the "5 meter rule" should be strictly followed. The reasons for this are explained later in the chapter.

10BASE-T Shared Media Rules

10BASE-T requires that all collisions be resolved within 512 bit times, or one slot time. In a 10BASE-T shared network, each component, including the cabling, adds transmission delays, accounting for a shrinkage in the total network diameter. Today's technology allows for a worst-case 10BASE-T UTP network with roughly four-repeater hops and three populated segments. Why only four hops? In order to lock on to an incoming signal, each repeater eats up bits of the signal. This can be accounted for as a loss of bit budget or network diameter. Each cabling segment and repeater represents a certain transmission delay, and the total round-trip delay cannot exceed one slot time, or 512 microseconds. With current repeater technology, this results in 10BASE-T networks of no more than three, or sometimes four, repeater hops. So even though Ethernet's collision domain is specified at 2,500 meters, in 10BASE-T form it rarely exceeds 400 meters. 10BASE-F (Ethernet over Fiber) allows for much larger shared 10-Mbps networks due to the extended transmission length of fiber, but 10BASE-F is typically implemented as a switched connection.

10BASE-T Switched Media Rules

10BASE-T switched networks are no different than 10BASE-T shared networks except for the fact that a new network diameter calculation begins at each switch port. Since switches provide dedicated connections, there are no collisions and no collision domain exists to restrict diameter. 10BASE-T switches are only limited by the same EIA/TIA 568 rules that govern current installations—the 100 meter hub-to-node and 5 meter hub-to-hub rules. Therefore, a 10-Mbps switched network will work in any existing 10-Mbps network with no network diameter constraints.

100BASE-TX/T4 Shared Media Rules

As discussed in Chapter 3, *shared* 100BASE-TX and 100BASE-T4 networks require a much smaller collision domain—only 205 meters. This allows for a 100-Mbps shared network of two repeaters with 100 meter cabling to each node and 5 meter cabling in between repeaters. As can be seen, purely shared Fast Ethernet networks require exact compliance to EIA/TIA UTP cabling specifications. If a network diameter of over 205 meters is required, then switching hubs must be used somewhere.

Class I 100BASE-T repeaters and stackable hubs are further limited to only one repeater hop because they incur the additional delay of converting incoming analog data to the digital MII interface. 100BASE-TX-to-100BASE-T4 translational repeaters are Class I by definition. 100BASE-T Class II repeater and stackable ports are all of one type (either TX or T4) and therefore allow two repeater hops. Figure 7.1 shows maximum shared network diameters for Class I and Class II stackable hubs

Figure 7.1

Class I and Class II shared media network diameters are limited to 200 and 205 meters respectively.

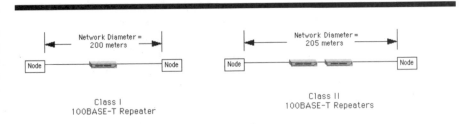

In general, 100BASE-TX is less critical than 100BASE-T4 regarding shared network restrictions because its bit budget has more flexibility. However, some 100BASE-T4 components will allow for extended cable lengths over 100 meters and/or more repeater hops due to innovative designs. A bit budget analysis must be done on any 100BASE-T installation that exceeds the IEEE802.3u specification (that is, over 2 repeater hops or greater than 205 meters in network diameter—refer to Chapter 3 for details). 100BASE-T4 is also lower frequency than TX and therefore less susceptible to noise and crosstalk. In general, wiring closets and other highly controlled areas are compliant with the EIA/TIA 568 specification, workgroups are often non-compliant because they are harder to control. A good understanding of your existing cabling infrastructure will help in determining how shared 100BASE-T is deployed in your network.

100BASE-TX/T4 Switched Media Rules

The previous section discussed the restrictions of shared 100BASE-T networks, which further illustrates the importance of switching to Fast Ethernet deployment. Rarely will 100BASE-T workgroups have more than one repeater hop in between switches. Shared 100BASE-T networks will most likely be deployed in workgroups connected to stackable hubs. This means that in a properly constructed shared/switched 100BASE-T network, *the 100BASE-T network diameter of 205 meters will never come into play.* Switching is imperative to the successful deployment of Fast Ethernet. In fact, the bulk of this chapter is dedicated to explaining how switched and shared 10- and 100-Mbps media can be blended together to form small and large LANs.

100BASE-FX Rules

Another necessity of today's LANs is the fiber optic connection. Fiber optic cabling is rarely used to connect hubs to desktops, but is commonly found in hub-to-server and hub-to-hub or backbone applications (see Table 7.1). Due to its ability to carry signals for distances of up to 2 kilometers, fiber allows multiple campuses to connect to the same backbone. Currently, it is common to find FDDI running on multimode fiber optic cabling, which is why 100BASE-FX is designed for the same type of multimode fiber. The 100BASE-FX specification, also categorized under IEEE802.3u, allows for many levels of extended distances, depending on the type of connection.

100BASE-FX is mainly used to extend networks to multiple floors or buildings. 100BASE-FX deployment beyond this function is a rarity.

Table 7.1

Types of 100BASE-FX Fiber Connection

TYPE OF 100BASE-FX CONNECTION	DESCRIPTION OF RULES
Shared-to-shared	In a true 100BASE-FX fiber repeater setting, the maximum distance from hub to node is 160 meters in accordance with the 100BASE-T bit budget. For this reason, 100BASE-FX repeaters will be in limited use.
Shared-to-switched	If one side of the connection is to a 100BASE-FX fiber switch, then the same 100BASE-FX repeater mentioned above will be able to send signals over 210 meters of fiber. Again, this will limit the practical use of the properties of 100BASE-FX.
Switch-to-switch	A 100BASE-FX switched port connected to another 100BASE-FX switched port is capable of transmitting over 412 meters of fiber optic cable. This will be the entry point for most 100BASE-FX backbone products.
Switch-to-switch full-duplex	The 100BASE-FX specification calls for a special full-duplex switch-to-switch connection that allows for 2 kilometers of fiber cabling in between switches. This allows 100BASE-FX to be run anywhere FDDI is used today. This represents the high end of the 100BASE-FX switch market.

Summary of Basic Rules

The general rules of 10BASE-T and 100BASE-T deployment are governed by the same specifications—the EIA/TIA 568 and the ISO 88023 standards. Each specification outlines basic guidelines on how UTP-based network technologies should be deployed. These include the following rules:

- 100 meter rule—100 meters UTP from hub to node

- 5 meter rule—5 meters UTP from hub to hub (recommended, but not necessarily for 10BASE-T)

In addition, 10BASE-T and 100BASE-T are available in the form of both shared and switched media equipment. Table 7.2 summarizes the various network diameter restrictions of each type, and also includes the diameters associated with 100BASE-FX.

An understanding of the general rules for switched and shared 10BASE-T and 100BASE-T deployment is essential before discussing how to implement them in a production network. The rest of the chapter is dedicated to the five steps towards Switched and Fast Ethernet deployment, the first of which is looking at an immediate improvement—adding 10-Mbps Ethernet switches.

Table 7.2

Network Restrictions for
10BASE-T and 100BASE-T

TECHNOLOGY	NETWORK DIAMETER SHARED MEDIA	NETWORK DIAMETER SWITCHED MEDIA	HUB-TO-HUB CABLE LENGTH SWITCHED MEDIA
10BASE-T	About 400 meters	Unlimited	100 meters
100BASE-TX/ 100BASE-T4	205 meters	Unlimited	100 meters
100BASE-FX	320 meters	Unlimited	400 meters
100BASE-FX Full-Duplex	N/A	Unlimited	2,000 meters

■ Step 1: Adding 10-Mbps Switches to Your Current Network

The first step toward upgrading your network to Switched and Fast Ethernet involves determining where to implement 10-Mbps switches. This section focuses on implementing 10-Mbps switches in two areas: the workgroup and the backbone.

In the workgroup, a 10-Mbps switch can be implemented effectively in two ways:

- Standard workgroup: A workgroup switch is used as a replacement for 10-Mbps repeaters in workgroups with clients and local servers.

- Switch of hubs: A workgroup switch is configured to provide 10 Mbps of dedicated bandwidth to individual stackable hub units.

  A 10-Mbps *backbone* switch can also be deployed in two fashions.

- Switched server farm: A backbone switch is configured as a central connection for server farms.

- Switched backbone: A backbone switch is configured as a 10-Mbps backbone hub, effectively providing the functionality of a multiport bridge.

These four basic deployment options are explored more thoroughly in the pages to follow. Since this is the first step in an overall deployment of Switched and Fast Ethernet, the performance gained will be moderate, but the timing of this implementation can be immediate.

10-Mbps Standard Workgroup Switches

Many clients, a few local servers, and a 10-Mbps repeater make up the typical workgroup of today. By adding a 10-Mbps switch, a shared workgroup can be converted to a higher speed switched workgroup. Consider the diagrams in Figure 7.2, where a workgroup has four clients and two servers connected through a 10-Mbps repeater. All nodes share the repeater's 10 Mbps of bandwidth. By replacing the repeater with a 10-Mbps switch, the available bandwidth of the workgroup can be increased several fold. In the switched example, each client has a dedicated 10-Mbps connection and each server has two dedicated 10-Mbps connections. Each server can provide up to 20 Mbps of data so the new workgroup bandwidth is 40 Mbps, or four times the original. In addition, the concept of simultaneous server access now becomes a reality with switches. One client can be accessing one local server while another is accessing a different local server. This type of switch deployment works well in small networks or isolated workgroups where most of the traffic is actually local.

Figure 7.2

10-Mbps switches in a standard workgroup

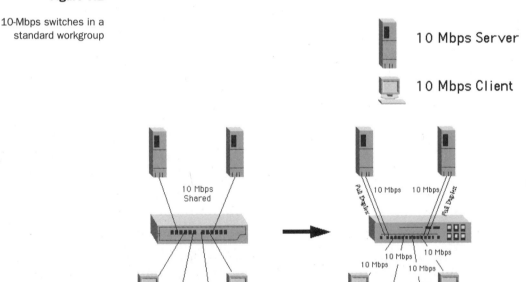

When does it make sense to install a 10-Mbps switch in this configuration? There are a few key indicators that will give you a good idea of whether or not 10-Mbps switching will help. These include counting the number of local servers in the workgroup and examining the amount of traffic that stays locally within the workgroup. Table 7.3 explains how these indicators are used to determine if 10-Mbps switching is needed.

Table 7.3

Determining Need for 10-Mbps Switching in a Standard Workgroup. If a Workgroup Exhibits One or More of These Features, Treat It as a Candidate for a 10-Mbps Switch Upgrade.

WORKGROUP FEATURES	DETAILED DESCRIPTION
Multiple local servers in the workgroup	If the workgroup only has one server, the cost of a 10-Mbps switch may not be worth the small performance gain. In cases where only one server is present in the workgroup, other features such as multiple server NICs, load sharing, and full-duplex are needed to increase performance.
Primarily local traffic	At least 80 percent of the activity is between the clients and local servers.
Large amount of traffic	The 10-Mbps shared workgroup is at least 20 percent utilized (> 2 Mbps).

Once the need for a 10-Mbps switch has been determined, the next question is what type of switch to deploy. Some key switch features to look for in this type of 10-Mbps switch deployment are full-duplex support, load balancing, and low latencies. Table 7.4 gives some ideas on what features to look for in a 10-Mbps switch.

Table 7.4

Optional 10-Mbps Workgroup Switch Features. These Features Allow 10-Mbps Switches to Provide Superior Performance.

SWITCH FEATURE	DESCRIPTION
Load balancing	Servers with multiple NICs, as shown in Figure 7.2, need special software to tell them how to balance the network traffic between the NICs. Don't attempt to connect multiple server NICs to the same 10-Mbps switch without this software. (Novell provides this function in a Netware Loadable Module, or NLM.)
Full-duplex	10-Mbps full-duplex switch ports coupled with full-duplex NICs in the server can increase the available bandwidth of the switch. Although full-duplex may only provide a small amount of additional throughput, it may be worthwhile for your application.
Low latencies	Workgroup switches should have low latencies, and therefore should be of the cut through or modified cut through variety. This helps in time-critical workgroup environments such as those involving video and audio playback.

It may seem like a bother to configure a server with full-duplex NICs and load-balancing software just to incorporate a 10-Mbps switch into the workgroup. It can be difficult, but in some cases it is the only option. For instance, in cases where servers are ISA based and not well suited for Fast Ethernet, this type of solution may work well. Also, this type of workgroup switching solution allows network administrators to make the most out of what equipment they already have. No new NICs are required for the clients (unless you opt for a client full-duplex scenario), and the 10-Mbps switch is a quick replacement for the 10-Mbps repeater. This may be ideal for a small network of only a few workgroups. However, as we will see next, a 10-Mbps switch also improves performance in larger networks based on 10-Mbps stackable hubs.

10-Mbps Switch of Hubs

Many large networks are configured with stackable hubs. Stackable hubs are typically used when connecting a large number of users in a workgroup. In this case, a 10-Mbps switch can be used as a *switch of hubs*, as shown in Figure 7.3, to improve the performance of a 10-Mbps stack. Instead of sharing a stackable backplane bus, each unit of the stack is provided with 10 Mbps of dedicated bandwidth from the switch. Once again, this is accomplished with little impact to the network infrastructure. In fact, a 10-Mbps switch can often be physically placed right on top of the existing stack.

Figure 7.3

Upgrading a 10-Mbps stackable hub with a 10-Mbps switch. This is often referred to as a "switch of hubs" configuration

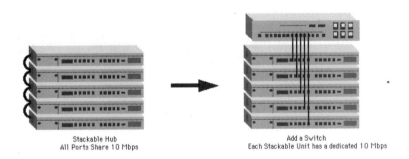

Stackable Hub
All Ports Share 10 Mbps

Add a Switch
Each Stackable Unit has a dedicated 10 Mbps

The performance gained is typically proportional to the number of switching ports used. In the example of Figure 7.3, the performance gained is five times (50 Mbps versus 10 Mbps). The main things to look for when using a switch in a switch of hubs configuration are port densities (are there enough switched ports for each stackable unit?) and the implications to network management. Since the management module in the main stackable unit can no longer "see" all network traffic (the switch blocks it), an alternative type of management must be used. For more on the management of switches in this configuration, see Chapter 9.

10-Mbps Switches in a Server Farm

A server farm, also referred to as a server closet, is defined as a collection of servers that reside on the backbone of a network. Servers in server farms are usually high-end systems that service a great number of users. Most servers in server farms are accessed indiscriminantly by a large number of users, so the traffic patterns are fairly constant, as opposed to those of servers in the local workgroup. Data tends to come in regularly from all sorts of sources. Installing a 10-Mbps switch in a server farm is yet another way to improve network performance with 10-Mbps switching. Adding a 10-Mbps switch in a server farm or server closet provides each server with dedicated bandwidth. The switched architecture also allows for multiple connections to the backbone in order to handle the increased traffic flow from the server farm. Figure 7.4 shows how a typical 10-Mbps shared server farm is upgraded by adding a 10-Mbps switch. The connection to the backbone is scalable by connecting additional 10-Mbps dedicated lines to the server farm switch. The trick of scaling the connection to the backbone is to weigh the amount of traffic typically generated by the switched server farm with the number of backbone connections. For instance, if the server farm typically generates an average load of 20 Mbps with peaks of 30 Mbps, then three 10-Mbps backbone connections should be used. In the case of multiple backbone connections, the switch must incorporate some sort of traffic balancing, similar to the load balancing of the workgroup scenario, to allow for the most efficient use of the switched ports.

Figure 7.4

Converting a shared 10-Mbps server farm to a 10-Mbps switch. Each server has 10 Mbps of dedicated bandwidth.

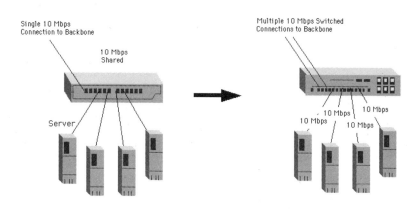

Because the data stream contains traffic from many different nodes, the possibility of corrupted packets is higher than normal. Therefore, store-and-forward switches with some measure of error checking and packet filtering are preferred in server farm applications. Error checking reduces the amount of work the server NIC and network operating system have to do to filter unwanted packets. Most mid-range to high-end servers are capable of supplying much more than 10 Mbps of data, so a 10-Mbps switch deployment in this scenario may be only a short-term solution. However, a 10-Mbps switch can be used to fill the gap while Fast Ethernet or other high-bandwidth deployment plans are solidified.

10-Mbps Switched Backbone

Many networks claim to have a backbone constructed entirely of 10-Mbps repeaters. This is not a true backbone because the entire network shares the available media. A backbone is truly deployed when traffic is divided by advanced network components such as bridges, routers, or switches. Backbones with bridging, routing, or switching create "firewalls" between sub-LANs because they can filter unwanted traffic. A 10-Mbps switched backbone can be extremely useful in improving the overall performance of a 10-Mbps shared network. The deployment of a switch in such a network is analogous to the switch-of-hubs concept used for stackable hubs. Each independent 10-Mbps repeater is connected to a dedicated 10-Mbps pipe, as shown in Figure 7.5.

Figure 7.5

Upgrading a 10-Mbps shared network with a 10-Mbps switched backbone. Total network bandwidth has been increased by a factor of four.

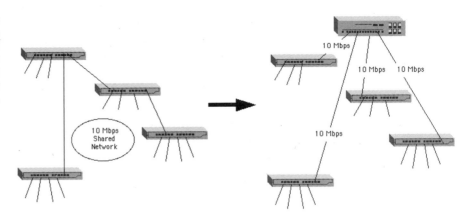

The theoretical network performance of the example in Figure 7.5 has been increased from 10 Mbps to 40 Mbps by adding a single switch. It is very similar to adding four bridges to the network to isolate traffic between segments. In addition, backbone switches can be cascaded together with multiple 10-Mbps switched connections or 10-Mbps full-duplex connections to improve throughput between backbone switches. This type of deployment allows a complete backbone to be built from 10-Mbps backbone switches. This architecture is scalable as long as additional hub-to-hub connections are available and the hub traffic balancing can handle the traffic levels. An example of this is shown in Figure 7.6.

Figure 7.6

10-Mbps switching hubs can be configured for multiple hub-to-hub connections. These connections may also be full duplex.

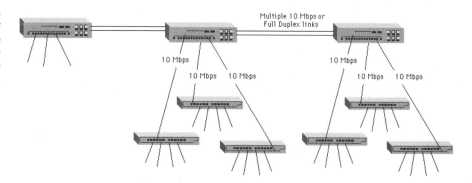

10-Mbps Switches Are Only the First Step

Although there are many ways to improve network performance with 10-Mbps switches, there are definite tradeoffs associated with deploying this technology. For example, there are many network management issues associated with switching that must be addressed. Also, depending on how your networking traffic grows, 10-Mbps switches may only support your network for a short time before high bandwidth devides are required. However, even with these potential drawbacks, the advantages of 10-Mbps switches are numerous. Increases in performance can be attained with little or no impact to the current network architecture. For instance, NICs rarely need to be replaced when 10-Mbps switches are deployed. Also, 10-Mbps switching is relatively inexpensive compared with other switching alternatives, such as switched Fast Ethernet and ATM.

In general, 10-Mbps switches enhance network performance in four areas, which are summarized in Table 7.5.

Table 7.5

Summary of 10-Mbps
Workgroup Switch
Deployment Examples.

10-MBPS WORKGROUP SWITCH INSTALLATION TYPE	DESCRIPTION	DEPLOYMENT ISSUES
Standard workgroup	Provides dedicated pipe(s) to local clients and servers in any given workgroup	Helps when most traffic is local Workgroups with multiple local servers benefit the most Full-duplex NICs and switch ports give added benefit Load balancing software is sometimes needed
Switch of hubs	Provides dedicated pipe to individual repeaters or stackable hub units	Improves performance in almost all cases Switch can be physically stacked with rest of stackable units May impact stackable hub management strategy
Switched server farms	Provides dedicated pipe to each server in a server farm. Also provided for multiple 10-Mbps connections to backbone.	Look for store-and-forward backbone switches with error checking capabilities. Full-duplex connections increase bandwidth to backbone Traffic balancing features needed in switch if multiple connections are made to the backbone.
Switched backbones	Provides same functionality as multiple bridges. Dedicated bandwidth throughout the backbone.	Like the switch of hubs concept in many ways Allows for some scalability of backbone bandwidth. Full-duplex hub-to-hub connections increase backbone bandwidth if switch has traffic balancing features.

■ Step 2: First Deployment of Fast Ethernet

The second step in deploying Switched and Fast Ethernet is putting the first Fast Ethernet network components in place. The natural entry point for Fast Ethernet in most networks is at the desktop and server. This is primarily because most Fast Ethernet NICs are 10/100, which means they can operate at either 10 Mbps or 100 Mbps. A 10/100 NIC installed today will typically be run at 10 Mbps for some time before a Fast Ethernet hub is purchased. This section describes how to prepare new desktops and servers with 10/100 NICs and how to plan your network architecture to accommodate a mixture of 10-Mbps and 100-Mbps workgroups.

Enable New Desktops and Servers with 10/100 NICs

There are a wide assortment of desktops and servers connected to 10-Mbps Ethernet ports today. With such a wide variety, it is practically impossible for new 10/100 cards to fit into every existing system. That is why a practical plan for deployment of Fast Ethernet begins with installing desktop and server 10/100 NICs in newly purchased or newly installed systems. As discussed in Chapter 6, older systems based on the ISA or PCMCIA bus are not ideal for Fast Ethernet upgrades, therefore older desktops and laptops should retain their 10 Mbps-only NICs. The next section (Step 3) will discuss how to connect these systems to your new Fast Ethernet network.

Consider the simple network shown on the left side of Figure 7.7. In its current state, each existing desktop and server is connected by a 10-Mbps NIC, represented by a PC. The network hubs are 10-Mbps repeaters. Now, two new servers and four new clients are to be added to this network to connect new employees to the LAN. These systems are enabled with 10/100 Mbps NICs and connected to the existing 10-Mbps network, as shown on the right side of Figure 7.7. These new systems should be EISA, PCI, S-Bus, or some other high-speed bus popular in servers and desktops. By adding 10/100 NICs now, you are preventing an expensive, time-consuming future NIC upgrade. Most network servers are so critical that they can't afford to be powered down. Most desktops are too numerous to allow for a mass replacement of NICs once they are installed.

When to Use TX versus T4

The type of 10/100 NIC to install depends primarily on the type of cabling used for the particular LAN. With Category 3 UTP, 100BASE-T4 is the only option. As many LANs will have some amount of Category 3 UTP, 100BASE-T4 may end up as the predominant 100BASE-T media type. With Category 5 UTP, either 100BASE-TX or 100BASE-T4 deployment is possible. The best guideline to follow when choosing between TX and T4 is to determine what supports the majority of your cabling. If two-thirds of your LAN is Category 5 but the other third is unknown, then 100BASE-T4 is your safest bet. Since most cabling infrastructures today are a combination of Category 5 UTP and Category 3 UTP, this makes T4 the typical workgroup choice. Some hub products make the selection between TX and T4 invisible to the user by providing TX and T4 ports on the same hub.

Figure 7.7

A 10-Mbps shared network before (left) and after (right) adding new systems with 10/100 NICs. All clients and servers in these examples are running at 10 Mbps even though some have 10/100 NICs installed. This provides a network that is primed for a Fast Ethernet hub upgrade.

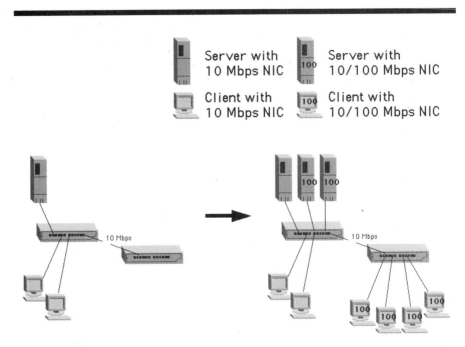

When in doubt, install what your cabling dictates. If you don't know what category your cabling is or how many pairs are available, consult your cable contractor or try one of the many portable cable testers discussed in Chapter 4. Table 7.6 outlines the various TX and T4 options dictated by your cabling infrastructure.

When to Use Specialty NICs

Specialty NICs include *intelligent NICs* and *multiport NICs*. Intelligent NICs have an intelligent processor or subsystem that offloads the host CPU from many of its tasks. Intelligent NICs should be used mainly in four areas:

- Multisegment Fast Ethernet servers

- Application servers where CPU power is at a premium

- PC-based routers such as Novell's Multi Protocol Router (MPR) software

- SFT III-compliant links such as Novell's Mirrored Server Link (MSL)

Outside these four niche areas, intelligent NICs are not very beneficial.

Multiport NICs combine serveral NICs into one by providing up to four UTP ports on one card. Multiport NICs are useful in systems where expansion slots are scarce. Many PCI systems have only two or three PCI slots

Table 7.6

Cabling Options

CABLE TYPE	CONNECTOR TYPE	NUMBER OF PAIRS AVAILABLE FOR LAN	100BASE-T SIGNALING SCHEME TO DEPLOY
Category 3 or 4 UTP (voice grade)	RJ45	2	100BASE-T not deployable
Category 3 or 4 UTP (voice grade)	RJ45	4	100BASE-T4
Category 5 UTP (data grade)	RJ45	2	100BASE-TX
Category 5 UTP (data grade)	RJ45	4	100BASE-T4 or 100BASE-TX
Type 1 STP	DB9	2	100BASE-TX
Coaxial Cable	BNC	n/a	100BASE-T not deployable

available for expansion cards. As PCI slots start becoming more plentiful, multiport NICs will slowly become less popular. Multiport NICs should only be used when external switching hubs are too expensive for your budget.

10/100 NICs and the Patch Panel Approach

Many large networks have network closets that house the connection from each office to a particular hub. This is typically accomplished with a patch panel (see Figure 7.8). A patch panel allows maximum configurability of the network. For instance, the network administrator can re-architect the network layout from the closet by switching the connections on the patch panel. A patch panel approach is very effective for converting from 10 to 100 Mbps. Suppose a network has several users with 10/100 NICs operating at 10 Mbps. If those systems are known, a quick restructuring of the patch panel wiring will condense these users onto one hub. Of course, this assumes there are no other reasons for the users to be separated. When any given 10 Mbps hub has all 10/100 NICs attached, it is a prime candidate for Step 3, adding a Fast Ethernet hub.

Figure 7.8

A patch panel

When Not to Enable New Desktops and Servers with 10/100 NICs

We have already heard several times that ISA-based desktops and PCMCIA based laptops will not gain much from the addition of a 10/100 Mbps NIC. Therefore, any new systems based on these buses may be configured with a classic 10-Mbps NIC. In Chapter 3, we discussed exactly how to get the best possible performance from these systems with 10/100-Mbps switches. If the system has particularly slow subsystems, like a slow server hard disk, then you may determine that a 100-Mbps NIC is not needed. For instance, a server with a higher-speed bus, like an EISA bus, but with a slower processor (Intel 80386 or lower) may not be a good candidate for 10/100 NICs. A good rule of thumb is to not deploy 10/100 NICs in any system that will be phased out of your network in the next year.

■ Step 3: Convert Workgroups to Fast Ethernet

The next logical step after installing 10/100 NICs is to find a way to convert them from 10-Mbps operation to 100-Mbps operation. This is best done by first converting workgroups from 10 Mbps to 100 Mbps. Workgroups can be converted using 10/100 Mbps switches or 100-Mbps repeaters, depending on the situation. In some cases, tradeoffs will need to be made to merge the new Fast Ethernet LAN with the existing 10-Mbps environment.

Four main types of workgroups are eligible for conversion to Fast Ethernet. Each requires a slightly different approach to achieve the best performance gain.

- *Existing workgroup*—10-Mbps-only NICs. Clients only (no local servers).

- *Existing workgroup with local servers*—10-Mbps-only NICs. Many clients and some local servers.

- *Newer workgroup*—10/100 Mbps NICs. Clients and/or local servers.

- *Newer power workgroup*—10/100 Mbps NICs. Clients and/or local servers.

If implemented correctly, each Fast Ethernet upgrade provides increased performance with minimal interruption to the network.

Existing Workgroups with No Local Servers

Replacing every NIC in your network would be a seemingly insurmountable task. Therefore the best Fast Ethernet workgroup solution for *existing* networks is one which allows you to leverage installed 10BASE-T NICs. Most existing workgroups can achieve a significant benefit from the addition of a 10/100-Mbps switch. For existing workgroups made up entirely of clients, a 10/100 switch with many 10-Mbps ports and a few 100-Mbps ports for connections to other workgroups and hubs is desirable. Consider the leftmost workgroup in Figure 7.9, which contains only 10-Mbps clients and a 10-Mbps repeater. In Step 1 of this chapter, we saw how a 10-Mbps switch could be deployed in this situation to enhance workgroup performance. A 10/100 switch can enhance performance even more and without the inconvenience of multiple full duplex uplinks to the backbone and special traffic balancing features. Figure 7.9 shows how a standard 10-Mbps shared workgroup can be upgraded with a 10/100 switch. A good example of this type of workgroup switch is the FastSwitch 10/100 AG from Grand Junction Networks.

Now what do you do with the newly acquired 100-Mbps uplink? Since Fast Ethernet won't be deployed in your backbone until Step 4, you may have to live with a 10-Mbps uplink for a little while. Performance won't approach ten times current levels until the Fast Ethernet backbone connection is completed. Therefore, it is wise to purchase a 10/100 switch with 10-Mbps performance features like traffic balancing. A good way to approach this problem is by investing in a 10-Mbps switch with an upgradeable option for Fast Ethernet. One such switch is the Kalpana Etherswitch-15. The Etherswitch can be bought as a 10-Mbps-only switch with space for two Fast Ethernet modules. The Fast Ethernet modules can be purchased when the rest of your Fast Ethernet network—specifically, the backbone—is in place. Figure 7.10 shows this type of switch deployment.

Figure 7.9

Upgrading an existing workgroup to Fast Ethernet without replacing the 10-Mbps NICs in the desktops

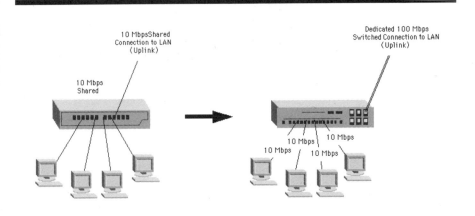

Figure 7.10

Leveraging 10-Mbps switches in a workkgroup. First a 10 Mbps shared workgroup is shown (left). Next, it is upgraded with a 10-Mbps switch (center). Finally, a Fast Ethernet uplink module is added to the switch (right).

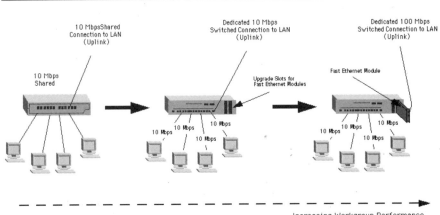

Increasing Workgroup Performance

Note that the 10/100 switch upgrade applies to existing workgroups that already have 10-Mbps NICs installed—where it would not make sense to upgrade existing systems with 10/100 NICs. A workgroup with mostly ISA-based clients is a classic example of where to deploy 10/100 switches in this manner. Another good example is a workgroup with a peer-to-peer NOS like Windows for Workgroups 3.11. When the wire in a workgroup of this type is over 20 percent, then it could be a prime target for a 10/100 switch upgrade. Areas where loading is typically high are in workgroups with not only many clients, but also local servers. This is discussed next.

Existing Workgroups with Local Servers

A slight variation on the previous scenario includes the addition of local servers in the workgroup. In most workgroups with local servers, the majority of the traffic (more than 80 percent) is between those servers and clients in the workgroup. This is often referred to as a *standalone* or *isolated* workgroup. 10/100 switches with more 100-Mbps ports are preferable in these situations. Each local server can be connected to a 100-Mbps pipe, and each client gets its own dedicated 10-Mbps pipe. This is also referred to as *Personal Ethernet* because each user gets their own dedicated Ethernet line. This is shown in Figure 7.11.

Figure 7.11

A 10/100-Mbps switch upgrade in a workgroup with local servers. Clients get dedicated 10 Mbps. Servers get dedicated 100 Mbps.

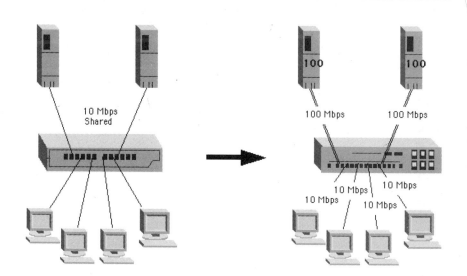

There are two types of 10/100 switches available to deploy in an isolated workgroup. The first and most obvious type is a switch with many 10-Mbps ports and more than a few 100-Mbps ports. A good example is the Bay Networks 28115, which has 16 ports that can be configured for 10 or 100 Mbps and two ports dedicated to switched 100 Mbps. This type of switch will give excellent performance and configurability, but the expense may be a little high for broad workgroup deployment. Another way to get similar workgroup performance is to use an architecture like that of the Grand Junction FastSwitch 10/100 AG. The AG has 24 switched 10-Mbps ports, one switched 100-Mbps port and four 100-Mbps shared ports. This allows several servers to share the same 100-Mbps bandwidth and still provide each client with 10 Mbps of bandwidth. The single switched 100-Mbps port connects the workgroup to the LAN backbone. This architecture, diagrammed in Figure 7.12, is less expensive than switching 10/100 on a per port basis.

Figure 7.12

Grand Junction
FastSwitch 100 AG
workgroup hub
architecture. This
workgroup switch
combines 100 Mbps and
10 Mbps parts in a very
cost-effective way.

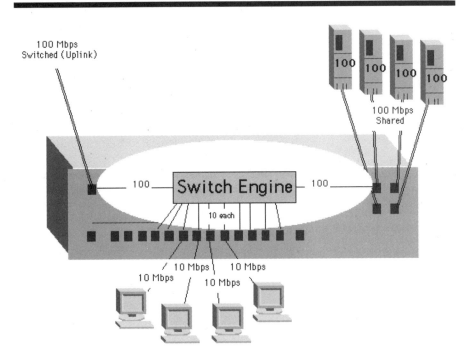

For the 10/100 switch to be of any use in this type of environment, the
servers must be outfitted with 10/100 Mbps NICs. This means the servers
must be capable of supporting 100-Mbps data rates. If the local servers are
ISA based, a 10/100 Mbps switch may not dramatically increase performance. A 10-Mbps switch may be more appropriate. However, if the local
servers do have high-speed bus types, such as PCI, EISA, or S-Bus, and 100-
Mbps-capable NICs, the performance increase can be ten times or greater.

New Workgroups

Up to this point, we have discussed upgrading existing workgroups where the
clients are restricted to 10-Mbps NICs. Next we will discuss how to implement
Fast Ethernet in new workgroups. The term *new workgroup* implies that the
systems in that workgroup were recently added to the network. In Step 2, we
discussed how to make sure each new system is installed with a 10/100-Mbps
NIC. The combination of many new systems being added to the network and
the inclusion of 10/100-Mbps NICs makes it very easy and inexpensive to upgrade to Fast Ethernet. The most cost-effective way to upgrade a workgroup
is with a 100-Mbps standalone or stackable repeater. The users will instantly
jump from sharing 10 Mbps to sharing 100 Mbps—a tenfold performance
improvement. This is how it can be done.

Small Workgroups

A small workgroup can be classified as 20 users or fewer. Depending on how you plan to increase that small workgroup, you may elect to connect them with a 100-Mbps standalone repeater or a 100-Mbps stackable hub unit. As described in Chapter 6, the standalone repeater will be cheaper in the short term, but the stackable hub offers greater flexibility for future growth. Let's look at an example of how a new workgroup is installed using a 100-Mbps standalone repeater. In this example, a new group of users is to be added to a small network. We have already seen how *existing* systems can be connected using a 10/100 switch. Now *new* systems can be connected using a 100-Mbps repeater. Figure 7.13 (A) shows a small network with just a few 10 Mbps repeaters, clients, and servers. Figure 7.13 (B) shows the new network after the addition of new users.

Figure 7.13

Network before (A) and after (B) adding a new Fast Ethernet workgroup. Older clients with 10 Mbps NICs are connected to a 10/100 workgroup switch. New clients with 10/100 NICs are connected to a 100 Mbps repeater.

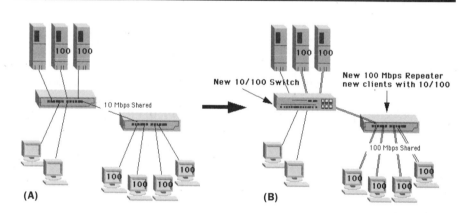

The newer clients share 100 Mbps of bandwidth with the newly 100-Mbps-enabled servers. The existing clients get 10-Mbps dedicated connections. The number of users on the network has doubled, the available bandwidth has gone from 10 Mbps to 100 Mbps, and no desktops were opened unnecessarily. Only new desktops were connected at 100 Mbps, thereby lowering the impact of deploying Fast Ethernet.

Large Workgroups

When deploying new users in a large network, Fast Ethernet stackable hubs or chassis hubs are the right choice. Large networks typically are upgraded from the network closet, where new users are connected through patch panels to rack-mounted stackable hubs or chassis hubs. Figure 7.14 shows a typical large 10-Mbps Ethernet installation of several racks of stackable hubs and a chassis hub.

Figure 7.14

A typical large 10-Mbps wiring closet installation including stackable hubs and chassis hubs.

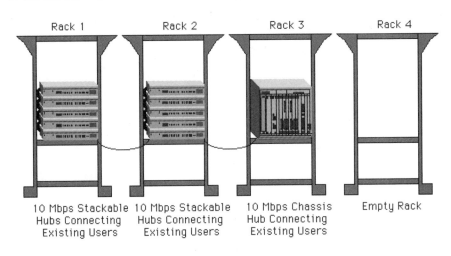

10 Mbps Stackable Hubs Connecting Existing Users   10 Mbps Stackable Hubs Connecting Existing Users   10 Mbps Chassis Hub Connecting Existing Users   Empty Rack

New users can be added to this network by installing 100-Mbps stackable hubs and connecting the new users to them. The new users can be connected to the existing 10-Mbps network via a 10/100 bridge or a 10/100 switching module in the chassis. Additional new users with Fast Ethernet can be connected via a new Fast Ethernet module for the chassis hub. The upgraded network is shown in Figure 7.15. In this example, a 10/100-Mbps speed matching bridge is used to connect the 10-Mbps and 100-Mbps networks,. Another way to bridge between 10 and 100 Mbps is to add a 10/100 Mbps-switching module to the chassis hub. A good example of this is the Bay Networks 5000 10/100 module (due in late 1995).

Figure 7.15

Adding new Fast Ethernet users to a large 10-Mbps wiring closet.

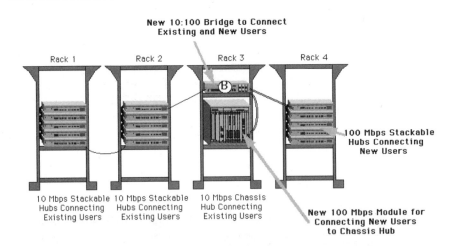

New 10:100 Bridge to Connect Existing and New Users

100 Mbps Stackable Hubs Connecting New Users

10 Mbps Stackable Hubs Connecting Existing Users   10 Mbps Stackable Hubs Connecting Existing Users   10 Mbps Chassis Hub Connecting Existing Users

New 100 Mbps Module for Connecting New Users to Chassis Hub

New Power Workgroups

A small but growing percentage of new workgroups fall into the classification of *power workgroups*. This classification indicates that the workgroup puts so much local traffic on the network, that even a 100-Mbps repeater cannot handle the workload. A good way to determine a power workgroup is to measure the network utilization. If it is above 30 percent and over 80 percent of that traffic is local, then it may qualify as a power workgroup. Some examples of power workgroups are CAD workstation clusters, groups of multimedia systems, and desktop publishing centers.

Clients and servers in power workgroups can be connected with higher-end 100-Mbps switches such as the Bay Networks 28115. Each client in the workgroup is given a dedicated 100-Mbps pipe. Servers are also given 100-Mbps connections, or in some cases, 100BASE-TX full-duplex connections. The connection to the backbone is typically not so critical, since most of the traffic is local, but it too is 100-Mbps switched. Figure 7.16 shows a Fast Ethernet power workgroup deployed with a 100-Mbps switch.

Figure 7.16

Power workgroup connected via a Fast Ethernet switch. Each client and server gets 100 Mbps of dedicated bandwidth.

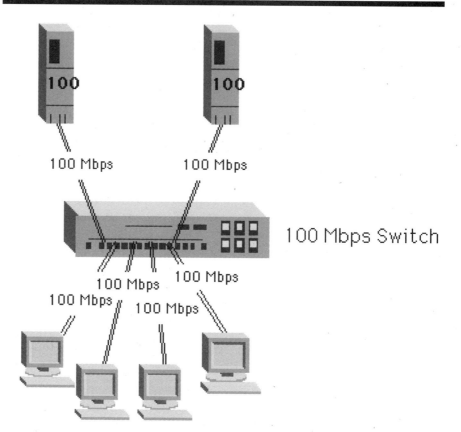

When a 10-Mbps-Only Switch Is Acceptable

You may be thinking, "But I don't have any power workgroups on my network. My network utilization is about 30 perecnt and I only need a small performance boost." In this case, now may not be the time for Fast Ethernet deployment in your network. Step 1 (10-Mbps switching) may be the answer to your current LAN bandwidth needs. Here are a few hints on how to determine if 10-Mbps switching is enough power for your LAN.

If

- The total number of users on your LAN is under 40

- You only run basic file transfers on the network from file servers

- Your current traffic rate is under 20 percent (less than 2 Mbps)

- Your customers do not complain about network performance or response time

then 10-Mbps switching may be the final step needed in your high-speed deployment strategy.

No matter what you deploy, always be on the lookout for increasing network traffic and plan your network architecture in such a way that you can easily migrate to Fast Ethernet (Step 3 and beyond) if the need arises. This includes deploying Fast-Ethernet-ready 10-Mbps switches and 10/100 NICs in all new desktops and servers.

Workgroup Switch Recommendations

10/100-Mbps switches will help in the deployment of high bandwidth to your existing client and server base. 10/100 switches are jacks of all trades in that they can provide 100 Mbps dedicated connections for backbones, servers, and power users, 10 Mbps dedicated connections for clients, and both 10- and 100-Mbps connections for repeaters. Some workgroup switches actually allow for 10-or 100-Mbps speeds on a per port basis. The 10/100-Mbps workgroup switches should have similar characteristics to the 10-Mbps switches discussed in Step 1. They should have low port-to-port latencies, substantial buffering, and minimal error checking features (this is better accomplished in other parts of your network). Also, as described in Chapter 6, workgroup switches should be manageable by standard SNMP applications.

As a low-cost alternative to switches, workgroup repeaters or stackable hubs are a cost effective way to deploy Fast Ethernet to users with new systems and 10/100 Mbps NICs. Table 7.7 illustrates the types of workgroups and the appropriate Fast Ethernet workgroup solution.

Table 7.7

Workgroup Switch
Deployment
Recommendations for
Four Basic Types of
Workgroups

WORKGROUP TYPE	DEFINING CHARACTERISTICS	RECOMMENDED FAST ETHERNET UPGRADE PATH (AND EXAMPLES)
Existing workgroup with no servers	All nodes are clients Clients are legacy systems with 10-Mbps-only NICs (usually ISA)	199
Existing workgroup with local servers	Mostly client nodes Some local servers attached to workgroup hub Clients are legacy systems with 10-Mbps-only NICs (usually ISA) Servers have higher-speed bus (EISA, PCI, S-Bus, and so on)	10/100 workgroup switching hub (Grand Junction FastSwitch 100 AG)
New workgroup	Mostly client nodes Local servers may be attached to workgroup hub Clients are new systems with 10/100-Mbps NICs Servers are new systems with 10/100-Mbps NICs	100-Mbps standalone repeater for small workgroups (NetWorth MicroHub 100 TX)) 100-Mbps stackable hub for large workgroups (3COM Linkbuilder FMS 100)
New power workgroup	Clients and servers are new high-end systems or workstations Clients and servers have 10/100-Mbps NICs Workgroup traffic level is above 20 percent Most traffic is local (more than 80 percent)	100-Mbps Workgroup Switch (Bay Networks Lattisswitch 28115)

■ Step 4: Converting the Backbone to Switched and Fast Ethernet

The next step after implementing Switched and Fast Ethernet in the workgroup is to either 1) create a new backbone, or 2) convert your existing backbone to Fast Ethernet. First, we will discuss what defines a backbone and what type of backbones exist. Then we will discuss how to deploy Switched and Fast Ethernet in those backbones. If the previous steps have been implemented correctly, the backbone conversion should be straightforward. Also, by upgrading the backbone, your *entire* local area network will have increased performance instead of just the workgroup.

There are many different backbone implementations that can be upgraded to Fast Ethernet from 10-Mbps Ethernet. Two of the more common types include distributed backbones and collapsed backbones.

A *distributed backbone* is one that couples major sub-LANs via a chaining technique. A *sub-LAN* is defined as a floor, site, or other physical collection of workgroups. For instance, in a ten story building, the LAN may incorporate all ten floors, plus the basement where the servers are kept. Each floor of the building is a sub-LAN and each sub-LAN is made up of several workgroups. As usual, the workgroups are concentrations of clients and local servers. A diagram of a distributed backbone is shown in Figure 7.17. Note the resemblance to an actual human backbone, which is where the name comes from. Distributed backbones include FDDI rings, Token Rings, and even switched backbones.

Collapsed backbones are typically deployed when delays through the switches or routers in a distributed backbone become to great. This is done by purchasing one high-end router for the basement and connecting each major Sub-LAN to it directly. In a collapsed backbone, a packet from one sub-LAN must only go through the high-end router to reach any other sub-LAN. Collapsed backbones are also employed with FDDI Rings, Token Rings, 10-Mbps switches, and high-end routers. A collapsed backbone is also shown in Figure 7.17.

Server farms are another type of deployment typically tied into the backbone. As shown above in Figure 7.17, server farms are classically defined as a collection of servers connected directly to the backbone. Server farms can also be of many shapes and sizes, but are usually grouped into two categories: *file servers* and *application servers*. File server farms typically are accessed randomly and provide file sharing and directory services to anyone on the LAN. File servers are subject to high-bandwidth spikes and bursty traffic, but their overall average utilization usually remains low. Application server farms are under more constant bandwidth demand because they are providing e-mail, database, and multimedia services. The average traffic generated by application server farms is typically large. This chapter will discuss what kind of deployment suits each type of server farm.

Distributed Backbone with Switches

The distributed backbone deployment of today can incorporate a wide variety of solutions. On the performance scale it can range anywhere from

Figure 7.17

The two types of backbones: distributed and collapsed

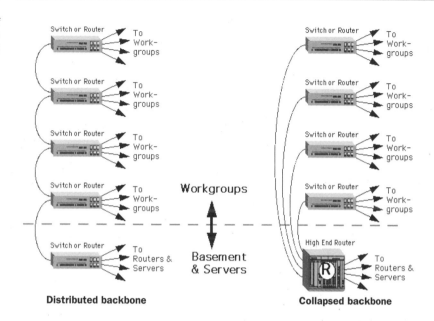

Distributed backbone   **Collapsed backbone**

10BASE-T to 100-Mbps FDDI. In a distributed backbone, a high-end router is not necessary, as each individual sub-LAN is connected via a particular hub, switch, or router. Therefore, the cost of a distributed backbone is usually lower than that of a collapsed backbone. The performance of a distributed backbone may be worse, however, due to high transmission latencies. In the example of Figure 7.17, a packet originating from the basement must pass through four backbone switches before reaching a destination on the top floor. The advantages and disadvantages of a distributed backbone architecture are summarized in Table 7.8.

Table 7.8

The Pros and Cons of Distributed Backbones

ADVANTAGES OF A DISTRIBUTED BACKBONE	DISADVANTAGES OF A DISTRIBUTED BACKBONE
Less expensive than a collapsed backbone	Lower overall performance than a collapsed backbone
Implementable in shared or switched environment	May encounter high transmission latencies

This section will focus on how to upgrade an existing 10-Mbps distributed backbone to Fast Ethernet, and also how to prepare for future backbone additions. Figure 7.18 shows a LAN with a 10-Mbps shared distributed backbone. Next, Figure 7.19 shows how this 10-Mbps LAN would progress through Steps 1, 2, 3, and finally Step 4. By implementing Fast Ethernet in the backbone, Step 4 marks the deployment of Fast Ethernet throughout the LAN.

Figure 7.18

Typical distributed backbone (10-Mbps bridged). Distributed backbones sometimes suffer from long latencies due to many switch or router "hops."

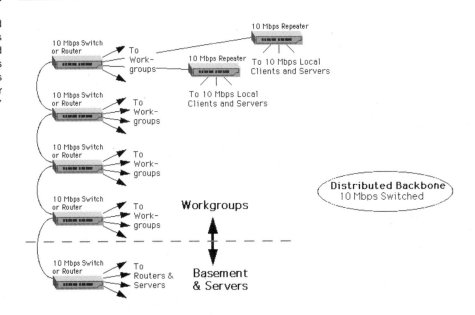

To complete the last figure, 100BASE-T switches have been added to the backbone. This nullifies any 100BASE-T network diameter constraints because switches don't suffer from collision domain restrictions. Therefore, a 100BASE-T distributed backbone of any size can be built with 100BASE-T switches. 100BASE-T switches also provide 100 Mbps dedicated bandwidth in and out of each backbone switch. The performance improvement over 10-Mbps shared can therefore be anywhere from 10 to about 100 times, depending on the loading of the backbone. The 100BASE-T switches added should have backbone switch features described in Chapter 6, such as enhanced packet filtering, error checking, advanced network management, and optional 10-Mbps support. The Bay Networks Lattisswitch 28115 100BASE-TX switch provides this type of functionality. Each of the 16 ports on the 28115 can be configured for 100BASE-TX or 10BASE-T operation. In our example, one workgroup hub is a 100-Mbps repeater and should be

Figure 7.19

Distributed backbone after Fast Ethernet deployment. Note that each step of Switched and Fast Ethernet deployment is shown.

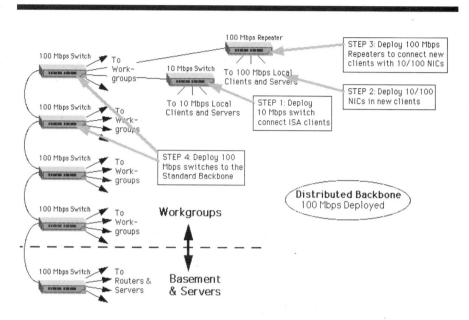

connected at 100 Mbps on the backbone switch. The other is a 10-Mbps switch and should be connected to a 10-Mbps port on the backbone switch (or a 10/100 switch could be used in its place). The Bay 28115 also provides two 100BASE-TX full-duplex ports for connecting backbone switches. This feature alone can provide an additional twofold bandwidth improvement in the backbone.

In this example, UTP wiring is used because the switch-to-switch connections of a multiple story building are unlikely to be greater than 100 meters long. This doesn't hold true for a physically spread-out distributed backbone. Consider a multiple-building site where each building is 500 meters from the next. In order to connect these buildings to the same 100BASE-T backbone, 100BASE-FX fiber connections must be made. 100BASE-FX can transmit over 2 kilometers of multimode fiber.

A drawback to deploying a 100BASE-T distributed backbone is the long latencies encountered in hopping from switch to switch. In cases where you'd like to deploy real-time LAN products such as video conferencing, a 100BASE-T collapsed backbone may be the better choice. The advantage of a distributed backbone, however, is lower cost 100BASE-T switches for each floor or site.

Collapsed Backbone with Switches

A collapsed backbone is not much different from a distributed backbone. In fact, the sub-LANs and workgroups are structured the same in either case. The things that change are the type of switches or routers installed in the backbone and the way they are connected. For instance, there is no such thing as a shared media collapsed backbone. Collapsed backbones are switched or routed by definition.

The issues with deploying Fast Ethernet into a collapsed backbone are of two varieties. First, determine what kind of router you have in your basement. Can it be upgraded simply with a Fast Ethernet module or will a whole new chassis-based router need to be purchased? Second, determine how your various sub-LANs are connected to the router and with what media type. It is highly possible that Fast Ethernet can be installed in your collapsed backbone with no rewiring at all.

When upgrading a collapsed backbone to Fast Ethernet, the basement router and some sub-LAN switches must be replaced together. However, not all sub-LANs need to be upgraded to Fast Ethernet at the same time. As soon as the new Fast Ethernet enabled router is in place, each sub-LAN switch can be replaced as the need arises. Figure 7.20 below shows a typical 10-Mbps collapsed backbone. Figure 7.21 indicates how part of the backbone can be converted to Fast Ethernet by adding one module to the basement router and one 100 Mbps switch to the sub-LAN.

Figure 7.20

A typical 10-Mbps collapsed backbone. The high-end chassis-bound router in the basement has many 10 Mbps modules.

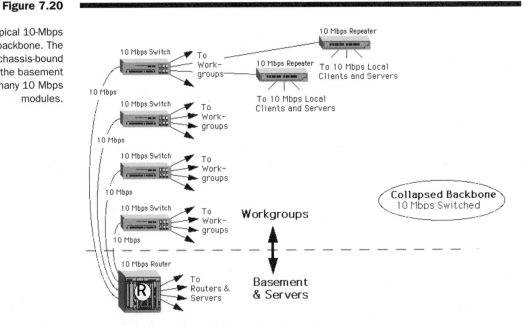

Figure 7.21

Backbone after adding a
new Fast Ethernet
module to the router and
a new Fast Ethernet
switch in one sub-LAN.
One sub-LAN at a time
can be added to a
collapsed backbone.

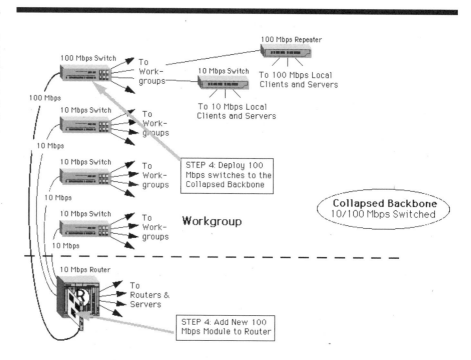

By upgrading the basement router with Fast Ethernet modules, you can deploy 100-Mbps collapsed backbones one step at a time. Of course, it is critical that the router support Fast Ethernet modules. One such router is the Cisco 7000. If the router at the center of your collapsed backbone is not upgradeable to Fast Ethernet, you will either have to purchase a new router (very costly) or only deploy Fast Ethernet in the workgroup. Whether you use a new router module or a brand new router, look for it to support fast and efficient routing between Ethernet and Fast Ethernet segments. In general, whatever features you look for in an Ethernet router, look for in a Fast Ethernet router as well.

Collapsed backbones are currently preferred over distributed backbones because of their performance benefits and lower packet latencies. However, a collapsed backbone requires a sophisticated piece of routing equipment, such as the Cisco 7000, which may be more expensive. Another problem that often arises with collapsed backbones is that because of large physical distances between sub-LANs, the sub-LAN connections commonly require cable lengths greater than 100 meters. UTP cannot be used in these situations. FDDI over fiber has been a common solution up until now, but 100BASE-FX provides a similar solution. For instance, if the example in Figure 7.22 requires a sub-LAN to be connected more than 100 meters away, a

100BASE-FX module can be inserted in the basement router and connected to a 2 Km fiber run. Be sure to consider that the sub-LAN switch (at the top of Figure 7.22) must also be capable of connecting to 100BASE-FX.

Figure 7.22

Using 100BASE-FX in a collapsed backbone

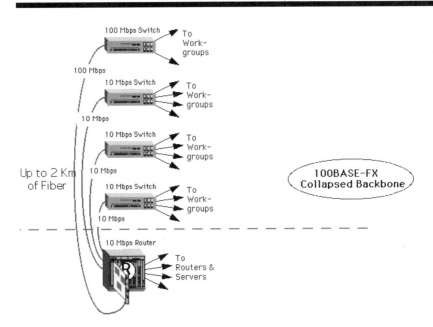

Server Farms

Server farms refer to clusters of servers that are connected directly to the backbone. These servers are also thought of as being *in the basement*, since they are hidden away from the everyday users. The benefit of placing critical pieces of the network, like servers, in the basement is that they can be more tightly controlled, monitored, and managed there. Servers such as these are often grouped into two categories—file servers and application servers.

File servers require high-speed disk subsystems, but little else. For instance, an 80486-based file server is likely to perform closely to a Pentium processor-based file server if similar hard drive subsystems are used in each. File servers also tend to be used randomly, with high bursts of network utilization when users open or close a file. For this reason, file server farms show large network utilization spikes but remain low in average bandwidth. As we have already seen, repeaters provide an excellent solution for this type of network. The trick is to determine how to distribute the shared bandwidth between servers. Consider below, where 16 file servers are part of a server farm on a 10-Mbps backbone. By measuring the amount of traffic generated by each server, you can determine how to upgrade them. Assume the servers put the following loads on the 10-Mbps repeater to which they are connected:

File Server 1	0.5 Mbps	File Server 9	0.5 Mbps
File Server 2	0.1 Mbps	File Server 10	0.2 Mbps
File Server 3	0.1 Mbps	File Server 11	0.1 Mbps
File Server 4	0.2 Mbps	File Server 12	0.2 Mbps
File Server 5	0.8 Mbps	File Server 13	0.1 Mbps
File Server 6	0.2 Mbps	File Server 14	0.1 Mbps
File Server 7	0.1 Mbps	File Server 15	0.1 Mbps
File Server 8	0.1 Mbps	File Server 16	0.1 Mbps
Total	**3.5 Mbps**		

When upgrading this particular file server farm to Fast Ethernet, you have the opportunity to optimize its configuration. First, replace the 10-Mbps NICs in each server with 10/100-Mbps NICs (if you already haven't done so as a result of Step 2). Next, consider that the best way to segment these file servers is to put the few high traffic servers together, separating them from the others. Each group is connected with a 100-Mbps repeater and attached to the network via a 100 Mbps switched pipe. This results in two server farms—one with servers 1, 5, and 9, and the other with the rest of the servers. Each server farm shares 100 Mbps of bandwidth through a Fast Ethernet repeater.

Application servers are also implemented as server farms. In this case, the bandwidth demands are usually too high and constant to use a repeater. A 100-Mbps backbone switch may be the best solution for an application server farm. The deployment is very similar to that of the file server farm, except each server gets its own dedicated 100-Mbps link. This way, when multiple users are accessing a database on an Application server, it can respond without regard for bandwidth constraints from other servers. This type of server farm deployment also allows for multiple servers to be accessed simultaneously. Unlike file servers, application servers get much better as the quality of the NICs, processors, expansion bus speeds, and amount of system memory improves. Pentium processors, the PCI bus, and intelligent Fast Ethernet NICs may be worthwhile investments for application servers.

When to Use TX, T4, or FX in the Backbone

One LAN administrator was quoted saying "I don't care if I have to use barbed wire in the backbone." Although this is a rather humorous way of putting it, the sentiment is typically true. The wiring infrastructure in the backbone or wiring closet is usually under the control of the LAN manager, unlike in the workgroup. Since the wiring can be made to adapt, it is less critical which type of 100BASE-T standard to use in the backbone. However, using existing wiring is always preferable, so either 100BASE-TX, 100BASE-T4, or 100BASE-FX may be selected. 100BASE-FX and TX tend to be good choices in backbones where FDDI or CDDI are used because of the similarities in signaling and cabling requirements. In LANs where the workgroups are all connected via 100BASE-T4 connections, there is no reason not to use T4 on a UTP backbone, as long as the four-pair requirements are met. In LANs that cover more than 20 floors or 2 miles of area, 100BASE-FX Fiber backbone connections are preferred.

Backbone Deployment Summarized

Deployment of Fast Ethernet in the backbone will allow your entire LAN to speak at 100 Mbps. By deploying Fast Ethernet in the backbone, you will have completed the lion's share of the upgrade from 10BASE-T to 100BASE-T. The performance gained should be evident in higher network traffic, faster network response times, and shorter packet latencies. Table 7.9 summarizes the important points of backbone deployment in each of these key areas.

■ Step 5: Completing the Switched and Fast Ethernet Environment

With 100BASE-T implemented in the backbone, there is little else you can do with Fast Ethernet to increase performance in the LAN. One place you can still upgrade is in the enterprise. In this context, the enterprise includes interconnect devices on the backbone that don't contribute directly to workgroup performance. This includes routers to the WAN and routers to other types of networks on your LAN, such as Token Ring and FDDI. After deploying 100BASE-T in this area, your Fast Ethernet LAN performance will not necessarily increase dramatically, but your LAN-to-LAN and LAN-to-WAN performance may increase. That is, the speed at which you can talk to dissimilar LANs such as Token Ring, FDDI, and remote LANs across the WAN may be much higher.

Table 7.9

Backbone Deployment
Issues

TYPE OF BACKBONE	FAST ETHERNET UPGRADE	ISSUES
Distributed backbone	Multiple 100BASE-T switches	A 100BASE-T switch is needed for each sub-LAN (floor, site, and so on) to be upgraded
		Distributed backbone can be implemented a piece at a time
		Packet latencies may be high
		Use 100BASE-FX for multiple building backbones
		Less expensive than upgrading a collapsed backbone
Collapsed backbone	Multiple 100BASE-T switches and a 100BASE-T router module for basement router	A 100BASE-T switch is needed for each sub-LAN (floor, site, and so on) to be upgraded
		A 100BASE-T router module is needed for basement router
		If basement router does not support a 100BASE-T module, a new router may have to be considered
		Collapsed backbone can be implemented a piece at a time
		Packet latencies should be low
		Use 100BASE-FX for multiple building backbones
		More expensive than upgrading a distributed backbone
File server farm	100BASE-T repeater	Upgrade all servers to 10/100 NICs
		Use one repeater for high-usage file servers
		Use another repeater for the rest of the file servers
Application server farm	100BASE-T Switch	Upgrade all servers with 10/100 NICs
		Connect each application server to a dedicated 100-Mbps pipe

Adding Fast Ethernet to Standalone Routers

The router used to concentrate a collapsed backbone is one of the most critical pieces of the LAN. This is why it is the focal point of upgrading a collapsed backbone to Fast Ethernet. However, there are probably other routers on the network that are less critical but could also be upgraded in performance. Fast Ethernet router modules can sometimes be used in these situations. For instance, Figure 7.23 shows the basement of a large networked site. The collapsed backbone router sits in the basement receiving many packets of data and concentrating on forwarding them. This router does not have time to filter and route packets to the WAN, so a standalone router is often used for WAN access Many networks use separate standalone routers for this task.

Figure 7.23

Standalone routers may need to be replaced with Fast Ethernet versions since they are not inherently upgradeable.

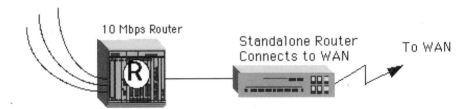

To upgrade these pieces of equipment, two tracks can be taken. The first strategy is to buy Fast Ethernet modules and install them in these routers as well. This strategy depends on two things. First, the modules must be available and second, the router must be of the modular type.

Another way to upgrade this network is with brand-new low-end Fast Ethernet routers. Many networks use smaller, nonmodular routers for these tasks, and some even employ software or PC-based routing for this function. PC-based routing may actually cost less than upgrading the modules in all your existing routers. In addition, Fast Ethernet and other network types can be specified up front, allowing for the manufacturer to configure the router to your specifications. An example of a software-based router is shown in Figure 7.24.

■ Summary

Many LANs may be different than the examples discussed in this chapter; therefore, this five-step plan should be thought of as a guide rather than a strict set of instructions. The steps are outlined in such a way that their execution can be planned over a long period of time, with steady performance

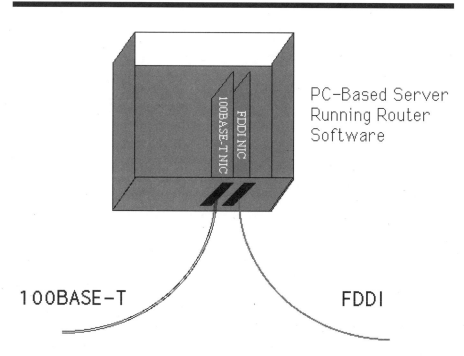

Figure 7.24

Fast Ethernet PC-based routing (FDDI-to-Fast Ethernet). PC-based routing offers an economocal alternative to expensive chassis-based routers.

gains. This will result in an interesting phenomenon—the more users that are added to the network, the more Fast Ethernet will be deployed. The performance of the newer users will be dramatically better than the existing users remember. When the existing users are upgraded to 10/100 switches, they too will enjoy the increased performance of Fast Ethernet.

In the next chapter, we will apply the lessons of Chapter 7 to some specific deployment examples, including building brand new 100 Mbps networks, attaching Fast Ethernet networks to FDDI, and upgrading a 10-Mbps branch office.

- *Example 1: Deploying in a Brand New Network*
- *Example 2: Deploying in a LAN with an Existing FDDI Backbone*
- *Example 3: Deploying a 10-Mbps Switched Backbone*
- *Example 4: Deploying in a Branch Office*
- *Reality: Every Network Is Different*

8

Deployment Examples

IN THE LAST CHAPTER, A FIVE-STEP DEPLOYMENT PLAN OUTLINED some guidelines for migrating from 10-Mbps shared Ethernet to Switched and Fast Ethernet. This chapter takes those basic principles one step further with practical examples. Each example described is a case study of a real network.

The four specific examples we will discuss are as follows:

1. *Deploying Switched and Fast Ethernet in a new network:* This example describes how you can build a new network using state of the art Switching and Fast Ethernet products. Deployment examples cover client, server workgroup, and backbone issues.

2. *Deploying Switched and Fast Ethernet in a LAN with an existing FDDI backbone*: This example describes how to convert or add on to an existing FDDI backbone. Issues such as adding Fast Ethernet workgroups to an FDDI backbone and expanding an FDDI backbone with 100BASE-FX are discussed.

3. *Deploying a 10-Mbps Switched backbone*: In some networks, Fast Ethernet may be overkill. A simple 10-Mbps Switched backbone may be all that is needed. This example illustrates the upgrade process from a 10-Mbps shared network with no backbone to a 10-Mbps Switched backbone.

4. *Deploying Fast Ethernet in a branch office*: A branch office is a classic small LAN. There are different issues for this type of 100BASE-T installation, such as cost of equipment and routing to the WAN.

In general, this chapter will apply what we've discussed in the previous chapters to real-world deployment examples. Although every network is different, there should be some similarities between your LAN and one of the instances discussed in this chapter. These examples should help crystallize the concepts and principles discussed up to this point.

■ Example 1: Deploying in a Brand New Network

Rarely do you have the pleasure of building a new network from the ground up with few constraints on the type of network used. Even when this does happen, the budgetary considerations of a new network sometimes prove to be a bit stifling. 100BASE-T addresses this problem with the best price performance of any high-speed networking technology available today. This example highlights the issues involved with building a brand new 100BASE-T network, including how to deal with the individual nodes, workgroup hubs, and backbone switches.

In order to work through this example, we must make some assumptions. First, the new network is to be installed in a building with four floors. Each floor is a square with 120-meter-long walls. There are to be roughly 200 offices per floor and a CAD/CAM workstation cluster on the top floor. The building has a basement where most of the servers and other critical network components will be placed. Brand new Pentium processor PCI PCs will be purchased for the top three floors, but the bottom floor will be using older

Intel 80386 ISA-based PCs. There are two wiring closets for each floor located directly opposite each other. Since you are planning for future growth and upgradeability, you have chosen to run 4-pairs of Category 5 UTP to each office and 62.5/125 micron two-strand fiber optic cabling for the backbone. This building is shown below in Figure 8.1.

Figure 8.1

New building ready for
Switched and Fast
Ehternet

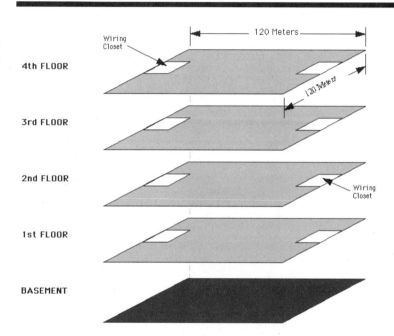

The Backbone Solution: A 100BASE-FX Switched Backbone

From sizing your formidable task, you discover that a 100BASE-T shared network won't be able to cover the entire area of the building. Not only is the building four stories tall, but the size of each floor is over 100 meters. This large size also makes a pure UTP installation messy, since UTP must strictly follow the 100-meter rule. The only way to ensure less than 100-meter UTP drops to each office would be to situate the wiring closet for each floor in the center of the building. This is not practical, since the wiring closets are already on the sides of the building.

With these facts in mind, a good solution for the backbone is Switched 100BASE-FX. By choosing switched 100BASE-FX, you are allowed to connect to any other FX switch over fiber runs of up to 2 kilometers. Also, this network can be easily upgraded in the future since a 100BASE-T backbone switch is highly scalable. You decide to install a high-end 100BASE-FX backbone switch in the basement and develop a collapsed backbone. The switch should be modular in nature with a chassis and several slots for 100BASE-T modules. As a higher performance option, you may decide to deploy a 100BASE-FX router, like the Cisco 7000, instead of a switch. In each wiring closet, place a 100BASE-TX switch like the Bay Networks LATISSWITCH28115. The 28115 has 18 100BASE-TX switched ports, two of which are upgradable to 100BASE-FX. This will come in handy later when you deploy 100BASE-TX to the workgroups on each floor. Also, your connection to a T1 WAN link is done through the basement chassis hub via a T1 chassis(or another type of WAN) module. The 100BASE-FX backbone deployment is shown in Figure 8.2.

Figure 8.2

Deployment of a new 100BASE-FX switched backbone A chassis-based router is installed in the basement and is connected to the wiring closets via 100BASE-FX free cabling.

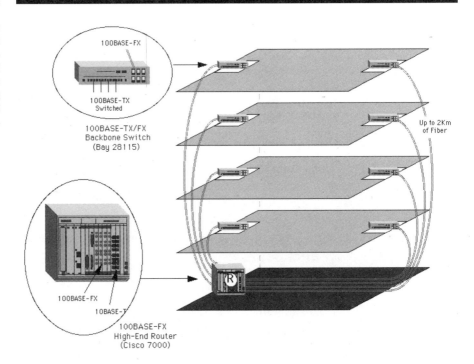

The Workgroup Solution: A Combination of Switched and Fast Ethernet

Now that your 100BASE-FX Switched backbone is in place, you can address the deployment of 100BASE-T to the workgroups. The top three floors will all have new PCI-based PCs so each of these can be outfitted with a 10/100 NIC. The first floor is using legacy ISA-based PCs, so they have to be installed with legacy 10-Mbps ISA NICs. For this building, you have chosen 100BASE-TX for the 100-Mbps option on your PCI NICs and 10BASE-T as the option for your 10-Mbps-only NICs.

100BASE-TX Stackable Hubs

Because there will be many connections on each of the top three floors, you elect to deploy 100BASE-TX stackable hubs such as the 3Com LinkBuilder FMS 100. Each of the stackable hubs is connected to one of the 100-Mbps switched ports of the 100BASE-TX switch installed in the wiring closet. In turn each one of the stackable hub ports is connected to a Category 5 UTP wiring segment that runs from the individual offices on the floor. You may want to expand this network in the future—increase the number of PCs per office, for example—so you want to make sure to have room to grow. For this reason, you should buy 100BASE-TX stackable hubs, which can be stacked at least six units high. Start by buying only four units per stack, which leaves room for the workgroups to expand beyond their current size. Each stackable unit has sixteen 100BASE-TX ports, so each stack of four units can service 64 users. Therefore, only four stacks of 64 ports each are needed to service 200-plus users.

There are two wiring closets per floor, so you can connect one-half of each floor to the stackable hubs in one closet and the other half to the other closet. Each workgroup of 64 users shares 100 Mbps of bandwidth, and each workgroup is allowed a 100-Mbps dedicated port into the 100BASE-TX switch in the wiring closet. Therefore, two sets of stackable hubs should be placed in each wiring closet. There are also some local servers for each workgroup; connect these directly to the stackable hub for that workgroup. The 100BASE-TX stackable hub deployment is shown in Figure 8.3.

By studying the prospective users of the new network, you discover that in any given workgroup, about 50 percent of workgroup traffic stays local—that is, it never gets forwarded on to the backbone. Therefore, you deduce that the 100BASE-FX backbone link to the wiring closet needs to support 50 Mbps of data from each workgroup in that wiring closet. Since there are two workgroups per closet on floors 2, 3, and 4, the backbone needs to support only a maximum of 100 Mbps. The Switched backbone connection provided by the 100BASE-FX switch supports this rate. If more workgroups are added or the existing workgroups are segmented so that there are less users per stackable hub, then an additional Switched 100BASE-FX connection may be needed for that particular wiring closet.

10/100 Workgroup Switches

The workgroup situation on the first floor is very different. Since the bulk of the systems are ISA-based PCs, the majority of the connections will be

Figure 8.3

Deployment of new 100BASE-TX workgroups. 100-Mbps switches are connected to 100-Mbps stackable hubs in the wiring closet. This is ideal for clients with 100 Mbs NICs.

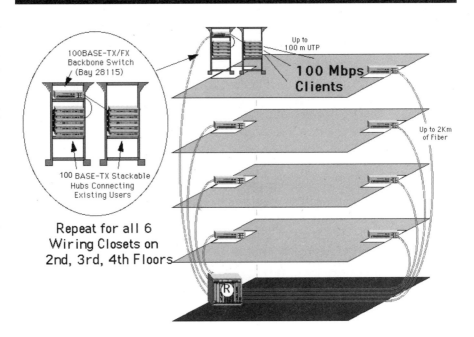

10BASE-T (ISA doesn't support 100-Mbps data rates very well). As we saw in the last chapter, 10/100-Mbps switches work well in workgroups with legacy 10BASE-T clients. However, the network installation shouldn't preclude the possibility of adding newer PCI-based systems equipped with 10/100-Mbps NICs. The workgroup strategy for the first floor also has to account for local servers, which should have 100-Mbps NICs.

This type of installation is best handled by 10/100 workgroup switches. Each workgroup switch has two or more 100-Mbps switched ports and multiple 10-Mbps ports. A good example of this type of switch is the Grand Junction FastSwitch 100 ES. The ES is available with up to nine 100-Mbps ports and twenty-four 10-Mbps ports. Every client is connected to a 10-Mbps dedicated port on the 10/100 switch. Since each switch has twenty-four 10-Mbps ports on each hub, a total of eight switches are needed to connect the 200 clients on the first floor—four switches in each wiring closet. One of the 100-Mbps switched ports on the ES is connected to the previously deployed 100-Mbps switch in the wiring closet. The first floor installation is shown in Figure 8.4.

There is one potential problem, however, with this first floor deployment scenario. Each workgroup switch collects data from twenty-four 10-Mbps clients. In this scenario, a workgroup switch could easily be forwarding 100

Figure 8.4

Deployment of new
100BASE-TX workgroups
with 10-Mbps ISA clients.
10/100 workgroup
switches are used to
connect 10-Mbps clients
to 100 Mbps networks.

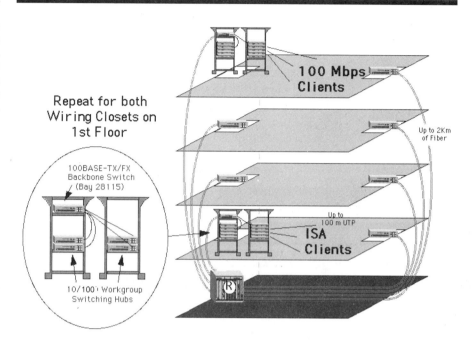

Mbps of data at any given time. Since there are a total of eight workgroup switches, each providing 100 Mbps of bandwidth, there is the potential for 800 Mbps of traffic to be forwarded to the backbone. The 100BASE-FX backbone provides only one 100-Mbps link, so it may become *oversubscribed*. Oversubscription occurs in switched environments when the sum of all data rates on the low-speed ports exceeds the data rate of the high speed port. In order to prevent oversubscription, one of two things must be done. Either more switched backbone connections must be run to the first floor—a costly effort—or the 100-Mbps switch on the first floor must be equipped with a congestion control feature. A switch can use congestion control to tell its connections that it is in a state of oversubscription. The Bay Networks 28115 is a good example of a switch with this capability. In this example, congestion control will allow only 100 Mbps of combined traffic to flow from the eight workgroups to the 100BASE-FX backbone connection.

Local servers and clients with new systems can still connect at 100 Mbps through one of the nine 100-Mbps ports on the FastSwitch 10/100 ES workgroup switch. Each new system deployed on the first floor should include a 10/100 NIC so it can eventually be connected to a 100-Mbps port.

Cost Analysis

The cost of deploying Fast Ethernet in this new network example will be somewhat higher than the cost of deploying a similar 10BASE-T solution. However, the performance gained is roughly ten times that of 10BASE-T. It should be noted that the cost of deployment for 100BASE-T will drop fast over the next few years as competition and silicon integration allow network vendors to sell 100BASE-T at costs close to 10BASE-T. For any new network, cost is easily determined by analyzing the cost of the network equipment in each case. Below is a cost worksheet that compares the cost of deploying 10BASE-T and 100BASE-T. This worksheet can be used as a starting point to determine how much 100BASE-T will cost. In Table 8.1, the equipment from this example is used. To analyze the cost of your new network, create a similar table and plug in the associated equipment costs. For general reference, the cost of this complete 100BASE-T network, at the time of this book's publication, is roughly three times that of a 10BASE-T network.

■ Example 2: Deploying in a LAN with an Existing FDDI Backbone

Many networks today feature an FDDI backbone ring. FDDI provides a high-speed, robust, semi-fault-tolerant technology which is ideal for backbones. However, FDDI is considered expensive and difficult to maintain and manage. 100BASE-FX, on the other hand, is not designed with built-in fault-tolerant hardware; however, many 100BASE-FX switch and router products provide this function in software. 100BASE-FX and 100BASE-TX are less expensive than FDDI and provide the same effective data rate—100 Mbps. In addition, 10BASE-FX allows for full-duplex connections of up to 200-Mbps data rates. In most cases, it is unwise to replace existing FDDI backbones with 100BASE-T. However, 100BASE-T can be used as an inexpensive extension to an existing FDDI ring.

This example examines the issues of adding 100BASE-T to a network that already has an FDDI backbone. 100BASE-FX can be used to extend the fiber backbone and 100BASE-TX or 100BASE-T4 can be used to distribute data from the FDDI ring down to the workgroups. We will first look at using 100BASE-T to improve the throughput of an FDDI ring to the workgroups.

Adding 100BASE-T Workgroups to an FDDI Ring

In this example, assume that an FDDI backbone exists with 10BASE-T-to-FDDI routers (or advanced bridges) providing the connection from the FDDI ring to the workgroups. This is shown in Figure 8.5. In this figure, each

Table 8.1

Example Cost Worksheet
for Justifying 100BASE-T
Deployment

NETWORK EQUIPMENT	100BASE-T EQUIPMENT	EQUIPMENT EXAMPLE	100BASE-T COST	10BASE-T EQUIPMENT	10BASE-T COST
Backbone switch	100BASE-FX chassis-based back-bone switch or router	Cisco 7000		10BASE-T backbone switch	
	8 - 100BASE-TX backbone switches with 100BASE-FX Port	Bay Net-works Lattis-Switch 28115		8 - 10BASE-T backbone switch (non-modular)	
Workgroup switch (2nd-4th floor)	4 - 100BASE-TX stackable hubs (4 units each)	3Com Link-Builder FMS 100		4 - 10BASE-T stackable hubs (4 units each)	
Workgroup switch (1st Floor)	8 - 10/100 switches	Grand Junction FastSwitch 100 ES		8 - 10BASE-T repeaters	
Workgroup NICs (2nd–4th floor)	600 - 10/100BASE-TX PCI NICs	Intel Corp. Ether-Express PRO/100		600 - 10BASE-T PCI NICs	
Workgroup NICs (1st floor)				200-10BASE-T ISA NICs	
Total	100BASE-T Cost			10BASE-T Cost	

workgroup shares 10Mbps of bandwidth provided by an FDDI-to-10-Mbps Ethernet switch such as the Cisco Catalyst.

When adding new workgroups to this network, 100BASE-T should be considered. Assume this particular network uses Category 3 UTP cabling for each workgroup. In this case, 100BASE-T4 is the logical selection for 100-Mbps connectivity to the desktop. In Figure 8.6 some new desktops have been connected to a 100BASE-T4 stackable hub. This workgroup now needs to be connected into the FDDI backbone. Several products are available which perform this type of connection. One type of product is a standa-lone FDDI-to-100BASE-T4 router, soon to be available from 3Com as part of the NetBuilder II Router product line. Since this is a multiport device, its

Figure 8.5

A 10BASE-T network with an FDDI backbone. 10BASE-T workgroups access the FDDI ring via routers.

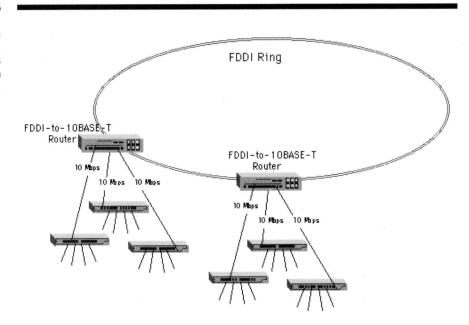

addition allows for multiple 100BASE-T4 workgroups to be connected to the FDDI backbone. As in Example 1, intelligent logic within the router may use congestion control mechanisms to prevent the 100BASE-T4 work-groups from oversubscribing the FDDI ring with too much traffic.

Figure 8.6

Adding 100BASE-T4 workgroups to an FDDI backbone. 100BASE-T4 is routed to FDDI much like 10BASE-T.

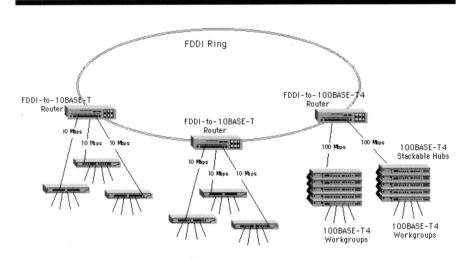

Extending an FDDI Ring with 100BASE-FX

Another way to add 100BASE-T to an FDDI ring is to consider extending the fiber backbone. In the previous example, the network utilized a distributed FDDI ring, which, in turn, had many FDDI to 10BASE-T connections. A simple way to extend the backbone to 100BASE-FX or 100BASE-TX is to add an FDDI-to-100BASE-T router in a strategic location. By doing this, the backbone can be extended in a star configuration from the location of the router. If this router is modular in nature, the FDDI ring can be routed to 100BASE-FX, 100BASE-TX, 100BASE-T4, or 10BASE-T via the addition of new router modules. In the example shown in Figure 8.7, the FDDI backbone has been extended to 100BASE-FX via a standalone router.

Figure 8.7

Adding a 100BASE-FX backbone to an FDDI backbone allows for the extension of fiber backbones to 100BASE-T.

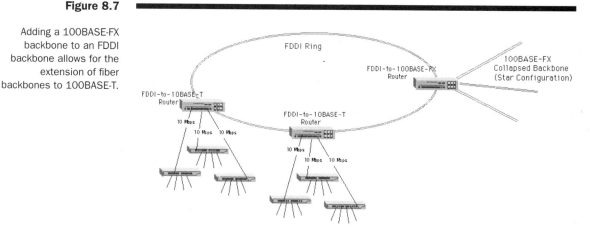

■ Example 3: Deploying a 10-Mbps Switched Backbone

In this example, we will examine a case where many clients and servers make up a 10-Mbps shared network. The majority of the systems, roughly 50 users, are clients. The rest, about six systems, are servers. This particular network, shown below in Figure 8.8, is experiencing average wire utilization above the 40 percent mark. This has caused some concern in the IS group and a small amount of funds have been budgeted to do something to reduce wire utilization and add bandwidth. An analysis of the network showed that most of the traffic was to and from two of the servers (A and B).

By applying the rules learned in step 1 of Chapter 7, it was determined that most of the traffic problems could be alleviated by adding a 10-Mbps backbone switch to this network. Each hub will now have its own dedicated

Figure 8.8

A typical 10-Mbps Shared Network

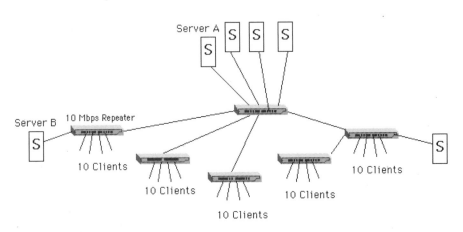

segment with 10 Mbps of bandwidth to share among all clients. The servers are also logically relocated on the network. The two busy servers are each given their own dedicated 10-Mbps connection and the other four servers share a 10-Mbps connection. The newly configured network is shown in Figure 8.9 below.

Figure 8.9

The same network after adding a 10-Mbps backbone switch. The performance of the network has increased by a factor of eight.

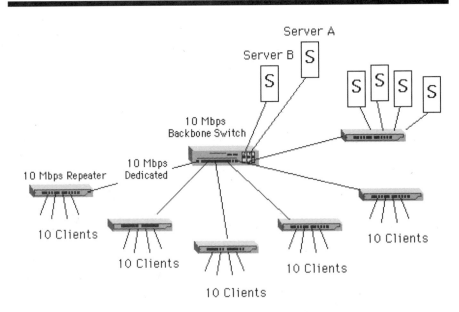

The new backbone switch should have extra features, such as error-checking and advanced packet filtering, so collided frames and runt frames are not propagated throughout the network. This is a great example of where a well-placed 10-Mbps switch can boost network performance without adding Fast Ethernet. Overall, each of the five workgroup segments share their own 10 Mbps of bandwidth so the total network performance could go up by a factor of five.

Of course, with the addition of switching hubs comes new challenges in network management and troubleshooting. These issues are addressed later in the book.

■ Example 4: Deploying in a Branch Office

The last example addresses the concept of deploying Fast Ethernet in a branch office. The term *branch office* is often used interchangeably with *small network* or *isolated network* in that the number of users is typically small and the amount of traffic is very localized. In addition, a branch office usually has a connection to a WAN link where information is sent and received from a remote place, such as corporate headquarters. The WAN links are mostly used at certain points in the day, such as the close of business for a bank branch office. The following list points out some of the common traits of a branch office.

- Small number of users—typically less than 50

- Physical network diameter is small

- Replacement of network components is easier and less disruptive

- Majority of daily traffic is localized

- There are one or more WAN connections

- WAN connection use is typically high during specific times and low at other times

The branch office is a situation where a shared Fast Ethernet solution excels. Since a branch office can be thought of as one large workgroup (although it is separated from the corporate backbone by the WAN link), the rules of workgroup deployment apply. Think back to Case Study #1 where new workgroups were deployed using 100BASE-T stackable hubs. Stackable hub deployment applies in this example just as well. Consider the branch office shown in Figure 8.10. There are eight users, two local servers, and one router that provides a connection to the WAN.

In this particular example, assume the branch office is an older building with a mixture of Category 3 UTP and Category 5 wiring. However, it is unknown how much of each is installed. One thing you do know from the previous LAN administrator is that four pairs are available to every desktop. In

Figure 8.10

A 100BASE-T4 branch office. Branch offices usually have a smaller number of users and a need to access the WAN regularly.

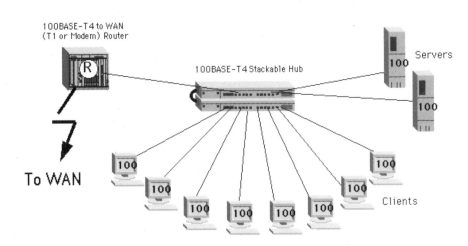

this case, 100BASE-T4 should be used throughout the network because of the uncertainty in cable quality. The clients and servers are then equipped with 10/100-Mbps 100BASE-T4 NICs. The nodes are all connected via a 100BASE-T4 repeater or stackable hub. In this example a Networth Fast-Stack 100 is used.

A simple 100BASE-T4/WAN router can be used to connect to the WAN. Typical WAN connections are T1 or modem based and therefore much slower than even 10-Mbps Ethernet. The routing capabilities of this device will prevent local traffic from being propagated on the WAN and wasting valuable WAN bandwidth. This is especially critical in this example, where the branch office is sharing 100 Mbps of bandwidth and the WAN link is made up of several 1.5-Mbps T1 lines. Performance of this LAN/WAN router is not critical in this case, because the WAN links are slow compared with the LAN links. In situations like this, PC-based routing can be used. PC-based routers, such as Novell's NetWare MPR (Multi-Protocol Router) software provide the right level of performance at low cost and high flexibility. In this example, a router is created using a standard PC, a 100BASE-T4 NIC, several T1-based NICs, and routing software.

■ Reality: Every Network Is Different

Real world examples allow us to gain insight into deployment issues, but in reality, every network is different. Although your entire network will not be exactly like one of the four cases discussed in this chapter, it is likely that parts of your network will be similar. These examples are designed to illustrate basic principles and highlight the deployment issues associated with Switched and Fast Ethernet. The examples discussed in this chapter should not be used as strict rules, but rather as guidelines for your own Switched and Fast Ethernet deployment strategies.

So far we have looked at what defines Switched and Fast Ethernet and how to deploy it in your network. In the next two chapters, we will discuss what to do with your Switched and Fast Ethernet network once it is installed—specifically, how to manage and troubleshoot a network that is very similar to, yet very different from, your 10-Mbps Ethernet network of today.

9

Managing Switched and Fast Ethernet Networks

I N THE PREVIOUS THREE CHAPTERS, WE MADE VARIOUS SUGGESTIONS for solving the bandwidth dilemma facing many of today's networks. However, this is only part of the solution. If the network, with all the new switching and high bandwidth capabilities, cannot be managed effectively, then it is not of much use to anyone. The obstacles that switching presents to network management are not easily surmounted. In fact, it may be years before all the necessary standards are in place to make switched network management coherent across multivendor products and services. However, don't be discouraged from making an investment in switching technology today. Even with its difficulties, the performance benefits associated with switching are too great and cost effective to bypass.

Since this book will not cover basic network management concepts, we'll assume the reader has an understanding of network management and is familiar with terms such as *SNMP, MIB, RMON,* and *DMI.* For more background in the area of general network management, books such as *The Simple Book: An Introduction to Internet Management*, by Marshall T. Rose, and *The Ethernet Management Guide*, by Martin A.W. Nemzow, may provide a more fundamental approach to network management. The purpose of this chapter, however, is to help you understand how to go about managing a Switched and Fast Ethernet network and what features to look for in management products. We'll start by describing two distinct types of management, network management and desktop management.

■ Network Management

In order to define the concept of management, we must first distinguish between network management and desktop management. *Network management* defines the management of network elements such as switches, routers, bridges, and gateways. To perform network management, protocols such as the Simple Network Management Protocol (SNMP) are used to affect the communication of management information between the managed elements of a network and the network manager. SNMP acts like a protocol stack, similar to TCP/IP, in that it sends and receives specific messages across the network that only SNMP-enabled devices can understand. The information used in this communication is stored in what is called a Management Information Base (MIB). Most administrators of large networks use SNMP to access management information stored in a network component's MIB. This approach, however, does nothing to manage one of the most important aspects of a network—the end node.

■ Desktop Management

How do you manage a desktop PC? Attendees of networking trade shows over the past three to four years have probably noticed that the term *desktop management* is being used to describe products that can do just that. To date, there are two types of desktop management. One method utilizes SNMP consoles that have been modified to meet a need for which they were not designed—managing desktop PCs. The second involves new prestandard and nonintegrated software utilities that solve a few of the desktop management problems without providing a look at the broad picture.

The reason SNMP desktop agents have to be modified to manage desktops is that a broad diversity of components make up the desktop environment.

Prior to managing any device, an SNMP console has to have the MIB for that device precompiled into its kernel. In the desktop environment there are tens of thousands of software types or hardware devices that could conceivably be located on a desktop computer. Even in the strictest and most tightly controlled MIS environment, there are dozens of different software and hardware applications that could be used on a desktop—and each one of them may require a separate MIB for the management console. This makes it extremely tough on the management software because it has to keep up with all the latest MIBs.

One of the most recent ideas in desktop management is in the SNMP Host Resources MIB. The Host Resources MIB allows an SNMP management station to access information about the end node in a predetermined way. This makes it possible for SNMP management consoles to learn node-specific information such as processor type, memory amount, and driver versions. However, this approach was introduced after other standards had already been designed. For instance, other innovative solutions to the desktop management dilemma, such as the *Desktop Management Interface* (DMI), had already been proposed and accepted by many networking vendors.

The Desktop Management Task Force (DMTF), which originally proposed the DMI, includes major networking vendors such as Intel, Bay Networks, Novell, IBM, Microsoft, and others, and has a lot of industry momentum. For instance, PC vendors like Compaq, Dell, and Hewlett-Packard are shipping PCs that are DMI-enabled. The potential advantage of DMI is that its database, called the *Management Information Format* (MIF) file, is in an understandable language format. This means the remote management console does not need to have the MIF compiled prior to management. When the console looks at the DMTF agent, the agent informs the console of all the management options on the workstation and when there is an option that may be managed by changing a parameter, all the parameters are also supplied in real-time by the DMTF agent. Also, because the MIF is written in an understandable language format, there are no codes or technical abbreviations to confuse the manager. If a workstation's video display has changed from VGA to SVGA, the option will be presented in those terms.

Although many MIS managers are not as concerned about the desktop as they are about the hub port to which it is attached, most will agree that the desktop is becoming more and more important with each advance in networking technology. Therefore, the future will undoubtedly see network and desktop management combine to form a comprehensive set of management capabilities. Until then, however, MIS professionals will have to plan their network management scheme around both.

■ Classic Management in a Shared Network

In a completely shared network, management is a relatively simple thing. Each and every packet on the wire is seen by each and every node on the wire. An event that happens in one part of the network is propogated to the rest of the network. If a problem occurs on the shared network, it can be easily isolated and remedied. Networking engineers have been working for several years to perfect the art of managing a shared network's infrastructure. Software-based traffic analyzers are available that provide full packet decode and analysis on networks (for more information on such devices, see Chapter 10).

One of the biggest advantages of a traffic analyzer is also its biggest weakness. Traffic analyzers examine network events on a packet-by-packet basis. Although a traffic analyzer can tell you how many bits are on the wire, it can only be used to manage the shared network segment to which it is attached. A traffic analyzer cannot see events on the other side of a switch, bridge, or router. Sniffers and analyzers are used quite frequently in today's shared networks because one can be connected to one of many shared segments. The types of management provided by these machines are warnings of disappearing connections, mysteriously slow networks, colliding packets, and malfunctioning network interface cards. However, in a network where the number of segments increases almost daily, expensive analyzers become too few and far between to cover all segments.

Software analyzers are only part of the total cost of managing networks these days. Network costs include support, troubleshooting, and replacing hardware and software. In fact, cost is a key factor in the management of networks today. Information from a recent Gartner Group study indicates that the cost of managing and supporting a networked PC is greater than the original cost of the PC, NIC, hub port, and associated network software combined.

With the way hardware costs are dropping, it shouldn't be surprising that every study done in this area shows that hardware costs are lower than support costs. Since hardware- and software-based analyzers are expensive and don't provide effective management for multisegment networks, many people have turned to SNMP-based network management. As mentioned previously, SNMP provides an efficient way to collect statistics from various network components instead of monitoring the actual traffic on the wire. In a sense, SNMP manages the network elements instead of the network itself. The network elements are then responsible for keeping their own statistics in a MIB compliant database. The SNMP approach lends itself much more readily to switched networks, as we will see in the next section.

■ The Impact of Switching on Management

SNMP will become even more important in your switched network management strategy. Once you've decided to introduce switching into your network, the next question becomes how to manage the new switched network. There are many problems associated with managing a switched network, including traffic statistics gathering, protocol analysis, and event/alarm generation. With a dedicated connection to specific nodes, management applications have to rely on the switch itself to collect and forward all data relevant to the network traffic associated with those nodes. This was quite a problem in the early days of switching because each switch vendor implemented this function in a slightly different way. What was really needed was a standard way to access network information from a switch through standard network management techniques. The obvious solution was to define an SNMP-based way of monitoring switch information, and as you will see, the RMON MIB was part of an ever-evolving answer.

The area of Switched Ethernet is where SNMP management consoles provide a unique and invaluable solution for resolving traffic-related problems. SNMP has developed a standard for managing network devices utilizing *Remote Monitoring* (RMON) capabilities, which allows network engineers with properly configured SNMP management consoles to view packet information on a port-by-port basis. The RMON MIB includes many new groups of statistics that were not part of the original SNMP standard MIB and are critical to switch management. These groups, standardized in RFC 1271, are outlined in Table 9.1.

With RMON and its associated database, the RMON MIB, network engineers can remotely monitor traffic coming in and out of distant ports. They can now get a global perspective *and* an individual perspective on large numbers of ports immediately and without having to set up sniffers on each of the segments one at a time. SwitchMan, an RMON-based switched network management application, can graphically display statistics and event generations based upon information stored in groups of the RMON MIB. A sample screen from SwitchMan is shown in Figure 9.1.

SNMP and RMON are invaluable tools for managing switched networks. The nature of SNMP allows it to transcend network elements such as bridges, switches, and routers that normally block traffic. Since SNMP and RMON rely on their own protocol and packets of information, the management information of the network can be collected from any point on the network.

Although RMON is invaluable to managing switched networks, it doesn't come for free. In many of today's network devices, RMON is supported by a separate piece of hardware and additional software. In many cases, full RMON support for a switching hub is roughly $200 per port. This

Table 9.1

The RMON Management Information Base (MIB) Includes Nine Groups. Each Group Includes Information Pertinent to Remotely Managing a Switched Network.

NUMBER	RMON GROUP	FUNCTION	DESCRIPTION
1	Statistics	Measures utilization and error statistics for each monitored device	Reports statistics for an entire device, such as how many errored packets a switch has seen on all ports combined
2	History	Reports statistical samples within a given time period	Allows managers to view statistics in 30-second or 30-minute intervals
3	Alarm	Compares the results from the History report to a known threshold and generates an event if the threshold is exceeded	Generates alarms based on preprogrammed thresholds. For instance, if the number of CRC errors exceeds a predefined limit, then an alarm signal will be generated. An RMON manager can receive this alarm and determine if it is important.
4	Hosts	Measures statistics on each host on the network. A host is determined by a source address.	Keeps statistics in a matrix based upon source address, not necessarily on a per-port basis.
5	HostTopN	Keeps a record of each host with the highest counter in each of a group of statistics	Keeps a list of the leaders in each of many statistics groups (CRC errors, runt packets, and so on)
6	Matrix	Measures statistics on packets that are transferred between two specific addresses	Keeps information on how much traffic is going from whom to whom based on the source address
7	Filter	Stores frames and data that pass a dynamic filter mechanism	Stores information about frames that pass a predefined set of filters
8	Packet Capture	Stores frames that pass a dynamic filter mechanism	Stores packets that pass a predefined set of filters. This could include a "catch all packets" setting.
9	Event	Controls the generation of events based on network information	A special SNMP RMON event packet can be generated based on results from other group information and statistics

SwitchMan is an RMON-based management application available from Bay Networks. SwitchMan allows for individual switch ports to be monitored and managed from a single SNMP console.

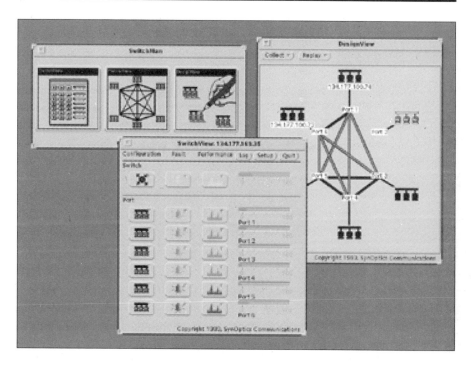

price doesn't even include what it costs to upgrade your SNMP management console to support the RMON MIB. That price will inevitably fall until RMON support is inexpensive enough to include with the switching hub as standard equipment. However, that day may be several years away.

So what should you do to enable this type of management in your switched network? First of all, start by purchasing network components that have SNMP management agents. If the components are upgradable to the new SNMP version 2 standard, then consider it a bonus. Second, any switching or routing device should have support for the RMON MIB. This will allow RMON-ready management consoles to effectively manage the ports on those switching devices. Third, any desktop or server NIC you purchase should come with an SNMP agent and associated MIB. A NIC that supports a DMI MIF file as well allows for a wider range of management options. These three items are probably the most critical pieces of a manageable switched network and are summarized in Table 9.2.

Table 9.2

Network Component
Management Features.
These Features Will Aid in
the Management of a
Switched Network.

TYPE OF NETWORK COMPONENT	RECOMMENDED MANAGEMENT FEATURES
All network components (NICs, Workgroup hubs, and Interconnect)	SNMP Agent (NICs may have optional DMI MIF support)
Switches, Bridges, or Routing Devices	SNMP Agent with support for the RMON MIB

■ The Impact of Fast Ethernet on Management

The brevity of this section should tell you something. Managing Fast Ethernet devices and desktops share the advantages and disadvantages of managing their classic 10-Mbps Ethernet siblings. Since the frame format, data format, and network access rules have not changed for Fast Ethernet, many of the network management applications will not need to change. Adding a new Ethernet device requires compiling a new MIB into your SNMP management application. Adding a new Fast Ethernet device also requires adding a new MIB—it's really that straightforward. One of the only changes that will occur is that the extra percentage of network bandwidth required to send SNMP packets will be much less at 100 Mbps than it was at 10. If this seems anticlimactic to you, then consider yourself pleasantly surprised.

SNMP and RMON will allow for more management in switched networks, but what about Fast Ethernet networks? First of all, if you have installed Fast Ethernet in your network, then it is highly likely you already have some sort of switched or routed backbone in place. If you don't then your network is of the shared variety and easily managed with classic tools such as software-based Fast Ethernet traffic analyzers. In the switched case, Fast Ethernet exacerbates the management problem because now you effectively have to manage a network at two different speeds: 10 Mbps and 100 Mbps.

The Fast Ethernet management solution is to use desktop management in conjunction with network management. This returns as much control as possible over desktop computers to centralized management locations. Fast Ethernet desktop management can be deployed with DMI-compliant MIFs at the desktop and server. Fast Ethernet Network Management is done in much the same way as 10-Mbps switched network management. SNMP MIBs are purchased with the various Fast Ethernet network elements (switches, bridges, routers, NICs, and so on) and each new MIB is compiled into the SNMP management console. The management information can be gathered via RMON capabilities on both the managed elements and the SNMP management console. If implemented correctly, an entire Switched Ethernet and Fast Ethernet network can be managed via SNMP in this fashion.

■ What Are the Potential Pitfalls?

The preceding text paints a rosy picture for managing a Switched and Fast Ethernet network. However, there are still many reasons why this style of management may not be implementable in your network today. Take, for example, the dilemma posed by a new 10/100-Mbps network interface card. In the first implementation throughout a network it would be fairly simple to manage them with SNMP, assuming that the card had a MIB associated with it and that the desktop users could afford the memory usage for another TSR on their workstation. As time goes on most new drivers released by the manufacturer would require a new MIB on the console. Later, when 10/100-Mbps NICs became a commodity item, the purchasing agents would start buying the cheapest cards available and the MIBs may need to be revised yet again.

Of course, MIS managers could put their foot down and insist on using a single vendor's solution regardless of the price—a sure way for an MIS manager to get into trouble. In reality, MIBs for network interface cards are quickly outdated and rarely upgraded. The reason for SNMP's inadequacy in this situation is that it was designed to make the maximum use of networking bandwidth by having the managed device send alerts or respond to commands by receiving or passing short and simple sequences of numbers (Object IDs) to the SNMP management console. The only piece of information that a management console might see about a device is its Object ID: 122.6.101.4.9.2. Unless the MIB is up to date on the management console and the operator of the management console knows exactly what version of what object he or she is looking at on the remote device, control of the remote device will not happen.

Using SNMP management consoles to manage network devices also has pitfalls. Since each device being managed requires an associated MIB, it is easy to see how enterprise-wide SNMP management consoles such as Hewlett-Packard's Openview can be quickly overcome with the overhead of all those devices. Typically, an SNMP management console can support about 1,000 objects—possibly fewer depending on the MIPs available on the management station. SNMP applications also may have limitations based upon the way their databases are constructed and the application is written. The SNMP-based network management solution for the MIS manager is still limited for these reasons; however, innovative new management applications that can effectively manage up to 10,000 objects are appearing on the horizon.

■ Summary

Network and Desktop Management are two areas that will prove vital to the future of Switched and Fast Ethernet networks. Without a strategy for both areas, a high-speed switched network could soon get out of control and come to a screeching halt. Currently, standards such as SNMP (and SNMP version 2) and DMI are providing solutions for network and desktop management, respectively. However, a crossroads for these two standards is coming soon that will force both vendors and customers to choose the technology that will best be able to manage both the network devices and desktops.

New technologies such as Switched Ethernet and Fast Ethernet will solve some problems on the networked desktops of tomorrow but they will exacerbate others and perhaps even create new ones that we haven't thought of yet. One potential area of concern is the rapid modification of the various device SNMP MIBs and how SNMP management consoles assimilate those modifications. The recent addition of the RMON MIB has added a new dimension to the management of switched networks, but has also started yet another MIB upgrade frenzy.

In any case, the MIS organizations of the world are actively seeking out the solutions that will save them the money they are currently spending. Network management will continue to be one of the most expensive parts of operating a local area network, and Switched and Fast Ethernet will only add to the management costs. However, the networking industry has always managed to manage itself. With each new innovation in networking hardware technology comes an equally impressive new method of control. Industry-backed standards efforts such as RMON and DMI will evolve to support the management needs of your new networks.

■ Desktop Management: A Better Definition

In the introduction of this chapter, a cursory definition of Desktop Management was provided. As this is a new concept for a lot of people, this extra section is intended to provide a better understanding of desktop management and its role in today's networks. If you already understand the concept of desktop management or feel the detail already provided is sufficient, then continue on to Chapter 10. If you would like more background on desktop management, then these few extra pages may be interesting to you.

Desktop management is loosely defined as a method of managing networked PCs and workstations from a centralized location. An example of a Desktop Management suite is Intel's LANDesk Manager. LANDesk Manager, shown in Figure 9.2, provides many of the desktop management application discussed in this section. Each application is supported with an appropriate icon, representing part of the greater suite of applications.

Figure 9.2

Intel's LANDesk Manager is a desktop management suite that supports many applications focused on managing networked desktops. LANDesk does not focus on managing other network elements such as hubs, bridges, routers, or switches, but snaps into SNMP-based management applications that do.

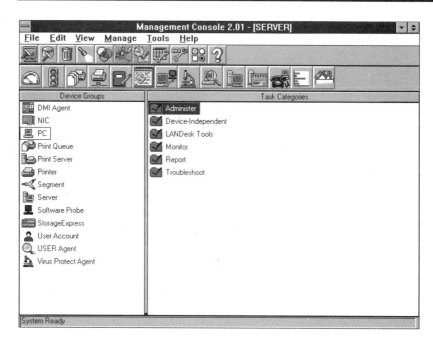

In general, desktop management provides many basic services, including the following three groups.

- Asset and Applications management
- ·Services management (Server Monitor)
- Services management (Help Desk)

Asset and Applications Management

For the most part, managers responsible for asset and applications management are interested in the areas of software distribution, software license metering, and inventory. In any area of the network where there are capital outlays (including the purchases of equipment and applications), asset management applications are needed. Managers have an interest in making sure that the capital expenditures are used efficiently and maximize return on investment. Reports are extremely important to people with these responsibilities.

MIS departments want to be able to manage desktop workstation software assets from a centralized location. To do that, they need to be able to know what's on the network, how much of it is being used, and how to get more of it into place—all from a centralized location.

There are three primary tools used to manage personal computing assets on the network: software license metering, software distribution, and inventory.

Software License Metering

In the marketplace of 1995, the following are desireable features of software license metering:

- The ability to meter applications that are run from shared network drives. (There may be some disagreement in this area; many products today allow the metering of applications run from local hard disks, but the license enforcement organizations consider any software installed on a local hard disk to constitute the use of a license regardless of whether or not the application is currently loaded into memory.)

- A very small TSR or agent on the desktop (it is preferable to have no agent whatsoever)

- Metering licenses across servers

- The ability to define application suites and meter multiple executables as if they were all part of one application

- A substantial and centralized alerting system to handle threshold violations

- Substantial reporting of the status of metered applications.

- The ability to prevent the copying or hiding of applications to be metered

- Multiple options of what to do when a metered application threshold is violated, including preventing access, placing users in queues to wait for access, and allowing overflow.

- The ability to create high-priority users who can go to the head of a queue if necessary

- The ability to create exempt users who will always have access to metered applications, regardless of the status

- The ability to give warnings at different levels of threshold usage

- The ability to meter applications (such as Lotus Notes) where the executable spawns other executables (including DLL files) and then exits, but leaves the application running in the form of the spawned files

- The ability to take a single metered application and assign different levels of usage to different groups

- In a wide area network, the ability to have licenses follow time zones so that multinational companies can purchase a set number of licenses and have people around the world use them

- Powerful reporting as defined by real-time information and timely summaries

One of the few areas of controversy in the metering world is whether or not it is acceptable to modify an application with a software "stub" that attaches itself to an executable file and allows metering applications to identify the stub. The problem with this is that they look and feel like viruses to many virus detection technologies. Another problem is that they require modification to executable code after the vendor has shipped the product and in many cases, this creates an unsupportable condition when application vendors are asked to support products that have been modified.

Of course, there are many reputable metering applications that use "stubs" in their technologies, so care must be taken when examining a metering solution to make sure it meets the standard practices and policies of an MIS organization.

Also in dispute in metering is whether or not it is a good idea to meter files located on the desktop's local disk. As discussed earlier, many international licensing organizations and individual license agreements are written such that the installation of an application on a local hard disk of a personal computer constitutes a license, regardless of whether or not it is loaded into memory.

Software Distribution

The problem of software distribution is becoming more and more acute with every passing year as personal computers become more powerful and the applications written for them become ever more complex and large. The latest office productivity suites require stacks of disks to install and occupy sometimes well over 100MB of disk space.

The problem is how to provide the users with the tools that make them productive without shutting down the entire MIS department in the process. MIS organizations are finding out that the installation of software packages alone could occupy the time of all technical engineers, managers, and help desk people. Alternatives include letting the users install software themselves, or installing the software on the servers and letting users run it over the network. The latter is often preferred because it also allows for a higher degree of revision control.

Some of the interim solutions to which companies have subscribed are only purchasing machines with preinstalled hardware, contracting with outsourcing organizations who can train hourly workers to do the repetitive and mind-numbing task of installing software on local workstations and offer it as a discount service, and the tried-and-true standby—waiting for a distribution tool to distribute the software.

Even when a company has obtained a software distribution application, that's only half the battle. It generally takes a long time to define what is going to be distributed to the remote workstations. For instance, your average application makes dozens of changes to a local hard disk when being installed, and your average distribution application needs to be programmed in a fourth-generation programming language in order to be able to take into consideration all the different hardware environments on which an application might be installed. Some distribution applications come with prebuilt distribution packages. Microsoft, for example, in their Systems Management Server application, provides prebuilt distribution applications for all the Microsoft business applications; but if a user needs to use SMS to distribute an application provided by another vendor then days or weeks are needed to develop the script.

A better way to develop application distribution packages is to have the computer do the work for you. Have the computer prepare a database of the way a workstation is configured, install the product or make changes to the workstation, and then prepare a second database of the machine's configuration and automatically create a distribution package using the differences.

Some other things to look for in software distribution are

- The distribution program automatically builds the uninstall package when you build an installation package.

- It incorporates either the "Push" or "Pull" method—meaning that the software should be forced onto the user or have the user be able to acquire the software when needed at his or her convenience.

- It is able to configure the pushing software mechanism so that some users can reject if desired and other users have no choice.

- It integrates the problem resolution system back into the redistribution queue so that users who had problems can get software redistributed.

- It implements version control so that newer Windows drivers are not overwritten by older Windows drivers.

- It has automatic sensing of whether or not the machine to be distributed to is qualified to accept the software (that is, does it have enough room? Is Windows installed?).

- It schedules distributions during off-hours.

- It installs packages to servers for end use as shared applications.

- There is no extra TSR.

- It creates profiles of different workstations or types of workstations so that jobs may be intelligently installed.

- It creates a log of each workstation distribution job so that jobs may be intelligently uninstalled.

- It is integrated with an inventory system so that queries may be done to determine potential candidates for the software application.

- It has powerful reporting as defined by real-time information and timely summaries.

- It is integrated with an alerting system.

Inventory

There are not as many complex issues in inventory analysis and control as there are in software distribution. The following are points to consider in an inventory system:

- It should operate without a TSR.

- It should log a complete list of hardware and software (including version number).

- It should automatically log changes to hardware and software on your network and have that tied into an alerting system.

- It should query for workstation-specific attributes.

- Information should be accessible by software distribution.

- The system should have extensive reporting capabilities—both on-screen and off-screen.

- It should keep contents and be able to update critical files (AUTO-EXEC.BAT, CONFIG.SYS, .INI files, and so on) for multiple generations so applications can restore critical files to desktops.

- It should be able to detect software versions in many different ways: from a preexisting comparative database including file sizes, dates, names, version numbers, and so on; from version information in file headers; and others.

- It should be able to produce a map showing location of significant applications on the hard disk.

- It should automatically log inventory changes on your network.

- It should export to common-format database file formats (such as SQL).

- It should be able to read management files from standard applications (such as SNMP consoles and DMI MIF browsers).

- It should be able to produce standard management file formats (such as SNMP and DMTF).

- It should use a flexible database that allows for distribution on a wide area network.

Services Management—Server Monitor

To a large degree, the types of tools involved with technical infrastructure include SNMP management consoles and software and hardware-based protocol analyzers that were discussed earlier in this chapter. Another type of tool that belongs in the domain of this type of network administrator is the critical node monitor, or server monitoring tool. Server monitors, found in management applications such as Microsoft's Systems Management Server (SMS) and Novell's NMS and ManageWise, often monitor both server software and hardware. Software and file information are monitored to ensure that proper service is provided to each user. Hardware is monitored to keep the server hard disk subsystem from getting too hot or becoming too fragmented. Other applications that a server monitor should be capable of include the following:

- Be able to monitor several different types of network operating systems from a single console

- Monitor the wide range of technologies in a file server, such as disk utilization, resource utilization, network utilization, processor utilization, and all areas associated with them (the most useful server monitoring tools will monitor over 100, and some do close to 300)

- Not add to the network traffic overhead of the wide area network

- Have a real-time graphical parameter display

- Maintain a historical analysis log

- Integrate with an alerting system that can e-mail, page, fax, or call a LAN administrator

- Be able to store and forward alerts so that if a server receiving alerts disappears from network, alerts are not lost

- Have a centralized repository for alerts

- Be based on standards and able to communicate with standards-based consoles

- Have substantial reporting capabilities

- Be able to provide its monitoring functions as background processes

- Be able to produce reports showing relative performance of different devices on the network based not only on network utilization, but also on the ability to communicate (in other words, if the server underutilized but cannot communicate with the network because the network cable is unplugged)

Services Management—The Help Desk

When a help desk engineer leaves his or her desk to go to an office, the time spent in transit is nonproductive. The goal of any desktop management system designed to assist the help desk engineer should be to allow him or her to resolve as many problems as possible without having to leave the center of responsibility.

The key technologies necessary to eliminate wasted time are substantial remote diagnostic utilities that include the ability to analyze the resources that desktop computers use—whether on the workstation itself or shared from remote file servers or workstations. This must be capped off by significant remote control technology that allows full mouse, keyboard, and video remote control of the many different types of machines and operating systems from a single console.

According to one MIS help desk administrator, 60 percent of the calls that came in to the help desk were resolved using a system like the one described above. These are calls that would, in the past, require help desk administrators to travel to the remote user's office. The biggest reason the administrator cited for quick resolution was that end users would identify a problem as something wrong with the computer when, in reality, it was generally a process that the user had misunderstood or forgotten. Many help desk administrators, when asked how many times they'd been asked to respond to a call about a computer or printer being broken and eventually had ended up showing the end user how to use the software, simply smile and say, "Too often."

Remote diagnosis and troubleshooting are blossoming technologies in the world of desktop management. Some technologies to look for in this area are

- Control, view, and diagnose any desktop workstation on your network (including servers)

- Take full control of remote computers, including monitor, mouse, and keyboard

- Instantaneously view and control multiple workstations

- Be able to see real-time status on TSRs in memory, CMOS settings, BIOS settings, network interface card settings, and statistics—in other words, be able to provide a complete diagnostic scan on any local device as if the administrator was on that workstation

- Be able to manipulate and change diagnostic settings

- Be able to edit and restore configuration files

- Keep an audit trail of remote control activity

- Include significant security features to prevent unauthorized access by remote control

- Be able to see values inside of standards management bases (either SNMP MIB, or DMI MIF)

- Access and control jobs in print queues belonging to users

- Access and control printers that are being accessed by users

- Be able to show historical usage for users utilizing printing resources

- Provide alerts when printing services fail

- Scan for viruses (with integration into alerting system and reporting)

- Help desk database for user trouble tickets

Although not specifically mentioned in all of the areas of desktop management, the need for standards-based management products is absolutely vital. New technologies such as Switched and Fast Ethernet will solve some problems on the networked desktops of tomorrow but will exacerbate others and perhaps even create new ones that we haven't thought of yet.

In any case, the MIS organizations of the world are actively seeking out management solutions that will save them the money that they are currently spending on desktop management. Hopefully, advances in areas like desktop management will keep up with similar advances in networking technology, like Fast Ethernet. Because without many of these cost-saving desktop management tools, desktop computers will not be able to reach their full potential.

- *Troubleshooting Products: Hardware*
- *Troubleshooting Products: Software*
- *Troubleshooting Techniques in a Shared Environment*
- *How Troubleshooting Differs in a Switched Environment*
- *How Troubleshooting Differs for Fast Ethernet*
- *Summary*

10

Troubleshooting

THE LAST CHAPTER OF THIS BOOK ADDRESSES THE TROUBLESHOOT-ing issues associated with upgrading your network to Switched and Fast Ethernet. Quick and efficient troubleshooting may be a lifesaver, depending on the state of your network and the amount of users depending on its services. When do you need to trouble-shoot your network? The obvious answer is when there are prob-lems, such as downed servers, downed connections, and increased traffic levels. However, the best troubleshooting is done proac-tively and on a consistent basis. By the time users are complaining about network problems it may be too late to quickly respond and correct the situation. Many of the problems in today's networks could be prevented, or at least predicted and planned for, if a small amount of troubleshooting were done in advance.

This chapter focuses on how traffic analysis-based troubleshooting methods change with the addition of Switched and Fast Ethernet. The chapter does *not* cover other, more general topics such as how to troubleshoot a faulty NIC, examine a NET.CFG file, optimize a NetWare server, or resegment a network. These issues are thoroughly discussed in many other books and change only slightly when moving to Switched or Fast Ethernet networks. A good example of a book of this nature is *The Ethernet Management Guide* by Martin A.W. Nemzow.

In contrast, this book delves into various hardware and software changes necessary to upgrade current diagnostic equipment to 100BASE-T. Also explored are some common problems to expect when deploying Switched and Fast Ethernet. Before addressing the troubleshooting methods applicable to Switched and Fast Ethernet networks, it is a good idea to cover the basics of troubleshooting today's 10BASE-T networks. Therefore, we start by classifying current troubleshooting products.

■ Troubleshooting Products: Hardware

Troubleshooting hardware products consist of diagnostic equipment such as LAN analyzers, LAN sniffers, traffic generators, cable testers, and other standalone devices. These hardware products are designed to analyze anything from packet filtering to cable integrity. Their common identifier is that they are used independently of the servers and clients on the network. For this reason, hardware troubleshooting products offer superior performance but are often difficult to learn and use.

LAN Analyzers (Sniffers)

LAN analyzers or "sniffers," such as the Network General Expert Sniffer, can be directly attached to a shared network and will "see" all packets traversing that particular network segment. Not only can the sniffer see all packets, but it can also break down and store each packet in its internal memory. The LAN administrator can later examine packet details such as frame type, CRC-integrity, and source address. The sniffer can also be used to collect network statistics such as how many collisions occurred, how many runt packets there were on the network, and how many broadcast packets were sent. In addition, an analyzer is a good tool for determining how much traffic is coming from each node on the network. This last feature is one that makes a LAN analyzer an invaluable troubleshooting tool.

Traffic Generators

A *traffic generator* is a device that can generate a preprogrammed data pattern on the network. Traffic generators can be standalone devices, or they can be integrated into LAN analyzers like the Network General Expert Sniffer. A traffic generator may not seem like a useful tool for a LAN administrator who is constantly trying to reduce network loading, but it can be helpful when doing modeling of a future network. For instance, assume you are planning to add three more users to a six-user network and you want to examine how the added traffic will affect network performance. By properly modeling the amount of traffic generated, you can perform an experiment with very reliable results. Some traffic generators allow you to catch all traffic from a specific node and then use that traffic pattern as the generated traffic. This can give an accurate indication of how additional clients will affect the network. This is illustrated in Figure 10.1.

Figure 10.1

Using a traffic generator to simulate additional users is useful in determining what effects future growth will have on your network.

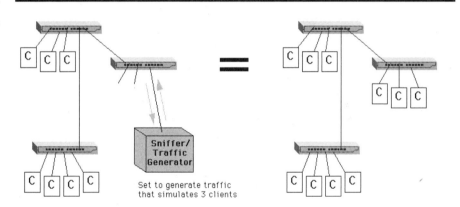

A traffic generator will also be useful in simulating the addition of constant-stream services on your network. This includes real-time applications such as video distribution and video conferencing. For instance, assume you know that a network video service, such as Intel's CNN at Work, will add a constant 300 Kbps of traffic to your network. You can use a traffic generator to model the impact of this application on your production network without actually purchasing the video product.

Hand-held Frame Analyzers

Hand-held frame analyzers, like the FrameScope 802 shown below in Figure 10.2, provide simple LAN analyzer-like troubleshooting features. These devices oftentimes allow for link testing, traffic statistic gathering, and traffic utilization monitoring, and they even break down frames by protocol.

Hand-held frame analyzers are especially useful in switched networks where connecting a LAN analyzer to every switched hub is neither physically or economically feasible. The FrameScope 802 shown here connects directly to UTP cabling, making it a very quick way to troubleshoot a large number of ports. One of the drawbacks of a hand-held device is that the user interface screens are typically small and monochrome, resulting in data that is harder to read and understand.

Figure 10.2

The FrameScope 802 from Scope Communications provides many LAN analyzer troubleshooting functions in a hand-held device.

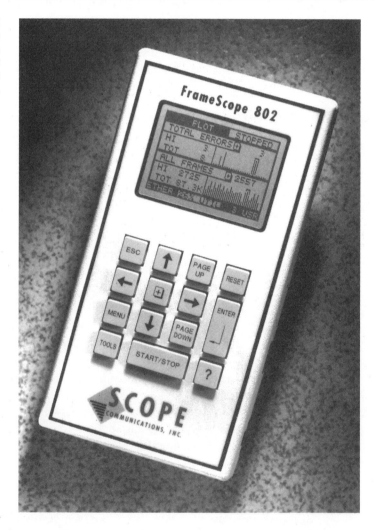

Hand-held Cable Testers

One of the main considerations when deploying Fast Ethernet is cabling. If you plan to use 100BASE-T4, cable category is not important, but the number of pairs available is critical. If you choose 100BASE-TX, then only two pairs are needed; however, the entire cabling plant—including the patch panel—must be Category 5 certified. This presents a problem because it now becomes important to determine if you have Category 5 UTP wiring and/or four pairs available to the LAN. There are several products that will assist in network cable studies. Most fall into the 100MHz cable tester category. An example is the Microtest PentaScanner, which performs many functions. This hand-held device can be used to help determine cable type, amount of pairs available, and cable integrity. For more on cable testers, see Chapter 4.

■ Troubleshooting Products: Software

Software products can also be used to troubleshoot networks and are commonly cheaper and easier to use than their hardware counterparts. Since they are typically used on a PC or workstation, they do not offer the same level of performance as a dedicated hardware product. With software diagnostic products, the amount of data that can be collected depends on the PC used, the NIC used, the drivers and NOS, and the amount of memory available to collect incoming data. Software troubleshooting products include software sniffers and LAN management products.

Software Sniffers: LAN Analyzer for Windows

If you don't have a few thousand dollars to spend on a hardware-based LAN analyzer, or if you want more functionality than a hand-held frame tester provides, then you may want to consider several software packages that can turn a PC into a respectable LAN analyzer. Novell's ManageWise is one such product. It runs as an application on a system with a NIC and NIC driver. Therefore, ManageWise doesn't care if the network is 10BASE-T, 10BASE-5, or 100BASE-T. It collects statistics and data as fast as it can, regardless of the network type. Although this software will run very well at 10-Mbps network speeds, be prepared to see dropped packets and missed frames at 100 Mbps. The software is just not built to handle data at those high speeds. ManageWise can provide a large assortment of basic diagnostic information for 100BASE-T networks, but a hardware product is required for individual frame capture and analysis. In general, a software-based analyzer can perform some functions well and some functions not so well.

The functions a software (PC-based) analyzer can perform well are

- Looking at frame statistics (Collision rate, runt packets, and so on)
- Counting the number of packets sent and measure traffic levels
- Collecting time-average information

The functions a software (PC-based) analyzer cannot perform very well are

- Performing data integrity checking and CRC checking
- Analyzing the protocol header of a frame
- Reporting on packet filtering (how much traffic is being generated from each node address)

LAN Management Suites

Another category of software troubleshooting products is LAN management suites. This category includes packages such as Intel's LANDesk Manager, and Microsoft's planned SMS for Windows NT. These products provide methods to get real-time graphical information on the traffic level and type of traffic on the network. The traffic analyzer in LANDesk Manager 2.0 allows users to monitor traffic levels and generate warnings when they get too high. The troubleshooting tools in LAN Management packages tend to be proactive in nature—that is, they will warn when network conditions look bad, but they rarely help the LAN administrator actually fix the problems. Usually more sophisticated equipment, such as a LAN Analyzer, is needed for this.

Troubleshooting Product Categories

As discussed, there are many types of diagnostic devices available to help you troubleshoot your network. These devices can be broken down into hardware and software devices. Table 10.1 recaps some of the basic features of each type of product.

■ Troubleshooting Techniques in a Shared Environment

A typical network environment may include several segments of 10-Mbps shared networks. Each of these segments shares 10 Mbps of bandwidth between all clients and servers on the segment. Therefore, when a problem occurs on one node, it usually affects all other nodes on the segment, and in some cases, all other nodes in the entire LAN. For instance, if one node on a shared LAN has a NIC that goes bad and starts transmitting bad data on the

Table 10.1

Troubleshooting Product
Categories and Their
Functions

TROUBLESHOOTING DEVICE	PRODUCT TYPE	CAN BE USED FOR	SHOULD NOT BE USED FOR
LAN analyzer/ sniffer	Hardware	Detailed packet analysis Detailed packet filtering Traffic source analysis Traffic level monitoring Collision frequency CRC, data integrity checking	Small networks where the cost of the analyzer is prohibitive Networks where special training cannot be justified
Traffic Generator	Hardware	Modeling addition of new clients or servers Modeling addition of new network services (such as video)	Modeling complex network scenarios (like the addition of new segments)
Cable tester	Hardware	Testing cable type (Category 3, 4, or 5) Testing number of pairs (2 or 4) Testing cable length and integrity	Certifying your cable plant
Software analyzers	Software	Traffic level monitoring Collison frequency	CRC, data integrity checking Detailed packet analysis Detailed packet filtering Traffic source analysis
Software network management suites	Software	Traffic level monitoring Warning of problematic network conditions	Determine cause and/or solution to network problems

wire, the other clients on that segment will not be able to send or receive data. However, because the problem can be seen anywhere on the segment, it is usually easily found, isolated, and remedied. Troubleshooting on a shared network can be done with a wide variety of devices, but a LAN analyzer can detect the most problems.

This section begins by discussing some basic shared network troubleshooting techniques like monitoring traffic levels and analyzing individual packets. The emphasis here will be to provide a clear understanding of the common problems found on a shared network. The next section then applies these common problems to Switched and Fast Ethernet networks, explaining how the isolation of the problems is different in those environments.

Traffic Level Analysis

High or erratic traffic levels are one of the leading causes of low network productivity. Too many nodes on any shared network can cause a level of traffic that may hinder the productivity of some network components. Also, the addition of nodes that transmit large amounts of data at frequent intervals, like powerful workstations, can increase traffic and decrease the overall performance of the network. Luckily, in a shared network this situation can be easily identified and remedied within a couple of days. Traffic monitoring software and hardware can provide constant updates of the overall traffic level and what constitutes the traffic. In Figure 10.3, a screen output of LANDesk Traffic Analyst shows how overall network traffic is monitored. The instantaneous traffic level is plotted as well as the average network traffic level. Other information, such as peak and low traffic levels can be monitored along with the times they occurred.

Figure 10.3

This screen capture of LANDesk Traffic Analyst shows how network utilization and individual packet information can be kept over time.

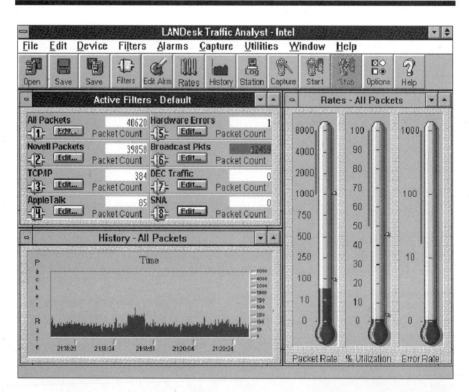

Traffic analysis provides basic information about the network and can be intrumental in identifying certain types of problems. Two common problems that cause high levels of traffic are newer, faster nodes and too many stations on the segment. Both are discussed next.

Problem: Faster Nodes

In the past, it was rare to find a server or client system that could continuously transmit packets at the maximum Ethernet rate. These older cards could not sustain the minimum 9.6 microsecond Inter Frame Spacing (IFS) of the IEEE 802.3 specification. This resulted in many nodes on the network vying for the wire at different points in time. The variety of these old networks worked well for the CSMA/CD nature of the Ethernet specification because it was built around the probabilities that no two stations would get on the wire at the exact same instant.

With the advent of newer, faster systems and NICs, almost all nodes on the network could sustain the minimum 9.6-microsecond IFS transfer rate. This causes a multitude of problems, the foremost being the "Capture Effect" (wire hogging) and increased secondary collisions (frames that collide more than once). These problems are such that the network utilization goes up while the efficiency drops. New schemes such as dynamic, adaptive IFS algorithms may help marginally, but the basic problem will still occur.

In order to find this type of problem, the traffic level can be monitored and compared to previous levels. A network categorized by a large number of high traffic peaks and a higher overall average traffic load is probably suffering from this problem. Consider Figure 10.4, which shows traffic levels after adding state-of-the art NICs to a few nodes in the network. The additional peaks and higher average traffic level may indicate that some stations can obtain the wire for extended periods of time. Two potential solutions for this problem are to upgrade to a switched workgroup in the areas where these NICs are installed, or to increase the bandwidth of the workgroup by deploying 100-Mbps Fast Ethernet NICs and hubs.

Problem: Too Many Nodes

The other problem that plagues shared networks is too many nodes on the network. When too many nodes are on a single 10-Mbps shared network, the traffic reaches levels where network efficiency goes down. The efficiency is measured by taking the total number of packets on the wire and determining how many of them are valid data packets and how many are collisions. The more traffic on the wire, the more likely any one packet is a collision. A shared Ethernet network that is over 50 percent loaded will suffer from poor efficiency. The bottom line is that even though the level of network traffic appears to be high, users will complain about long network response times.

Figure 10.4

This figure shows traffic levels with many fast nodes on the network. Note the two extended spikes in network utilization. This may indicate that the newer nodes are much faster than the rest of the nodes on the network and could be causing traffic problems.

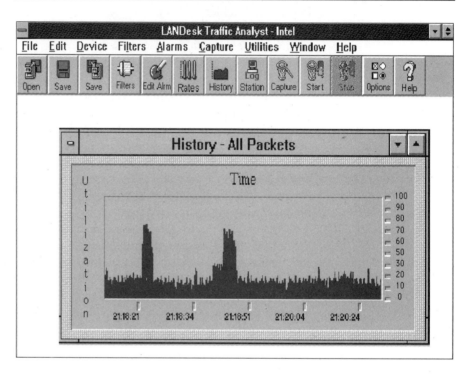

This problem is easily seen by most traffic analysts that can separate collisions from good packets. No details of the packets need to be seen. Figure 10.5 shows what a network with too many nodes (and too many collisions) will register on a typical traffic analyst.

In the past, this problem was remedied with Ethernet bridging or segmenting, short-term solutions at best. Adding switches or higher bandwidth devices is the best way to avoid this problem in the long term. The deployment of such devices was discussed in Chapter 7.

Individual Frame Analysis

Although monitoring overall traffic levels can give you a good indication of when your network is overloaded, it may not tell you when other problems are occurring. Traffic levels on the network may not be high, but the packets that are on the network could be problematic. Examples of these problems include the following:

- Imbalance in packet distribution

- Large number of broadcast packets

- Bad packets on the network

Figure 10.5

This shows the traffic level with too many nodes on the network. Note that the utilization is well above the 50-percent mark. This results in a network with less than optimum performance.

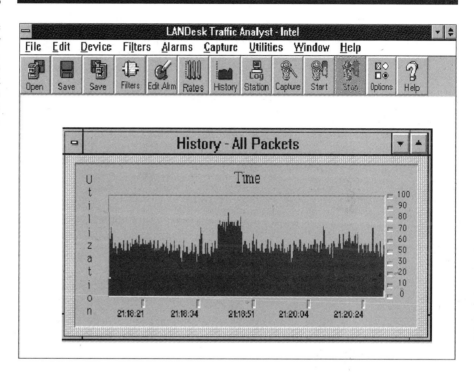

Sometimes the only way to find the source of these problems is to analyze individual packet statistics and contents. Usually, a high-performance device such as a LAN Analyzer is required for this purpose. In the sections that follow, each of the three problem examples will be characterized by how to diagnose them.

Problem: Improper Packet Distribution

Packet distribution statistics can tell you if one or more nodes are dominating most of the network bandwidth. By monitoring the source address of each packet on a shared network, one can create a distribution pie chart of who is using what portion of the network. Problems arise when an isolated client is using more than 5 percent of the available shared bandwidth for any extended period of time. This client is likely to be doing some LAN-intensive tasks, such as video conferencing or database queries, which require a lot of bandwidth. Clients like these, often referred to as *power users*, should be given their own dedicated switched hub port, or congregated together on a faster 100BASE-T network. In a normal shared environment, you should expect servers to be responsible for the majority of the packets.

Problem: Broadcast Storms

A broadcast packet is designed to reach all nodes on the network. Since a broadcast packet's destination address is FFFFFFFFFFFF, each individual node knows it must receive the packet. A bridge or switch does not act like a firewall for broadcast packets (as a router does). Bridges always forward broadcast packets, so they tend to flow freely throughout the network. Since these packets must flow to all nodes on the segment, there is a higher probability that they will collide. When many broadcast packets are being transmitted simultaneously on a network, the effect is called a *broadcast storm*. When many stations send broadcast frames at once, broadcast storms are more likely.

This is easy to detect by measuring how many broadcast frames are on the network at any given time. A packet distribution that shows a high number of broadcast frames concentrated in a small amount of time is likely a broadcast storm. A broadcast storm is usually found in networks with many NetWare servers (which send broadcast "keep-alive" packets every 30 seconds) or with TCP/IP networks (TCP/IP uses broadcasting extensively). In a shared network, a broadcast storm problem can be remedied by adding routers, adding switches with broadcast filtering capabilities, or upgrading to Fast Ethernet. The latter is preferred because it is the most long-term solution of the three.

Problem: Errored Packets

Errors in packets occur in various ways. Often packet errors are caused by sub-par cabling infrastructures, bad NICs, faulty hubs or interconnect devices, or noise interference. Packet errors can usually be detected by software analyzer products; however, to really troubleshoot the *cause* of the error, more sophisticated hardware-based analyzers may be required. The following section describes some of the more common errors found in today's Ethernet networks. Figure 10.6 shows where each type of error occurs in an Ethernet frame.

Runts (Collisions)

Runt packets refer to packets that are shorter than the minimum Ethernet frame length. This is currently defined as 64 bytes, including CRC, Destination Address, Source Address, Type/Length field, and data. If a frame is received with less than 64 bytes, then one of two things has probably occurred: The frame has collided somewhere on the network and the remaining portion of the frame is the collision jam signal; or the station that transmitted the frame encountered an underrun during the transmission process and the transmitted frame was cut short. Regardless of the cause, a runt frame is useless and must be discarded. Usually, runt frames of the underrun variety must be dealt with at the source—the transmitting station.

Figure 10.6

Locations of common packet errors including runts, CRC errors, late collisions, and misaligned frames

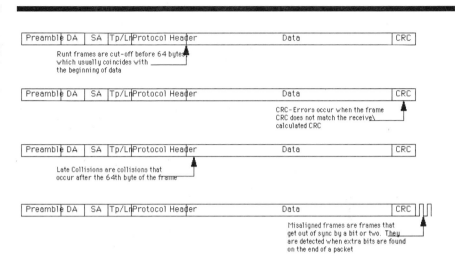

CRC Errors

The CRC is a 4-byte field at the end of every frame that tells the receiving station the frame is valid. When the frame is transmitted, it is fed bit by bit through a linear feedback shift register in the transmitting station. The output of the register is a 4-byte value that is appended to the end of the frame. During reception, the receiving station then computes the CRC just as the transmitting station did. The receiving station compares the value it obtains with the value received at the end of the frame. If the two values are equal, then no errors have occurred during transmission. When the values do not add up, the receiving station should report a CRC error and discard the frame.

CRC errors can be detected by most LAN analyzers. In any network, more than a dozen CRC errors a day should be cause for alarm. CRC errors usually indicate that a portion of the network is suffering from bad cabling, external noise, or excessive transmit jitter. All three conditions can be isolated by looking at the Source Address of the CRC-errored frame and tracing the path of the frame back to its original point of transmission. It is likely that one of the components along that path is at fault.

Late Collisions

Late collisions are almost never seen in today's 10-Mbps networks because they are a product of a shared network diameter that is too large. However, since the shared network diameter is much smaller in Fast Ethernet networks, people are more likely to connect networks that exceed the 205-meter network diameter rule. In networks such as these, late collisions may occur. If you are seeing late collisions on your network, recheck all the shared network diameters for compliance to the IEEE802.3 specification (see Chapter 3).

Misalignment

Misaligned frames are also very rare, but can occur when network conditions deteriorate. A misaligned frame is one that somehow gets out of sync with the receiving station's receive clock recovery circuit. A misaligned frame will actually be valid on the wire, but the receiving station will see it as a CRC error. Misalignment is reported if the frame ends with a CRC error and extra bits are also detected. These are called dribble bits and are shown in Figure 10.6.

Troubleshooting in a shared environment requires understanding of many problems and encompasses many techniques. Some of these problems are discussed in this section and are summarized in Table 10.2.

Table 10.2

Troubleshooting Techniques for a Shared Network

TYPE OF ANALYSIS	PROBLEM	TECHNIQUE FOR TROUBLE-SHOOTING	POTENTIAL SOLUTION
Overall traffic level analysis	Too many nodes	Look for shared media traffic levels near 50 percent	Segment existing network with bridges Add switching capabilities to current network Add more bandwidth to current network (Fast Ethernet)
	Fast nodes hogging bandwidth	Look for bandwidth "spikes" above 50 percent	Add switching capabilities to current network Add more bandwidth to current network
Individual packet analysis	Imbalanced packet distribution	Look for high percentages of packets from any given Node Address	Segment with active nodes should be connected to a switched port or upgraded to Fast Ethernet
	Broadcast storms	Look for many broadcast packets in a concentrated amount of time	Add routers as Broadcast "firewalls" Add more bandwidth to current network Add *Virtual LAN* Capabilities to network with switching hubs

Table 10.2

TYPE OF ANALYSIS	PROBLEM	TECHNIQUE FOR TROUBLE-SHOOTING	POTENTIAL SOLUTION
Individual packet analysis (continued)	Runt frames	Count the number of runt frames reported by LAN analyzer	Determine if the frames are collisions or underruns If collisions, try segmentation, adding switches, or adding more bandwidth If underruns, trace Node Address of the generating station or switch
	CRC errors	Count the number of CRC errors reported by LAN analyzer	Trace CRC errors back through network to original transmitting node. Problem may be anywhere along that path.
	Late collisions	Count the number of late collisions reported by LAN analyzer	Network diameter is probably out of specification. Recheck cabling distances and repeater hops—especially for Fast Ethernet.
	Misaligned frames	Count the number of misaligned frames reported by LAN analyzer	Trace misaligned frames back through network to original transmitting node. Problem may be anywhere along that path.

■ How Troubleshooting Differs in a Switched Environment

In a switched network, the problems and solutions of a shared network don't always apply. Each node may have a dedicated switched port so that bad packets from that node don't affect the rest of the nodes on the network. This feature is somewhat offset by the fact that troubleshooting switched networks is much more difficult. No longer can a LAN analyzer see all packets and determine which node is the cause of the problem. For this reason, the concept of measuring overall traffic levels and studying individual frame statistics is not straightforward in a switched environment. Several switching hub vendors have proposed ways to remedy this problem with innovative techniques such as internal traffic monitors and switch port aliasing. We will discuss these techniques and their effectiveness on traffic-based problems.

Traffic Level Analysis in a Switched Network

Monitoring traffic levels in a switched environment is not straightforward. If you remember the description of a switch, a packet is only forwarded to one port on the switch, so a LAN analyzer connected to one port of a switch will not necessarily catch all packets flowing through the switch. Many switch vendors have attempted to solve the traffic monitoring problem by designing statistic collecting modules into the switch. These modules are either based on SNMP (or RMON) statistics or a proprietary collection mechanism. For instance, the Bay Networks Lattisswitch 28115 switch keeps statistics on each packet and can report overall switch traffic levels to any SNMP agent or Bay Networks Optivity management software. Figure 10.7 shows an example of the Bay 28115 statistical capture screen.

Figure 10.7

The Bay Networks Lattisswitch 28115 screen displays many useful statistics about the switch traffic, but is only accessible via a dedicated station connected directly to the switch.

```
-------------PORT 1-----PORT 2-----PORT 3-----PORT 4-----PORT 5-----

RxFrm           0         45         0     1213320       0
BadCRC          0          0    .     0           0       0
FrmAlign        0          1         0           0       0
RX_bps          0   33453754         0     1123211       0
TXCngst         0         14         0           0       0
RXFifoOv        0          0         0          55       0
EPRXFrm         0       4554         0     1213320       0
HPRXFrm         0       4554         0     1213320       0
HPRxOvr         0          0         0           0       0
HPRetry         0         23         0           0       0
EPReject        0          0         0           0       0

-------------PORT 6-----PORT 7-----PORT 8-----PORT 9-----PORT 10----

RxFrm           0          0   3200980    1213320       0
BadCRC          0          0    .  44         0       0
FrmAlign        0          0        44         0       0
RX_bps          0          0  67023219        0       0
TXCngst         0          0      1448         0       0
RXFifoOv        0          0       724         0       0
EPRXFrm         0          0    320098         0       0
HPRXFrm         0          0    320098         0       0
HPRxOvr         0          0         0         0       0
HPRetry         0          0      3210         0       0
EPReject        0          0         4         0       0

CTRL-E:  Enter, Exit;  CTRL-T:  Toggle Page;  CTRL-C:  Clear; CTRL-P:  Main Menu
```

Traffic level problems can be diagnosed on a switch with the above techniques; however, problems such as faster nodes and too many nodes may not cause problems on a switched network. Unlike shared networks, switched networks do not suffer from throughput degradation caused by these two problems. In a workgroup switch, each new user gets a certain amount of dedicated bandwidth. As long as the high bandwidth connection to the switch can handle the traffic, there should be no traffic level problems. For instance, the switch in Figure 10.8a has six clients connected to 10-Mbps ports and a local server connected to a 100-Mbps port. Odds are the traffic level in this switch will not be more than the switch can handle. This is because even if all clients are sending a maximum amount of data, only 60 Mbps of the server link will be used. Now consider the same workgroup with double the number of clients, as shown in Figure 10.8b. In this case, the clients could possibly create enough traffic to cause an overall traffic level problem in the switch. The solution to this problem is to attach some of the clients to a repeater and connect the repeater into a switched port. If the sum of the total bandwidth of all the clients is not greater than the bandwidth of the server link, then the clients will never overrun the server with too much traffic.

Figure 10.8

(a) A switch without the potential for a traffic problem: Even if all six clients are transmitting at maximum rates, the 100-Mbps server connection will not be overrun.
(b) A switch with the potential for a traffic level problem: With 12 clients, the server could receive 120 Mbps of requests at the same time, resulting in an overrun situation.

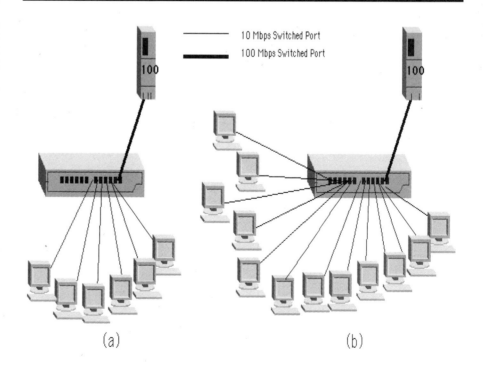

10 Mbps Switched Port
100 Mbps Switched Port

(a)   (b)

Sometimes, hardware in individual ports on a switch may fail. If this happens, the switch can suffer from increased traffic levels due to the faulty port. This can usually be detected by the switch's own internal management module, which periodically checks the integrity of each port.

Individual Frame Analysis

Individual frame analysis on a switch is also an interesting proposition. Packets do not get forwarded to all ports on a switch, so there is no logical place to simply plug in a LAN analyzer and view all packets. Switch vendors have designed many ways to overcome this troubleshooting drawback. Two ways are port aliasing and adding a repeater to monitor a port.

Port Aliasing

Port aliasing is a mechanism by which a switch monitors all traffic flowing through a given port and mirrors it to a special alias port. This allows a LAN administrator to examine switch traffic one port at a time. If problematic packets are coming out of a switch, they can usually be isolated in this fashion. Figure 10.9 shows how port aliasing works.

Figure 10.9

In port aliasing on a switch, the alias port can be set up to mirror the traffic on any given port of the switch.

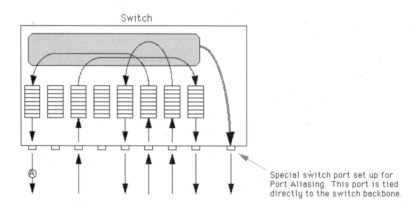

Special switch port set up for Port Aliasing. This port is tied directly to the switch backbone.

Port aliasing is useful in isolating some of the packet errors mentioned previously in this chapter. Below is a brief description of how each type of error manifests itself in a switched environment and how a typical switching hub deals with the problem.

Imbalanced packet distribution   A few nodes accounting for most of the traffic on a switch will not cause as big a problem as in a shared environment. Since the switch, and not the shared media, is the arbitrator between ports, it can intelligently determine the relative priority of each port. Because of this feature of switches, bandwidth hogging is rarely a problem in switched networks.

Broadcast storms   Switches that forward packets according to bridging schemes like store-and-forward and cut-through are especially susceptible to broadcast storms. Since broadcast packets are supposed to be for everybody, they are forwarded to every port on a switch. In effect, broadcast packets make switches act like repeaters so broadcast storms will have the same effect on switches as they do on repeaters. Switches with virtual LAN capabilities are able to filter broadcast packets from some ports; however, this will hardly solve a broadcast storm problem. As in a shared network, the best way to remedy a broadcast storm in a switched network is to decrease the amount of broadcast packets on the network. This often means going to the source of the packets.

Runt packets   Since switches help nodes avoid collisions, a runt frame is usually not due to a collision. However, frames that have underruns on the transmitting station will still show up as runt packets at the switch. Some switches may have a feature that allows them to filter out any runt frames, thus preventing them from being propogated through the switch.

CRC errors   Depending on the features of your switch, CRC errors may not be a problem. Some store-and-forward switches check the integrity of the CRC of every packet before forwarding it to a specific port. If this is the case, CRC-errored packets will never make it through the switch. If the switch does not do CRC checking, then the packet will be forwarded as normal. It is possible that a bad port on a switch could actually induce a CRC error. In this case, the end node or another switch will have to catch the error.

Late collisions   Collisions in general are less frequent in switched networks. If they occur at all, it is because they are propogated to the switch from shared networks that connect to a switched port. Switches will typically handle late collisions like they handle regular collisions—by dropping the packet.

Misaligned frames   To a switch, misaligned frames are seen as CRC errors. If the switch is capable of filtering CRC errors, then it will filter misaligned frames as well.

Adding a Repeater

Even if a switch does not have advanced troubleshooting features like statistic gathering modules and port aliasing, there are still a few tricks you can use to troubleshoot problematic switched networks. Adding a repeater is one such method. *Adding a repeater* refers to cascading a suspected problem node through a repeater into a switch, as shown in Figure 10.10. A port and a LAN analyzer are both connected to a repeater and the repeater is, in turn, connected to the switch port. In this fashion, any port on a switch can be monitored for bad frames and other error conditions.

Figure 10.10

Sometimes, adding a repeater to troubleshoot a switch is the only way to view the traffic going in and out of a switched port.

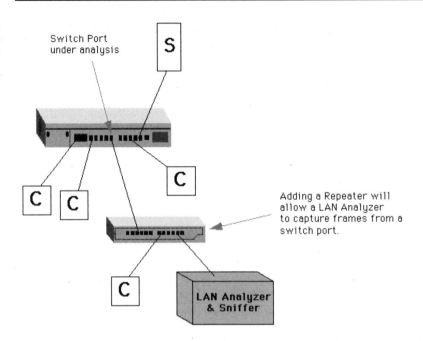

Troubleshooting in a switched environment involves many new techniques in order to obtain the same level of information found in a shared environment. Two basic troubleshooting methods, monitoring traffic levels and analyzing individual packets, take on a new meaning in a switched environment. In a shared network, this level of monitoring is accomplished with a software or hardware LAN analyzer. In a switched network, LAN analyzers must be paired with features of the switch itself to obtain similar information. Table 10.3 briefly summarizes the techniques used to troubleshoot a switched network.

■ How Troubleshooting Differs for Fast Ethernet

Fast Ethernet networks may be shared or switched and may incorporate 10-Mbps networks as well. This introduces some interesting challenges to the troubleshooting a Fast Ethernet network. In general, however, Fast Ethernet network problems can be diagnosed with the techniques discussed earlier in this chapter. The challenges involve enabling troubleshooting equipment for Fast Ethernet and preparing for any new problems Fast Ethernet may bring to your network. This section starts by briefly describing how to upgrade current software and hardware analyzer products to Fast Ethernet. It then finishes

Table 10.3

Troubleshooting
Techniques for a
Switched Network

TYPE OF TROUBLESHOOTING	METHOD FOR TROUBLESHOOTING	SWITCH FEATURES NECESSARY
Traffic level analysis	Monitoring switch statistics	Internal switch statistic-gathering module
Individual frame analysis (including checking for errored frames)	Port aliasing	Special switch hardware that allows for port aliasing
	Adding a repeater	No special switch feature required

with a detailed look at some of the problems to expect after deploying Fast Ethernet in your network.

Changing Diagnostic Hardware

Troubleshooting hardware products, such as LAN analyzers, hand-held frame analyzers, and traffic generators, can sometimes be upgraded to include Fast Ethernet diagnosis capabilities. Devices that can be upgraded are often products that can already handle some form of high-speed module, like FDDI or CDDI. Modules that do not have a Fast Ethernet upgrade are probably built around an architecture that is too slow to analyze 100-Mbps data rates. Most hardware-based products have an independent user interface that needs to be aware of the type and speed of the network it is monitoring. Therefore, sniffers and LAN analyzers will likely need a firmware upgrade when a new 100BASE-T module is added. The Network General Expert Sniffer is a product that has an ugrade module for 100BASE-TX. This particular analyzer, shown in Figure 10.11, can adapt to many high-speed technologies, such as Fast Ethernet, FDDI, and CDDI.

In general, diagnostic products will support 100BASE-TX, 100BASE-T4, and 100BASE-FX. If you have any thoughts of deploying more than one type of Fast Ethernet, be sure to determine if the network troubleshooting device you are considering will support all three.

Changing Diagnostic Software

Most diagnostic software is PC-based and relies on a NIC and device driver for its interface to the wire. For this reason, most software-based troubleshooting products are easily upgradable to Fast Ethernet by simply adding a new NIC and driver. However, most PCs are not powerful enough to receive, store, *and* analyze incoming data at 100-Mbps rates. Therefore, as in 10-Mbps,

Figure 10.11

The Network General
Expert Sniffer 100BASE-T
model will be available in
the second half of 1995.

software-based analyzers make better traffic level analyzers than they do individual packet analyzers. LAN management suites such as Intel's LANDesk Manager are also easily upgradable to Fast Ethernet. A simple NIC and driver replacement provides the path to 100 Mbps. Since LANDesk Manager doesn't examine every packet at the byte level like a LAN analyzer would, so its management applications can keep up with the 100-Mbps traffic.

There are a few things to watch out for in any software-based LAN diagnostic package. First, be sure the program is not hard coded for specific data rates, like 10 Mbps for Ethernet or 16 Mbps for Token Ring. Flexibility in the maximum data rate is needed for a smooth upgrade to Fast Ethernet. Second, determine which protocols are supported when you upgrade to Fast Ethernet. Although your 10-Mbps software may support IPX, TCP/IP, NetBios, and SNMP, new modules may not support the same variety. Last, make sure that any software-based product you purchase can run at both 10- and 100-Mbps speeds and will support 100BASE-TX, 100BASE-T4, and 100BASE-FX.

Potential Problems with Fast Ethernet

With the inclusion of Fast Ethernet in your network, there are a some new problems to consider. In addition to the common problems of 10-Mbps Ethernet, Fast Ethernet networks could encounter problems with network diameter, UTP cable type, mismatched 100BASE-T ports, and noisy environments. Each of these problems is discussed in further detail below.

Shared network diameter is too large   As described previously, a shared Fast Ethernet network can only have a diameter of 205 meters. If this network diameter is not followed, effects such as late collisions and undetected dropped packets may occur. Network diameters usually become too large in one of two ways. Either the two repeater rule or the 100-meter hub-to-node rule is not followed. Shared Fast Ethernet networks with diameters over 205 meters should be immediately enhanced with a Fast Ethernet switching hub or bridge.

100BASE-TX is running on Category 3 UTP   Another common problem occurs when a 100BASE-TX hub or node is connected using Category 3 UTP cabling, which will simply not work. Category 5, or data grade, UTP cable is required for 100BASE-TX. If this happens in your network, you will most likely encounter many CRC errors and lost packets. It is questionable if you will even get a good link integrity indication. 100BASE-T4 is the right Fast Ethernet choice for the portion of your network that utilizes Category 3 UTP cable.

100BASE-T4 is running on UTP with only two pairs   When 100BASE-T4 is used, four pairs of cable are required. Studies have shown that most networks have four pairs available for data, but that may or may not be true in your network. If you only have two pairs of your Category 5 UTP cable dedicated for LAN, then 100BASE-TX should be used. If you only have two pairs of Category 3 available for LAN connections, you may need to rely on 10BASE-T in those portions of your network.

100BASE-T4, 100BASE-TX, and 10BASE-T ports are mismatched 10BASE-T and 100BASE-T4 use a start/stop style of communications. That means that the voltage on the wire is zero when there is no transmission or reception occurring. 100BASE-TX, however, uses a special data pattern, called the TX Idle sequence, to designate idle times on the wire. One of the drawbacks of this difference is that if a 100BASE-TX station is connected to a 10BASE-T or 100BASE-T4 port, the TX Idle transmissions will jam the 10-Mbps hub with what amounts to "garbage" packets. You may have problems of this type if you mistakenly connect 100BASE-TX NICs to 100BASE-T4 or 10BASE-T ports. Connecting 100BASE-T4 to 10BASE-T ports is less problematic because although the two ends will not be able to communicate, there will be no garbage packets on the network.

Noisy Environments   In some noisy environments, such as 25-pair bundles and wiring near fluorescent lighting, 100BASE-TX may not work reliably. For that matter, 10BASE-T may not work either. If you are encountering problems which are isolated to a specific cable segment, you should have the noise level checked on that segment. In general, 100BASE-T4 and 10BASE-T are less succeptible to external noise than 100BASE-TX. 100BASE-FX is not succeptible to electrical interference since it is based on optical transmission. This property makes 100BASE-FX the best choice in extremely noisy environments.

■ Summary

Troubleshooting networks today can be a tricky business. With networks evolving toward switching hubs and high-speed alternatives such as Fast Ethernet, the chance for problems to arise becomes that much greater. This chapter has attempted to outline some of the common problems associated with Shared, Switched, and Fast Ethernet networks. In addition, we discussed hardware and software products that can be used to aid in the isolation of these problems.

Although troubleshooting Switched and Fast Ethernet networks may seem complicated at first, once the proper infrastructure is in place, diagnosis and resolution of network problems is usually straightforward. Hopefully, this chapter has provided some insight into how to prepare that infrastructure and how to approach common problems.

■ Appendix A

■ Fast Ethernet Vendors

Vendor Name	Product Type	Address	Phone Number
3Com	Hubs, NICs, switches, routers	5400 Bayfront Plaza Santa Clara, CA 95052	(408) 764-5000 1-800 NET-3COM
Accton Technology	Hubs, NICs	1962 Zanker Road San Jose, CA 95112	(800) 926-9288
Alantec	Hubs, NICs	70 Plumeria Drive San Jose, CA 95134	(800) ALANTEC
Asante Technologies	Nics, repeaters, stackables	821 Fox Lane San Jose, CA 95131-1616	(800) 662-9686
Auspex Systems	Aggregator	5200 Great America Parkway Santa Clara, CA 95054	(408) 986-2000
Bay Networks*	Hubs, switches, routers	4401 Great America Parkway Santa Clara, CA 95054	(800) 8 BAYNET
Broadcom	Silicon	10920 Wilshire Boulevard, 14th floor Los Angeles, CA 90024	(310) 443-4490
Brooktree	Silicon	9868 Scranton Road San Diego, CA 92121-37007	(619) 452-7580
Cabletron Systems	Hubs, switches, routers	35 Industrial Way Rochester, NH 03866-5005	(603) 332-9400
Chipcom Corp.	Hubs, switches, routers	118 Turnpike Road Southborough, MA 01722	(800) 228-9930
Cisco Systems	Switches, routers	1701 West Tasman Drive San Jose, CA 95126	(408) 526-4000 (800) 818-9202
CNet Technology	NICs, hubs	2199 Zanker Road San Jose, CA 95131	(800) 486-2638
Cogent Data Technologies	NICs	175 West Street Friday Harbor, WA 98250	(800) 4 COGENT
Cray Communications	Switches	Smedeholm 12-14 DK-2730 Herlev, Denmark	(45) 44530100

* Bay Networks is the merger of Wellfleet and Synoptic Communications.

Vendor Name	Product Type	Address	Phone Number
Cypress Semiconductor	Silicon	3901 North First Street San Jose, CA 95134-1699	(408) 943-2600
Data General	NICs	4400 Computer Drive Westborough, MA 01580	(800) DATA GEN
Datacom Technologies	Cable testers	11001 31st Place W. Everett, WA 98204	(800) 468-5557
Danya Communications	NICs	849 LeVoy Drive Salt Lake City, UT 84123	(801) 269-7200
Digital Equipment	NICs, silicon, switches	550 King Street, LKG 1-3/M07 Littleton, MA 01460	(800) 457-8211
Exar		2222 Qume Drive San Jose, CA 95131	(408) 434-6400 x3067
Farallon Computing	NICs, bridges	2470 Mariner Square Loop Alameda, CA 94501	(510) 814-5000
FastLan Solutions	Hubs	2320J Walsh Ave. Santa Clara, CA 95051	(408) 988-3667
Fluke Corporation	Test equipment	P.O. Box 9090 Everett, WA 98206-9090	(206) 347-6100
Fujitsu	Silicon, NICs	Kamikodanaka Nakahara-Ku Kawasaki 211 Japan	(81) 44-754-3234
Grand Junction Networks	NICs, hubs, switches	47281 Bayside Parkway Fremont, CA 94538	(800) 747-FAST
Hughes LAN Systems	Switches	2200 Lawson Lane Santa Clara, CA 95054	(408) 565-6000
Hyundai Electronics America	NICs, switches	510 Cottonwood Drive Milpitas, CA 95035	(408) 232-8674
IMC Networks		16931 Millikan Avenue Irvine, CA 92714	(714) 724-1070
Integrated Circuit Systems	Silicon	1271 Parkmoor Avenue San Jose, CA 95126	(408) 271-2510
Intel	Silicon, NICs	5200 NE Elam Young Parkway Hillsboro, OR 97124	(800) 538-3373
Interphase	NICs	13800 Senlac Dallas, TX 75234	(214) 919-9000

Vendor Name	Product Type	Address	Phone Number
Kalpana	Switches	1154 East Arques Sunnyvale, CA 90086	(408) 749-1900
LANCAST	Switches	10 Northern Blvd, Unit 5 Amherst, NH 03031	(603) 880-1833; (800) 9LANCAST
LANNET	Hubs, switches, stackables	17942 Cowan Irvine, CA 92714	(714) 752-6638
Micro Linear	Silicon	2092 Concourse Drive San Jose, CA 95131	(408) 433-5200
Microtest	Test equipment	4747 N. 22nd Street Phoenix, AZ 85016	(602) 952-6400
MITRON Computer	NICs	2200 S. Bascom Avenue Campbell, CA 95008	(408) 371-8166
National Semiconductor	Silicon, NICs	2900 Semiconductor Drive Santa Clara, CA 95052	(800) 272-9959
NCR Microelectronics	Silicon	2001 Danfield Court Fort Collins, CO 80525	(303) 226-9600
NEC Electronics	NICs	475 Ellis Street, MS MV5145 Mountain View, CA 94039	(415) 965-6000
Network General	Test equipment	4200 Bohannon Drive Menlo Park, CA 94025	(415) 473-2000
Networth	NICs, hubs, stackables, switches	8404 Esters Boulevard Irving, TX 75063	(800) 544-5255
Olicom	NICs, hubs	900 E Park Boulevard, Suite 180 Plano, TX 75074	(800) 2 OLICOM
Packet Engines	Switches	32578 Montgomery Court Union City, CA 95487	(510) 489-3162
Psiber Data Systems	Test equipment	4011 Camino Allegre, La Mesa, CA 91941	(619) 670-7456
Quality Semiconductor	Silicon	851 Martin Avenue Santa Clara, CA 95050	(408) 450-8053
Racal-Datacom	NICs, hubs	60 Codman Hill Road Boxborough, MA 01719	(508) 263-9929
Racore Computer Products	NICs	170 Knowles Drive Los Gatos, CA 95030	(800) 635-1274

Vendor Name	Product Type	Address	Phone Number
Raytheon Semiconductor	Silicon	350 Ellis Street Mountain View, CA 94043	(415) 962-7915
Rockwell International	NICs	7402 Hollister Avenue Santa Barbara, CA 93117	(805) 262-8023
SEEQ Technology	Silicon	47200 Bayside Parkway Fremont, CA 94538	(510) 226-7400
Scope Communications	Test Equipment	100 Otis Street Northboro, MA 01532	(508) 393-1236 (800) 418-7111
Standard Microsystems (SMC)	Silicon, NICs, hubs, stackables, switches	350 Kennedy Happauge, NY 11788	(800) SMC-4YOU
Sun Microsystems Computer Company	NICs	2550 Garcia Avenue Mountain View, CA 94043	(800) 821-4643
Texas Instruments	Silicon	12203 SW Freeway Stafford, TX 77477	(713) 274-2000
Thomas-Conrad	NICs, Hubs	1908 R Kramer Lane Austin, TX 78758	(512) 834-6335
UB Networks	Hubs, stackables, switches	3990 Freedom Circle Santa Clara, CA 95054	(408) 496-0111 (800) 873-6381
Unisys	NICs, switches	322 North 2200 West Salt Lake City, UT 84116	(801) 594-4310
Xircom	NICs	2300 Corporate Center Drive Thousand Oaks, CA 91320	(800) 438-4526
ZNYX	NICs	48501 Warm Springs Boulevard 107 Fremont, CA 94539	(510) 249-0800

■ Appendix B

■ References

Biagi, Susan. The Myth of Category 5. *Stacks*, July 1994: 18.

Costa, Janis Furtek. *Planning and Designing High-Speed Networks Using 100VG-AnyLAN*. Hewlett-Packard Professional Books/Prentice-Hall Professional Books. 1994.

Crane, Ron C. The Case for High Speed CSMA/CD (Ethernet) Network Links to Desktop. September 30, 1991.

Crane, Ron C. Transmission System Issues for 100 Mb/s Ethernet (802.3). October 10, 1991.

Derfler, Jr., Frank, and Les Freed. *Get a Grip on Network Cabling*. Ziff-Davis Press. 1993.

Derfler, Jr., Frank. *Guide to Linking LANs*. Ziff-Davis Press. 1993.

Derfler, Jr., Frank. *PC Magazine Guide to Connectivity*. Ziff-Davis Press. 1991.

Digital, Intel, Xerox (DIX). The Ethernet. September 30, 1980.

Fast Ethernet Alliance. Introduction to 100BASE-T Fast Ethernet. White Paper. June 1994.

Feldman, Robert. Proactive Management Tools. *LAN Times*. January 10, 1994.

Grand Junction Networks. Switched Ethernet. An Evolutionary Alternative to High Speed Networking. White Paper. March 1994.

Grand Junction Networks. Fast Ethernet, An Evolutionary Alternative to High Speed Networking. White Paper. October 1994.

Gunnerson, Gary. Switching Hubs: Switching to the Fast Track. *PC Magazine*. October 1994.

Hayes, James. Fiber Optic Testing. Fotec, Inc. Boston, MA. 1994.

Held, Gilbert. *Ethernet Networks, Design, Implementation, Operation, Management*. Wiley. New York, NY. 1994.

Henderson, Tom. Protocol Peacekeeping. *LAN Magazine*. May 1995: 129–137.

Hewlett-Packard. *Designing HP AdvanceStack Workgroup Networks*. June 1994: P/N 5962–7968E.

IEEE Standards Department. 802.3u Supplement to 1993 version of ANSI/IEEE Std. 802.3. Piscataway, NJ. May 1995.

IEEE Standards Dept. Draft Supplement to 1993 Version of ANSI/IEEE Std 802.3. Document # P802.3u/D4–D5. January 11, 1995.

IEEE. Draft Supplement 802.3u/100BASE-T to 1993 version of ANSI/IEEE Standard 802.3. Version 4. January 1995.

Laepple, Alfred, and Heinz-Gerd Hegering. *Ethernet: Building a Communications Infrastructure*. Addison-Wesley. Wokingham, England. 1993.

MacAskill, Skip. Full Duplex Ethernet Holds Its Own in Test. *Network World*. May 2, 1994.

Metcalfe, Bob. Computer/Network Interface Design: Lessons from Arpanet and Ethernet. *IEEE Journal on Selected Area in Communications*. Vol 11, No. 2, February 1993: 173–179.

Michael, Wendy H., William J. Cronin, Jr., and Karl F. Pieper. *FDDI, An Introduction*. Digital Press/Butterworth Heinemann. Newton, MA. 1992.

Morse, Steven. As Seen on TV: NetWare-Based Video Servers. *Network Computing*. December 1994.

Nemzow, Martin A. W. *FDDI Networking, Planning, Installation, & Management,* McGraw-Hill. 1993.

Nemzow, Martin A. W. *LAN Performance Optimization*. Windcrest-McGraw-Hill. 1992.

Nemzow, Martin A. W. *The Ethernet Management Guide, 2nd Edition*. McGraw-Hill. 1993.

Parnell, Tere. Comparison: Switching Hubs. *LAN Times.* February 13, 1995.

Raynovich, R. Scott. Is the Time Right for Fiber? *LAN Times*. April 10, 1995: 27–30.

Rose, Marshall T. *The Simple Book: An Introduction to Internet Management, 2nd Ed.* Prentice Hall. 1994.

Ross, Floyd, and James Hamstra. Forging FDDI. *IEEE Journal on Selected Area in Communications*. Vol 11, No. 2, February 1993: 181–190.

Saunders, Stephen. A Quick Read on LAN Problems. Hot Products Column. *Data Communications*. January 1995.

Saunders, Stephen. Bad Vibrations Beset Category 5 UTP Users. *Data Communications*. June 1994: 49–53.

Seifert, Rich. Ethernet: Ten Years After. *BYTE Magazine*. January 1991: 315–319.

Shimmin, Bradley F. Comparing Three Methods of Ethernet Switching. *LAN Times*. January 10, 1994.

Shipley, Buddy, and William F. Lyons. *Ethernet Pocket Reference Guide*. Shipley Consulting International. Silver Springs, Maryland. 1992.

Shoch, John F., Yogen K. Dalal, David D. Redell, and Ronald C. Crane. The Evolution of Ethernet. *Computer*. 1982.

Tansey, Thomas. Virtual LANs No Longer a Fantasy. *LAN Times*. March 28, 1994.

3Com Corporation. 100Base-T Fast Ethernet, A High-Speed Technology for Accelerating 10BASE-T Networks. White Paper. September 1994.

Tolly, Kevin, and David Newman. High-End Routers. *Data Communications*. January 1993.

Tolly, Kevin. 100VGNowhereLAN. *Data Communications*. November 1994: 37–38.

■ Index

Ziff-Davis Press Survey of Readers

Please help us in our effort to produce the best books on personal computing.
For your assistance, we would be pleased to send you a FREE catalog
featuring the complete line of Ziff-Davis Press books.

1. How did you first learn about this book?

Recommended by a friend . . . . ☐ -1 (5)

Recommended by store personnel . . . . ☐ -2

Saw in Ziff-Davis Press catalog . . . . ☐ -3

Received advertisement in the mail . . . . ☐ -4

Saw the book on bookshelf at store . . . . ☐ -5

Read book review in: _____ ☐ -6

Saw an advertisement in: _____ ☐ -7

Other (Please specify): _____ ☐ -8

2. Which THREE of the following factors most influenced your decision to purchase this book? (Please check up to THREE.)

Front or back cover information on book . . . ☐ -1 (6)

Logo of magazine affiliated with book . . . . . . ☐ -2

Special approach to the content . . . . ☐ -3

Completeness of content . . . . ☐ -4

Author's reputation. . . . . ☐ -5

Publisher's reputation . . . . ☐ -6

Book cover design or layout . . . . ☐ -7

Index or table of contents of book . . . . ☐ -8

Price of book . . . . ☐ -9

Special effects, graphics, illustrations . . . . ☐ -0

Other (Please specify): _____ ☐ -x

3. How many computer books have you purchased in the last six months? _____ (7-10)

4. On a scale of 1 to 5, where 5 is excellent, 4 is above average, 3 is average, 2 is below average, and 1 is poor, please rate each of the following aspects of this book below. (Please circle your answer.)

Depth/completeness of coverage	5	4	3	2	1	(11)
Organization of material	5	4	3	2	1	(12)
Ease of finding topic	5	4	3	2	1	(13)
Special features/time saving tips	5	4	3	2	1	(14)
Appropriate level of writing	5	4	3	2	1	(15)
Usefulness of table of contents	5	4	3	2	1	(16)
Usefulness of index	5	4	3	2	1	(17)
Usefulness of accompanying disk	5	4	3	2	1	(18)
Usefulness of illustrations/graphics	5	4	3	2	1	(19)
Cover design and attractiveness	5	4	3	2	1	(20)
Overall design and layout of book	5	4	3	2	1	(21)
Overall satisfaction with book	5	4	3	2	1	(22)

5. Which of the following computer publications do you read regularly; that is, 3 out of 4 issues?

Byte . . . . ☐ -1 (23)

Computer Shopper . . . . ☐ -2

Home Office Computing . . . . ☐ -3

Dr. Dobb's Journal . . . . ☐ -4

LAN Magazine . . . . ☐ -5

MacWEEK . . . . ☐ -6

MacUser . . . . ☐ -7

PC Computing . . . . ☐ -8

PC Magazine . . . . ☐ -9

PC WEEK . . . . ☐ -0

Windows Sources . . . . ☐ -x

Other (Please specify): _____ ☐ -y

Please turn page.

6. What is your level of experience with personal computers? With the subject of this book?

	With PCs	With subject of book
Beginner	☐ -1 (24)	☐ -1 (25)
Intermediate	☐ -2	☐ -2
Advanced	☐ -3	☐ -3

7. Which of the following best describes your job title?

Officer (CEO/President/VP/owner) ☐ -1 (26)
Director/head ☐ -2
Manager/supervisor ☐ -3
Administration/staff ☐ -4
Teacher/educator/trainer ☐ -5
Lawyer/doctor/medical professional ☐ -6
Engineer/technician ☐ -7
Consultant ☐ -8
Not employed/student/retired ☐ -9
Other (Please specify): _____ ☐ -0

8. What is your age?

Under 20 ☐ -1 (27)
21-29 ☐ -2
30-39 ☐ -3
40-49 ☐ -4
50-59 ☐ -5
60 or over ☐ -6

9. Are you:

Male ☐ -1 (28)
Female ☐ -2

Thank you for your assistance with this important information! Please write your address below to receive our free catalog.

Name: _____

Address: _____

City/State/Zip: _____

Fold here to mail.

3385-07-18

_____

_____

_____

NO POSTAGE NECESSARY IF MAILED IN THE UNITED STATES

BUSINESS REPLY MAIL
FIRST CLASS MAIL   PERMIT NO. 1612   OAKLAND, CA

POSTAGE WILL BE PAID BY ADDRESSEE

Ziff-Davis Press
ZD PRESS
5903 Christie Avenue
Emeryville, CA 94608-1925
Attn: Marketing